Chocolate Fell From the Sky

Hedda Martens

ISBN 978-1-947635-14-2 (Hardcover Edition)
    978-1-947635-15-9 (Paperback Edition)

Printed in the United States of America

First Printing December 2018

Published by Martens Books

Chocolate Fell From the Sky:

My Journey Through Life

By Hedda Martens

I think my mother is hovering over every little story that I am relating here. However, she would not want me to have "outsiders" read them. As far as the outside world knew, my mother had four perfect children, and all members of her immediate family were beyond reproach and led perfect lives.

I dedicate this book to all the members of my family, both past and present. Their experiences both shared with me and relayed to me in times of happiness, sadness, or excitement have made my life fuller than most.

—Hedda Martens

Acknowledgements

No adjectives can describe my gratitude and love for my daughter, Anna Davidson, who has worked countless hours arranging my words into meaningful order. She is my security and pride and joy each day we spend together. My dear friend, Debby Sullivan, has sat by Anna's side providing editing expertise and forward momentum when the task of creating a book seemed too daunting. A big thank you goes to my son-in-law, Bruce Davidson, who first saw a memoirs writing class advertised, signed me up, and took me to the very first class back in 2007. I must also thank the members of the class and especially our fearless leader, Rick Ohler, for finding my stories interesting and encouraging me to add details that I found myself saying aloud when we would discuss a piece. I thank Kateri Ewing for designing the book cover to reflect my life. To my dear friends John and Mary Glenn, I thank you for your many dinner invitations and visits. Finally, I thank my grandchildren, Carl and Erika, for being the main reason I was driven to write all these stories down in the first place.

Anna and Debby editing on the couch beside me.
I found this very comforting.

List of Stories

Prologue

A New Chapter in my Life

I moved to East Aurora in May 2007 and was most fortunate to find a lovely home at Woodbrook Condominiums. It was wonderful to be close to my dear daughter, Anna, and her equally dear husband, Bruce. My grandchildren, Carl and Erika, were a constant joy.

"I've signed you up for a memoirs class and you're going to write about your life," my son-in-law announced in September of 2007. We purchased a computer and printer. Carl, then eleven years old, came over to give me instructions. I wondered what I was going to write about and, with great trepidation, awaited the first meeting of the class. When Bruce dropped me off, I felt like the new kid in kindergarten, suddenly deserted by her mother.

The teacher, Rick Ohler, introduced everyone, but I confess that I did not register a single name. They all seemed familiar with one another and I was clearly an outsider. Some members read charming, well-written stories that made me wonder how I could keep up with them. Most of my memories were in German. To write in English might present some problems.

Halfway through the class, Rick asked a hitherto silent member, "John, what are you going to write about?" My story will be called "Behind the Stone Wall," John replied. I was enchanted by this romantic, mysterious title and wondered about the treasures hidden behind the stone wall. I had driven along Knox Road and envisioned a huge mansion surrounded by beautiful gardens. It was no surprise to me to learn that anyone living in East Aurora knew what lay behind those walls. Knox Farm State Park, the former country estate of Buffalo's renowned Knox family, became a New York State Park in 2001.

John's lovely wife, Mary, pointed out that she was just going to be a "listening" rather than a "writing" member of the class; however, Mary did go on to write many beautiful stories.

When class ended that first day, John and Mary invited me to join them for dinner. I had to decline since dear Bruce was waiting outside in the hall to take me home. I hoped that they would ask me again.

They did just that and our acquaintance soon blossomed into a most wonderful friendship. I have learned more and more about John and Mary's lives on Knox farm and their very strong connection to the Knox family. John and Mary are special, endearing people. I am fortunate and thankful to know them.

Since that first day in 2007, I have written many stories. Most of them follow in this book. I am grateful to all the members of the memoirs class for making me feel so welcome and at home in East Aurora.

Back row, left to right: John, Debby, Rick, Alison, Pat, Kateri, Ellen,
Mary Lou, Judy, Leita, Sally
Front row: Maureen, Hedda, Mary, Nancy

Confused and Totally Befuddled

Hedda (left) Says Goodbye to her Mother, Lisa, in May 1952

May 1952: After an eleven-day trip aboard the ship *Italia*, I arrived in New York City. My Onkel Hans, who had served as my sponsor, and who worked as a physician at the Tuberculosis Hospital on Murray Hill, Mt. Morris, NY, had come to New York City to meet me. We spent several days in the city and then took a beautiful drive up north along the Hudson River. I enjoyed the spectacular scenery and felt most welcome in my new home. My uncle was eager to show me the sights. He was obviously happy to speak German and to have a member of his family with him. He had left Germany in 1937. However, he expressed his concern, and I detected sadness, about my recent engagement to a German physician who had immigrated to Canada. My mother, his sister, had informed him of that event.

There were four letters waiting for me when we arrived in Mt. Morris: (1) my mother from Lübeck-Travemünde, Germany; (2) Prof. Hans Harmsen from Hamburg, Germany; (3) Stanley Abeyesinghe from London, England; and (4) Dr. Hermann Dillenberg from Regina, Saskatchewan, Canada.

Regrettably, I did not keep these letters, but I remember the contents almost verbatim.

My mother wrote: "My dear Hedda, I hope you had a good sea voyage and are happy to be in America. When I received the letter from Hermann Dillenberg, asking me for your hand in marriage, I was confused to say the least. (The letter was posted from Calais.) Didn't you say goodbye to Stanley just a few weeks ago here in Travemünde and now you are engaged to a total stranger? Since Dr. Dillenberg mentioned that he had been together with Prof. Harmsen as physicians in Rommel's Africa Corps, I traveled to Hamburg and spoke with Prof. Harmsen. He was very friendly and helpful. He assured me that Dr. D. was an honorable man, seeking a new livelihood as a bacteriologist in Canada and that you would be well taken care of. Do me, and yourself, a favor and discuss this rather new development with your uncle. Do not make hasty decisions, please! First, get settled in your new life in nearby Rochester and wait until Hinrich and I join you in December of this year, when we will also immigrate to the U.S.A. We miss you already. Love and a kiss, Mutter. P.S. Prof. H. told me that he met you when you came to ask for a new examination appointment for Brigitte in 1948."

Hans Harmsen wrote: "Hedda, it was a pleasure to meet your lovely mother this morning. I shall be in NYC around May 29. There is a meeting of WHO (World Health Organization) sponsored by the Rockefeller Foundation which I have been asked to attend. Please send me your uncle's phone number so we can set up a meeting. I am enclosing $200 for your expenses. I hope you can make it. We need to talk. Hans."

I felt miserable for not having shared my friendship with H.H. with my mother.

Hermann Dillenberg wrote: "My dear Hedda, I have arrived safely in Regina and am very pleased about the reception and my new position at the hospital. You know that I made a commitment to work here for at least two years. (Immigrants to Canada made these work commitments with their respective employers who sponsored them.) However, there is a chance for me to get a position at the University of Toronto, which would be ideal for you as well since it would be closer to your family in New York. I have fond memories of our trip together on the *Italia*. It was rather difficult to part when I had to debark in Halifax. Meanwhile, I made arrangements to come to Toronto for a brief visit and then hope to meet you at the border in Niagara

Falls. I learned that neither one of us can obtain a visa at this time to enter either the USA or Canada. But I am told that we can meet on the Rainbow Bridge and talk. I hope you will be able to get a ride. I am enclosing my phone number. Please call so that we can make the necessary arrangements. I am convinced that we made the right decision for a life together. Until soon, Hermann."

Hermann Dillenberg and I met aboard the *Italia* while the ship was still at anchor in Hamburg. My mother and brother had accompanied me to the harbor. Once aboard the boat, I quickly put my suitcase on the bed assigned to me (third class, dormitory style) and ran upstairs so that I could wave goodbye. Next to me stood Hermann. He asked me whether I would be so kind to alert him if I spotted a tall, lanky man, in a white shirt and not wearing a tie. When I told him that I too was looking for someone of that description, we started up a conversation. It turned out that we were both looking for Hans Harmsen, and we immediately got involved in a very good conversation. I spotted Hans in the crowd as well as my mother and brother and we waved. Hermann told me that he was serving as the ship's doctor and was provided with excellent accommodations. When he learned of my dormitory accommodations, he offered that I share his suite. I was only too glad and relieved to do just that. My newly acquired lodging brought with it the added luxury of dining at the captain's table. Not bad. We got on well together and, two days later, we decided to get engaged. A few days later, however, when Hermann suggested that we have the captain marry us, I felt that I could not do that to my uncle who was waiting for me in New York. Actually, I wanted to discuss the matter with Hans Harmsen. So we dropped that idea.

And now to the fourth letter, which came from Stanley, who never addressed me by my first name. Instead he consistently used a term of endearment. I met and fell in love with Stanley Abeyesinge, an artist from Ceylon, when I was working at the Student Movement House in London. He wrote: "London is empty and grey without you. We simply cannot say good bye. I shall go for some work back home to Colombo (Sri Lanka) which will last for about two months and then, before returning to London, I plan to see you in America. I am hoping that this is agreeable to you. I miss you, and will write to you again tomorrow. Forever, Stanley."

I decided to discuss all these problems with my uncle. In actuality, I had just come to know my uncle a few days ago when he met me in New York. I was a child when he left Germany for India. However, it felt comfortable and easy to tell him of my troubles. He listened intently for a long time. At the time, my uncle lived in one of the bachelor apartments on the fifth floor of the hospital and just when I was hoping for some comforting words from my uncle, another physician stopped in to meet me. It was not until the following day when my uncle simply said, "Go to New York and find out what Prof. Harmsen has to say." I followed his advice.

The following day, I took the train, I think it was called *Phoebe Snow*, from Mt. Morris to New York and found my way to the apartment of Ted von Borsig, Hans Harmsen's brother-in-law. Ted, a photo journalist, was out of town but Hans was waiting for me. We were very glad to see one another again and talked about everything under the sun, with the exception of the problem at hand, my engagement. The next day, Hans had to be at some meetings and we agreed to meet at around three in the afternoon at the Guggenheim Museum. I remember not being interested in any of the paintings and disliked the novel display of the art. In fact, it made me dizzy. From there, we took a quick look at the Frick Gallery and then took the ferry to Staten Island. The sunset provided a true romantic setting. However, once again, there was no mention of Herman Dillenberg, who was the reason for my coming to New York. I brought up the delicate topic over dinner when we were back in Manhattan.

Hans said, "He is a good friend of mine. The war brought us together. He is, I have no doubt, honest in his intentions and a very good bacteriologist. However, he will have to work very hard to establish himself in Canada and I cannot envision you in a small apartment waiting for his return tired from a long day's work. I think that both of you need time to establish yourselves before you take such a drastic step. You should go to the university and pursue your dream to become a teacher, which will be possible with your uncle's help. Express these thoughts in a letter and then there will be no need to meet at the border. As you know, I am very fond of you. Against my better judgment, I have pursued our whirlwind friendship/relationship ever since that fateful day in 1948 when we met in Hamburg. I have no right to say to you what I would like to say… We'll talk some more about this in the morning." We did not broach this delicate subject again.

I took the train back to Mount Morris, decided to part with Hermann Dillenberg, begin to look for a job in Rochester, NY, and start taking classes at the university. Hans and I continued our weekly exchange of letters. He traveled around the world as president of Planned Parenthood and shared with me his numerous publications which addressed a variety of topics, such as (1) the family as backbone of society; (2) birth control; (3) the displaced persons, refugees, and migrant workers whose unstable lives frequently resulted in criminal activities; (4) society's lack of support for gifted children; as well as numerous articles about the artist Ernst Barlach. Barlach's sculptures and artwork had been declared "degenerate" during the Hitler regime.

My mother and brother arrived in the United States in December 1952 and my sister, Emmeli, in June 1953. We were all trying to make a go of our new lives here. This was not always an easy task and serious social flaws that I observed were very disturbing to me. Fellow students viewed me with suspicion when they learned that I had spent time in the Hitler Youth Movement. This fact appeared to make me responsible for the horrible misdeeds of the Nazi (NAtionalsoZIalist) regime. Then I met two Jewish physicians at the Mount Morris Hospital who had gone to medical school in Holland and Switzerland respectively because some American medical schools did not accept Jews. Several golf clubs quietly observed the same rules. I could not believe that there was anti-Semitism in this country.

The world had wondered how it had been possible that a relatively unknown Austrian could become such a powerful tyrant, yet an equally undistinguished Republican U.S. Senator from Wisconsin, Joseph Raymond McCarthy, had given a speech in 1950 charging that the U.S. State Department was infiltrated by Communists. Initially, these charges were branded a hoax and a fraud. Yet McCarthy repeated his claims on national television and in 1952 the Committee on Government Operations was formed. He cleverly exploited the public's fear of Communism, made reckless accusations, artists and writers were blacklisted, and many careers were ruined (Eartha Kitt, the singer and actress, was among them). Fortunately, he lost his position and power in the Senate in 1954. He seemed to be a forgotten man when he died in 1957, unlike Hitler, who predicted that his name would go down in history.

When German soldiers returned from prison camps in the United States, they told unbelievable stories. They had been treated better than their black guards. It seemed incredible. Had the world not been appalled when Hitler would not shake hands with the great athlete Jesse Owens because he had upset the Aryan theory of white supremacy? I wondered whether equal rights and true tolerance were practiced in our new home. The former German POWs had reported the truth. When Benjamin Hooks, a civil rights leader, died in April 2010, it was reported in Newsweek that he was an Army sergeant who guarded European POWs. When it was time to eat, "Whites Only" restaurants would serve the prisoners, but not Sergeant Hook. Discrimination and fear continue in this country today.

My uncle, mother, three siblings, and I made the United States our permanent home. Although we pursued different interests, settled down in different places, we supported and helped one another through good as well as bad times.

I think that my mother would have preferred that I not yield to my daughter's and her husband's plea to write down stories of my life. My mother was vehemently opposed to spilling family secrets and of any indiscretions that might embarrass members of the family and friends. But then we might never have had the treasures of the many sagas, epic stories, novels, poems, and among others, the precious fairy tales told by Jakob and Wilhelm Grimm and Hans Christian Andersen who wrote about abandoned and abused children, false pride, conceit, and mendacity. I am certain that the authors either witnessed or experienced these tragic events themselves. Thomas Mann called his novels *The Buddenbrooks*, *The Magic Mountain*, as well as the novella, *Death in Venice,* fiction which allowed him to camouflage his own life.

Well, no publisher is promising me an advance. I am truly just writing for my family and friends who might be interested in a very ordinary life, depicting someone who has lived through the turbulent years of WWII, the "Rise and Fall" of Hitler, the departure from a beloved city and country, and the beginning of a new life in America. Countless people have come into my life; many have already gone. All have played an important role and made me who I am today. The most influential is probably my daughter's father, Hans Harmsen, who died in 1989.

Thus, I'll begin writing about my life. This is for my daughter, Anna, my son-in law, Bruce, my grandchildren, Carl and Erika, and everyone who is interested.

Here it goes…

My Family Tree

Hedda Martens

Taken in 1952 in Bremen prior to boarding the ship Italia *to America*

Born February 5, 1928

My paternal great-grandparents on my father's side:

Philipp Martens
4/5/1837-1899

Jenny Marie Witt
10/21/1845-1930

I was told that my grandfather Heinrich emulated Philipp with his
hard-working, honest business practices.
Jenny was referred to as the
"Most beautiful woman of Lübeck," in her eighties
with her white hair and dark brown eyes.

My maternal great-grandparents on my father's side:
(No Photo Available)

Carl Heinrich Friedrich Blunck   *Anna Christina Egge*
3/3/1847-1929   *12/24/1844-1920*

My paternal great-grandparents on my mother's side:

Ludolf, Great Aunt Käthe, my Mom Lisa, Grandmother Elise, Sophie, Aunt Käthe

Johann Ludolf Dethlefsen   *Sophie Margarete v.d. Fecht*
11/29/1830-1907   *4/24/1844-1925*

My maternal great-grandparents on my mother's side:
(No Photo Available)

Christian Bartelt   *Carolinn Wilhelmine Streck*
3/20/1819-?   *6/4/1824-?*

My paternal grandfather, Heinrich Matthias Martens, and his siblings:

| *Jenny Anna Catharina Martens* 1/19/1865-1903 | *Else Martens* 8/8/1874-1942 | *Philipp Paul Heinrich Martens* 10/10/1867-1940 | *Heinrich Matthias Martens* 7/20/1869-1951 |

Not pictured are
Robert Martens 2/14/1876-1930
Karin Martens 8/23/1879-1954

Jenny married a Swedish merchant, Maximum Hasselquist. They had one son, Arvid Pitter, who later became my godfather. Philipp became a well-known banker in Lübeck. Two of his children left Germany in 1937 for Venezuela and unfortunately lost contact with the rest of the family. Heinrich founded an insurance company in 1900 that still bears his name today. Else married a man from Sweden and was widowed at a young age. Heinrich provided for her and her son, Arvid. Robert was an export merchant.
Karin married and moved to Berlin.

My grandparents on my father's side:

Emma Blunck   *Heinrich Martens*
3/19/1875-1937   *7/20/1869-1951*

My grandparents on my mother's side:

Rudolf Johannes   *Elise Sophie*
Daniel Bartelt   *Dethlefsen*
4/28/1859-1923   *3/27/1871-1940*

My father, Carl Philipp, and his siblings:

Carl Philipp Robert	Lisa Anna Jenny	Anna Marie
Martens	*Martens*	*Martens*
9/18/1897-1936	*4/28/1899-1990*	*8/13/1906-1986*

My mother, Lisa, and her siblings:

Käthe	Rolf Henry	Hans Christian	Lisa Marie
Bartelt	*Bartelt*	*Bartelt*	*Bartelt*
4/19/1897-1988	*8/29/1906-1986*	*3/1/1903-1986*	*10/25/1901-1994*

My Family Tree

Me and my siblings:

Hedda, Emmeli, Hinrich, Brigitte

Emmeli Käthe Martens	*Brigitte Lisa Martens*	*Hinrich Robert Martens*	*Hedda Martens*
11/25/1922-2000	*12/22/1923-2007*	*b. 4/21/1934*	*2/5/1928-2018*

My aunt, Käthe, had one child with Wilhelm Hagen:

Rudolf Hagen
6/30/1927-2006

Rudolf, Wilhelm, Käthe

Rudolf with his mother, Käthe, 1941

My uncle, Rudolf (Rolf), had two children with Annemarie Heinz:

Annemarie, Rolf, Stephan
Stephan Bartelt
b. 11/29/1941

Christian and Rolf
Christian Bartelt
b. 5/26/1947

My sister, Brigitte, had three children with Ewald Boettrich:

Christian *Hans Nikolaus* *Matthias*   *Hans, Matthias, Christian, Brigitte*
Boettrich   *Boettrich*   *Boettrich*
b. 5/25/1953 *b. 2/8/1948*   *b. 8/9/1951*

I, Hedda, had one child with Hans Harmsen:

*Anna Lisa
Martens
b. 4/24/1967*

Anna and Hedda

Anna and Hans

My brother, Hinrich, had four children with Nancy Noyes:

Philip, Polly, Nancy, Hinrich, Clark, David

*Philip Robert
Martens
b. 4/13/1960*

*Polly Joan
Martens
b. 11/28/1968*

*Clark Matthias
Martens
b. 2/15/1964*

*David Christopher
Martens
b. 1/21/1959*

Hinrich added two children when he married Maria Hayden in 1975:

Hinrich and Maria

*Susan Jean
Bell
b. 4/2/1968*

*Adam Carr
Bell
b. 4/12/1966*

My cousin, Rudolf, had three children with Elfriede Meyer (Fidele):

Konstanze, Johannes, Fidele, Katharina, Rudolf

*Konstanze Elise
Hagen
b. 1/22/1963*

*Johannes Rudolf
Hagen
b. 6/8/1970*

*Katharina Elisabeth
Hagen
b. 4/25/1961*

My cousin, Stephan, had two children with Karin (Nina) Hemmersan:

Julie, Nina, Felix, Stephan

Julie Bartelt	*Felix Bartelt*
b. 4/19/1970	*b. 7/11/1972*

My nephew, Hans, had one child with Ellen Herling:

Hans, Lisa, Ellen

Lisa Ellen
Boettrich
b. 9/17/81

My nephew, Matthias, had one child with Sara Worl:

Matthias, Lydia, Sara

Lydia Boettrich
b. 3/8/1999

My nephew, Christian, had two children with Kathie Monroe:

Stefan, Christian, Kathie, Teresa

Stefan James
Boettrich
b. 2/8/1980

Teresa Virginia
Boettrich
b. 5/13/1982

My daughter, Anna, had two children with Bruce Davidson:

Anna, Carl, Erika, Bruce

Carl Robert	*Erika Rose*
Davidson	*Davidson*
b. 3/30/1996	*b. 3/27/1998*

My nephew, David, had two children with Kathy Gabel:

Grant, Kathy, Brian, David

Grant Michael	*Brian Alexander*
Martens	*Martens*
b. 12/15/1989	*b. 2/27/1992*

My nephew, Philip, had three children with Carol O'Brien:

Philip, Christopher, Max, Amy, Carol

Christopher Robert	*Max Hinrich*	*Amy Livia*
Martens	*Martens*	*Martens*
b. 2/14/1989	*b. 6/6/1995*	*b. 4/28/1991*

My nephew, Clark, had two children with Theresa Kantowski:

Peter, Clark, Theresa, Colin

Peter Norman	*Colin Nicholas*
Martens	*Martens*
b. 7/7/1995	*b. 7/7/1995*

My niece, Polly, had two children with Tom Culver:

Hannah, Tom, Polly, Marlena

Hannah Elizabeth Culver
b. 5/25/1997

Marlena Maureen Culver
b. 9/13/2000

My step-nephew, Adam Bell, had two children with Annette Vertino:

Katie, Annette, Adam, Jennifer

Katherine Terese Bell
b. 7/27/1997

Jennifer Jane Bell
b. 2/16/2000

My step-niece, Susan Bell, had three children with Don MacDougall:

Heather, Allison, Susan, Elizabeth, Don

Heather Lynn	*Allison Jane*	*Elizabeth Anne*
MacDougall	*MacDougall*	*MacDougall*
b. 6/15/1997	*b. 4/29/2000*	*b. 4/12/2002*

**My cousin once removed, Katharina,
had two children with Wolfram Merkel:**

Vera, Wolfram, Constantine, Katharina

Vera Maria Fidele Merkel	*Constantine Jürgen Rudolf Merkel*
b. 12/16/1994	*b. 12/23/1996*

My Family Tree

My cousin once removed, Konstanze, had four children with Helmy Abouleisch:

Mariam, Helmy, Soraya, Selma, Sarah, Konstanze

Mariam	Soraya	Selma	Sarah
Abouleisch	Abouleisch	Abouleisch	Abouleisch
b. 8/30/1986	b. 1/21/1990	b. 8/16/1992	b. 2/4/1985

My cousin once removed, Johannes, had four children with Jesana Hartmann:

Jesana, Jakob, Junis, Johannes, Clara, Elias

Jakob	Junis Rudolf	Clara	Elias
Hagen	Hagen	Hagen	Hagen
b. 8/20/2009	b. 2/8/2007	b. 7/5/2002	b. 6/15/2005

My cousin once removed, Julie, had three children with Dirk Schellack:

Julie, Freddi, Dirk, Leonie, Johanna

Jan Frederick (Freddi) | *Leonie Katharina* | *Johanna Sophie*
Schellack | *Schellack* | *Schellack*
b. 2/16/2005 | *b. 4/3/2001* | *b. 6/5/1999*

My cousin once removed, Felix, had one child with Otgonbayer (Oka) Tsedendamda:

Oka, Oscar, Felix

Oscar
Bartelt
b. 11/4/2016

My grand-nephew, Stefan, had two children with Urška Roš:

Stefan, Philip, Urška, Jakob

Philip
Boettrich
b. 3/17/2017

Jakob
Boettrich
b. 6/14/2014

My grand-niece, Lisa, had one child with Philip Gerhardt:

Philip, Jane, Lisa

Jane Eleanor
Gerhardt
b. 9/20/2016

My cousin twice removed, Sarah, had two children with Thomas Fischer:

Thomas, Nuria, Sarah, Layla

Nuria
Abouleisch
b. 7/1/2013

Layla
Abouleisch
b. 6/6/2011

**My cousin twice removed, Soraya,
had two children with Maximillian Boes:**

Suhaila, Max, Soraya, Noah

Suhaila
Abouleisch
b. 1/30/2015

Noah
Abouleisch
b. 5/10/2013

My Family Tree

Germany

Travemünde
See Insert on page 149
Lübeck
Rostock
Hamburg
Berlin
Heidelberg

.... Former Border between
East and West Germany

New York State

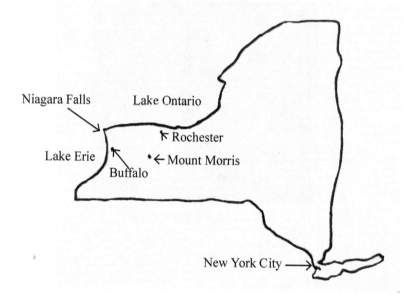

Niagara Falls
Lake Ontario
Rochester
Lake Erie
Mount Morris
Buffalo
New York City

My Grandfathers' Lives Intertwine

My Father's Father, Heinrich Martens
My Mother's Father, Rudolf Bartelt

Three prominent and relatively prosperous families residing in Lübeck would become related to one another. They were the Bartelt, Martens, and Blunck families. The construction company Blunck & Sohn was the best known firm in Lübeck. This company would be employed to build houses by each of my grandfathers.

In 1896, Rudolf Bartelt (1859-1923) hired Blunck and Sohn to build his family home on Hansestrasse. It was a magnificent building, containing fourteen spacious rooms. He was anticipating a large family. The house also had three small rooms in the attic for the household help and storage rooms for coal, wood, potatoes, plus a large room for laundry in the basement. The kitchen was also in the basement as was customary at that time. Each room had a beautiful ceramic stove which was heated with coal. It was a most labor-intensive household and by 1907, after four children (Käthe, my mother Lisa, Hans, and Rudolf) had been born, the household required three maids and one governess. Rudolf Bartelt, a captain and ship inspector, could well afford it.

On November 20, 1896, Heinrich Martens (1869-1951) married Emma Blunck (the daughter of the construction company owner). In 1903, the family of Heinrich Martens with three children, Carl Philipp, Lisa Anna, and Anna Marie, moved to an even larger and more pretentious house, also built by Blunck and Sohn. The Martens' residence was located diagonally across the street from the Bartelt house: Hansestrasse Nr. 4 and 17 respectively. Anna Marie Martens and Lisa Marie Bartelt were of the same age and became fast and best friends once school started for them. Lisa also became super close friends with her cousin Anna Marie Blunck. This friendship would last her entire lifetime. By the year 1900, Heinrich Martens had become the owner of three thriving companies: a wine dealership, an import business for dry goods, and an insurance agency. He too was well-to-do.

Hansestrasse 4: Bartelt Family Home

Hansestrasse 17:
Martens Family Home

My mother's father, Rudolf Bartelt, came from the small village of Ziegenort, located near Stettin (now Szezecin in Poland) on the Baltic Sea. His father, a sailor, left his wife, Caroline, and his two children, Rudolf and his sister Paula, in dire circumstances. While his mother worked as a seamstress, little Rudolf was hanging around the harbor, doing odd jobs for fishermen who rewarded him with some of their daily catch so that he could help to put food on the table. However, by the time he was twelve, he left home. Tall and strong for his age, he was hired as a lowly cabin boy on a larger ship with the Merchant Marine that transported cargo and passengers to and from Skandinavia and Russia. Some of his duties included attending to the captain's needs which enabled him to become familiar with the duties of a captain. He studied the maps, learned to read the compass, and the captain allowed him to assist in the bookkeeping and keeping track of the cargo and the passengers.

At age seventeen, Rudolf was sent to school. Sponsored by the shipping company, he studied ship building, engineering, navigation, and became a licensed machinist. Six years later, he went back to sea. This time he was hired as a mate. Soon after, he was encouraged to leave the sea once again to go to captain's school, which took an additional three years. His career as captain for Hapag-Lloyd, a huge shipping concern, began and he was finally in a position to ask for the hand of Elise Sophie Dethlefsen, whom he had met several years before. They moved to Lübeck into the newly built house on Hansestrasse.

Their home was filled with love and happiness. Daughters, Käthe and

Lisa, were followed by sons, Hans and Rudolf. Captain Bartelt was able to provide very well for his family. The children had a governess named Emma who was mainly responsible for making sure the children did their studies. Emma became a life-long friend to everyone in the family. Elise had many servants for all household work. In 1917, Rudolf was in Bremen when some newly christened submarines (U-boats) were launched and he allowed his son Hans to go with him on a trial run.

Lisa eventually married Carl Philipp Martens from across the street. On December 21, 1923, their first daughter, one-year-old Emmeli, was sitting on Captain Bartelt's lap when she suddenly fell to the floor. Rudolf Bartelt had suffered a fatal heart attack. Lisa, who was quite pregnant, went into labor, and Brigitte was born the following day on December 22, 1923. I am sorry that I never met my grandfather Bartelt, a most interesting and loving man.

My father's father, Heinrich Matthias Martens could have been one of the characters depicted in Thomas Mann's novel *Buddenbrooks*. He was a highly disciplined man. He regularly rose at 6:15 a.m. without requiring an alarm clock. After a cold shower and getting immaculately dressed, he sat down for a spartan breakfast: one slice of toast with butter and a cup of coffee, which his housekeeper served him at the right time. She helped him with his hat and coat. After lighting his cigar, he left his house promptly at 7:30 a.m. so that he would arrive at his office at 8:00 a.m. sharp. He returned home at 12:30 p.m. for a two-hour dinner break and resumed working at his office from 3:00 to 5:00 p.m. He watched carefully that not a single employee left the work place a minute before.

One of my grandfather's favorite phrases was: "Well, children, when I was your age, I…" Instead of reading books or, God forbid, playing, he was working. Throughout his life, he was disciplined and worked hard. He followed Bismarck's motto "Ora et labora" (pray and work), although neither was very religious. He attended the same boys' school as Thomas Mann who was six years younger. The Mann and Martens families had business dealings and my grandfather proudly related to us that he had been in the same room with the celebrated novelist on several occasions when both were children. My grandfather did not like school and left at age sixteen, when he apprenticed himself to a business in Berlin for three years and thereafter returned to Lübeck with the firm Boye & Schweighoffer until 1895. He then founded his own company dealing with a variety of goods. He imported wood and matches from Sweden; dry goods, such as raisins, from Italy; and wine from France.

After his marriage to Emma Blunck, he founded an insurance company in 1900 which still carries his name today. For many years, he operated three different import companies. The wine import company remained in operation until 1957.

Heinrich's 70th Birthday Gathering 1939
From left: Lisa (Hedda's mom), Hinrich, Lisa (Hedda's aunt),
Heinrich, Hedda, Anna (aunt), Brigitte, Emmeli

During his lifetime, his birthdays were always duly celebrated. I remember the special day when he turned seventy in 1939. His garden was beautifully decorated, his roses were, as he used to say "like a poem" (Sind meine Rosen nicht wie ein Gedicht?), and the food, especially the desserts and cakes, were wonderful. It was warm and the food was served inside. Grandfather had told us that a big surprise was waiting for us once we returned to the garden. I recall getting very anxious sitting through the endless speeches given by invited business partners, employees, and family. Every speaker included in their orations touching stories about my deceased father and grandmother. Finally, the big moment had come. What was the surprise? Five most beautiful bicycles were lined up in a row. Grandfather enjoyed giving us gifts on his special day. It was indeed a wonderful surprise. My brother Hinrich, who was five years old at the time, had already been practicing on a friend's bicycle and was very proud to show off his recently acquired mastery. My mother and sisters, Emmeli and Brigitte, and I were all grateful that we were now able to give our old hand-me-downs away.

Hinrich, Hedda, Brigitte, Emmeli, Mutter
with new Bicycles!

His 80th birthday in 1949 was very different indeed. A tired old man was sitting on the front porch of his stately home. The porch was decorated with beautiful flowers, and a small group of musicians came by to serenade him. Only his immediate family had come for a visit. There were his two daughters; his sister-in-law, Anna Wolff; and my mother, sisters, and brother; as well as Brigitte's eighteen-month-old son, Hans. My grandfather delighted in the fact that he now had a great-grandchild, and he was beaming when little Hans fearlessly ran up the stairs and greeted him.

Heinrich Matthias Martens 80 Jahre alt

Seinen 80. Geburtstag kann am morgigen Mittwoch der Seniorteilhaber der Firma Martens & Prahl, Heinrich Matthias Martens, feiern. Der Jubilar wurde als Sohn eines Lübecker Kaufmanns geboren und gründete 1900 die Kolonialwaren- und Versicherungsagentur Heinrich Martens. Die Versicherungsabteilung dieser Firma wurde später herausgelöst und an das Versicherungskontor Martens & Prahl angegliedert.   In.

Heinrich 80th year birthday notice in paper:
His 80th birthday was celebrated on Wednesday morning with senior members of the firm Martens & Prahl. The son of a Lübecker businessman, Heinrich founded the insurance company in 1900.

Hans with Heinrich, 80th Birthday

In the summer of 1945, when housing was desperately needed for the many refugees from the east, government quartermasters ordered that my grandfather remodel the downstairs by giving up his bedroom, his dining room, and dividing one of his two large rooms to the front to make an extra little bedroom for himself, while leaving the larger part to a couple. The housekeeper's room in the back was permitted. The large backyard had lost two beautiful shade trees. They had been cut down to use as firewood in order to keep the rooms heated. The beautiful upstairs rooms (where my sisters, Emmeli and Brigitte, were born) had already been transformed into an apartment after my grandmother's death in 1937.

13 Friedrich Wilhelm Straße
My Grandfather bought this house on December 12, 1917.
My mother and father lived there as newlyweds until 1924
when they moved to Hansestraße 4 and I lived there with my family
for six months following the bombing of our house in 1942.

By 1947, the western occupation zones were coordinating their policies, especially concerning economics. In 1948, the split between the Western Allies and the USSR had become complete, and when the Western Allies planned to take steps toward a West German constitution, the Soviet authorities unsuccessfully blockaded West Berlin (1948/49) as part of the Cold War. For all practical purposes, Germany had been divided into two states by 1949: The Federal Republic of Germany (West), which included the American, French, and British Zones; and the German Democratic Republic "DDR" (The Russian Zone). Berlin remained divided into East and West. The Nuremberg Trials had been held and Rudolf Hess, Hitler's one-time deputy, had been given a life sentence which he was to serve in Spandau, a huge prison in Berlin. (After a while, Hess was the only prisoner there, guarded by Russian, British, American, and French soldiers. Ironically, this prison was the only place where the Western Allies communicated peacefully with the Soviets.) My grandfather's place of business had been destroyed during the bombing raid in 1942. Heinrich had been able to find new quarters and in 1948 appointed my uncle, Rolf Bartelt, director of the firm so Heinrich could enter into semi-retirement.

Heinrich's parents were Philipp Martens, a businessman, and Jenny Maria Witt, who was Swedish. They had six children: Jenny Anna, Philipp, Heinrich Matthias, Else, Robert, and Karin. My grandfather, Heinrich, was very proud of his son, Carl-Philipp, who joined him in the insurance company. He also was very fond of his four grandchildren, Emmeli, Brigitte, Hedda, and Hinrich, as well as his daughter-in-law, Lisa Marie. He never recovered from his son's untimely death in 1936, but continued to support my mother with her four small children. His two daughters, Lisa Anna Jenny and Anna Marie ("Ama") did not have happy lives. Although both were attractive and equipped with a good dowry, they did not get married. Both were about to become engaged when my grandfather did not find their respective suitors good enough. The two daughters became nurses, a frequently chosen profession at that time for women who were not married by the time they were twenty-seven years old.

After my father's death, my grandfather searched for new partners. H.C. Koch owned a profitable wine dealership and invested in the Martens firm to attain partnership. However, he proved to be highly dishonest and was imprisoned. This was a heavy blow for my grandfather. He then selected Walter Prahl as partner and the firm was renamed "Martens & Prahl" which still exists today. Mr. Prahl, however, died in 1938 of tuberculosis. He left twin sons, "Plisch and Plum," who were twenty years old when they were reported missing during the Russian offensive in WWII. Their mother, Hedwig, hoped in vain that her sons might return, but that never happened.

My grandfather was a Freemason. Members of the Masonic Lodge believed in a Supreme Being; however, their anticlerical attitude caused strong opposition from the Roman Catholic Church. Their principles were traditionally liberal and democratic. They engaged in secretive, elaborate, symbolic rites and ceremonies, using instruments of the stonemason, such as a plumb, square, level, and compasses, while "building" King Solomon's Temple for allegorical purposes. Lacking a central Masonic authority, the jurisdiction was divided among autonomous national authorities, called Grand Lodges. Well-known members were Benjamin Franklin, John Hancock, Paul

Revere, George Washington, Voltaire, Goethe, Schiller, Haydn, and Mozart, whose opera *The Magic Flute* is an allegorical story, riddled with Masonic symbolism. Freemasonry was officially banned and forcibly eradicated by the Fascists and Nazi regime. My grandfather continued to meet regularly on Sunday mornings over a glass of beer with his friends. Their regular reserved table (Stammtisch) was always decorated with a small swastika flag to avoid arousing suspicion. We did not learn about his membership in the Freemasons until we attended his funeral, when three of his friends came forward and laid three yellow roses, forming the shape of a pyramid, on top of the coffin. These men told us about the forbidden lodge.

My grandfather did fly the swastika flag at his home when required. However, in his belongings, he had a printed notice that said, "Wir nie gehören dem Führer!" (We will never belong to the leader.)

*Heinrich's House Flies the
Swastika Flag*

My grandfather died on June 23, 1951, two days after suffering a stroke. Heinrich Martens was a highly respected, honest businessman, and a dear grandfather.

My Grandmother, Emma (Blunck) Martens

Emma Blunck

Emma's parents were Carl Heinrich Blunck (1847-1929) and Anna Christina Egge (1844-1920). They had six children: Ernst, Erich, Richard, Emma and her twin sister Louise, and Anna. Together with his son, Ernst, Carl Blunck (a well-known architect) founded the soon-to-be very prosperous construction firm, Blunck & Sohn. While her brothers, Erich and Richard, pursued careers in architecture, Emma and her sisters, as was customary at that time, stayed at home, doing needlework and essentially working on their dowries by monogramming bed linens, towels, napkins; learning to cook; and, of course, learning to run a household. In time, the three girls were married off. Louise's husband was a pharmacist, Anna's a surgeon, and Emma married a businessman, Heinrich Martens.

I have fond memories of Louise's ("Lite's") husband, Dr. Emil Stülcken. He owned a pharmacy in Lübeck, and had earned the reputation for concocting the best cough syrup anywhere, as well as drugs that were more potent against all kinds of pain. After the death of my father, he took my mother under his wings, maintaining a most caring correspondence long after her emigration to the United States. While visiting Lübeck in 1966, I called to ask whether I could visit with him. He was delighted and I was invited to come at 11:30 the next day. His daughter-in-law led me to his room, located behind the pharmacy. It was a spacious room, which now served as both bedroom and living quarters. There was his bed, his upright piano, several comfortable lounge chairs, and a very big writing desk. Onkel Emil was seated by his desk on an old wooden chair. However, as I entered, he got up to give me a welcoming hug. He was ninety-nine years old. On a separate table I saw several packs of cigarettes, all different brands. "Everybody in America smokes, I think. But I did not know which kind you prefer, so I got a selection from across the street." I was touched by his thoughtfulness, but I did not smoke at that time. "Why do you have several dictionaries on your desk?" I asked. I am still in awe of his response, "Well, I begin each day with reading a page in Greek as well as one in Latin. And then, you know that one of my sons moved to Australia, and I have to correspond with my grandchildren in English. Therefore, I am learning English." His wish that he would not live to be a hundred and endure noisy festivities was granted. This remarkable man died three months before that date. Oh, I forgot to mention that his piano playing was curtailed to just one hour a day, due to arthritis.

When Heinrich Martens came to court Emma, her father was not that enthused and wondered whether this young man could provide the lifestyle to which his daughter was accustomed. His engagement present, an attractive golden brooch with a diamond, was actually not good enough. However, they got married in 1896. They moved into a large house, built by Emma's father which, oddly enough, was situated diagonally across the street from the Bartelt house. Emma and Heinrich had three children: Carl Philipp Robert, Lisa Anna Jenny, and Anna Marie. Carl Philipp would become my father. His sisters had no children.

Emma's Engagement Brooch

Sadly, I did not see my grandmother often. She suffered from severe depressions and was often away in a sanatorium enduring what must have been painful shock treatments. She was unable to provide a happy childhood for her children who were cared for by housekeepers. It was not a happy home. Her daughter, Anna Marie, spent much of her time across the street with her best friend and playmate, Lisa Bartelt (my mother). My grandfather's business proved to be most successful and in 1917 he bought a new house in a beautiful residential district. Living in this upscale neighborhood brought prestige but not happiness. She once told my mother that the best day in her life was when she got the news that her son, Carl Philipp, was safe as a prisoner of war in England. However, my grandmother was unable to recover from her son's untimely death in September 1936.

Lisa Bartelt and Anna Marie Martens and Annemarie Blunck were classmates and good friends and eventually would all become related by marriage!

Reminiscing about the life of my Oma Martens makes me sad. She must have led a very lonely life, struggling with a disease over which she had no control. No medical intervention appears to have helped her. There are some family photographs including her, but I do not remember her from those gatherings. I do not recall ever sitting on her lap or getting a hug on the rare occasions that we met.

I found her diary with just a few notations, "Went to hear Rheingold with Carl Philipp. Asked our cook to prepare veal for dinner. Finished another placemat—intricate lace work. Carl Philipp and I…"

My Grandmother, Emma (Blunck) Martens

There are photos showing her on a winter vacation in the Harz Mountains. It was in 1934 when my grandparents took my sister Emmeli to learn to ski. Emmeli did not feel like talking about that trip when I asked her about it while looking at the photo. It must have been a difficult experience for my then twelve-year-old sister.

Emma and Heinrich

Emmeli with Heinrich, 1936

In March 1937 my grandfather, who was also grief stricken over their son's death, was advised to take a cruise with his wife. The two of them boarded a boat in Genoa, Italy, for a sea voyage around Sicily. Oma Martens died aboard ship on March 15, 1937.

Like my father, Oma Martens died two days before her birthday. For many years thereafter, I was always glad when the two days before my birthday passed and I was still alive and well.

I still have two small pieces of Oma's lace work, as well as the brooch with the "rather small diamond" that she received as an engagement present from my grandfather.

My Grandmother, Elise Sophie Bartelt

"Children, do not quarrel, you will both get a turn," our Oma Bartelt said from her hospital bed. It was in early June of 1940 when my cousin Rudolf and I visited her after school as we had been doing quite regularly for the past month. Our grandmother was suffering from diabetes. She had undergone several operations. It had begun with the amputation of her toe, soon after her foot, and finally her entire leg. Now it seemed that she would recover and the nurses had brought a wheelchair into her room, inviting us to take our Oma for a ride. What was the point of contention between Rudolf and me? We argued over which one of us would take the first turn pushing her along the hospital corridor. It seems surreal, even if one takes into consideration that we were only thirteen and twelve years old respectively. My grandmother was rather heavyset and it took two nurses to lift her out of her bed onto the wheelchair. Oma had decided that both of us would hold on to her chair.

For some time Oma had endured a lot of pain in her foot, unable to wear regular shoes. She got around on comfortable slippers. Once a week, Oma wanted to go to the nearby movie theater. Rudolf and I had the job of helping her to get to the "Puschen-Kino" (Slipper cinema). It took us half an hour to manage the trip. In reality it was a ten-minute walk. Once we arrived at the theater, we were allowed to take our grandmother to her seat. However, we then had to leave because the films were always "verboten" for youths under age fourteen. So Rudolf and I went home only to return ninety minutes later to retrieve our grandmother. I remember feeling very proud and important.

Further complications prevented Oma's recovery and my grandmother died on August 2, 1940. (When our house, actually it was my grandmother's house, was destroyed in March 1942, I overheard my mother saying, "It is good that Mutter did not live to see this destruction.") On that day, Rudolf and I promised one another never to argue again. We never did.

As best as I can, I will now write about the life of our wonderful grandmother. Elise Sophie Dethlefsen was born on March 27, 1871, in Krempe, a small town located near the mouth of the river Elbe near the North Sea. Her father, Johann Ludwig Dethlefsen (1830-1907) was a very well-to-do merchant. He had married Elise Lucia Boyens (1833-1865) with whom he had seven children: Andrea, Claudine, Andreas, Carl, twins Knud and Ludolph, and Ernst. Their mother died after giving birth to Ernst in 1865. In 1868, Johann Ludolf married Sophie Margarete von der Fecht (1844-1925). Five more children were born: Elise Sophie (1871-1940), Hans (1872-1874), Emilie (1878-1958), Marie (1877-1948), and Käthe (1881-1929).

Clockwise: Marie, Elise, Emilie, Käthe with their mother, Sophie Marie von der Fecht Bartelt

Emilie married a Catholic! He was a physician. They moved far away to a small town near Cologne, in the Rhineland, where everybody was Catholic. My grandmother used to say that Emilie's husband was inconsiderate by constantly impregnating his wife. They had eight children but only six survived. Käthe's husband was said to be disagreeable and did not enjoy family affairs as a consequence. Marie became an elementary school teacher. She was a much loved great aunt and visited us often. Marie taught in Trittau, a village located between Lübeck and Hamburg.

Elise Sophie married Rudolf Bartelt, a captain with a large shipping concern, in 1895. They moved to Lübeck and the construction company Blunck & Sohn designed and built a most beautiful house in the Hansestrasse. It was located near the railroad station, since the captain traveled frequently to Hamburg when boarding a ship and, in later years, as a ship inspector. The Bartelts were well off and could easily afford this big house, which was a lot to take care of and required two live-in maids.

As I have mentioned, my grandmother was born in 1871, a year that brought about enormous changes to what we now know as Germany. The "Iron Chancellor," Otto von Bismarck, who had been appointed premier by King Wilhelm I, managed to put an end to the German Federation of many duchies and principalities. The Austro-Prussian War left Austria defeated which was followed by Austria's expulsion from the North German Federation and the loss of Austria's right to rule over the duchies, Schleswig and Holstein. After the Franco-Prussian War (1870-1871) which resulted in the defeat of Napoleon III, Wilhelm I was declared Emperor of a United Germany in 1871. His reign would constitute the "Second Empire" which lasted until 1918 with the end of WWI and the abdication of Emperor Wilhelm II. (The "First Empire," also known as the "Holy Roman Empire," was founded in the year 800 by Carlus Magnus [Charlemagne] and lasted until 1648 with the conclusion of the Thirty-Year-War.) The "Third Empire" began in 1933 with Adolf Hitler, who proclaimed that it would last a thousand years. Fortunately, this was not the case. It ended in 1945, after twelve most difficult years.

My grandmother enjoyed a happy marriage and family life. They had four children: Käthe (1897), Lisa Marie (1901), Hans Ludolf Christian (1903), and Rudolf Henry (1906). At that time a nanny, called Emma, was added to the staff. Captain Rudolf Bartelt was able to provide very well for his family. In the early years, he was often gone on extensive voyages overseas but later, once he was promoted to inspector, he just commuted to Hamburg daily. The comfortable life for the Bartelt family changed drastically in December 1923 when Rudolf Bartelt suffered a fatal heart attack.

Rudolf's pension was modest and after time the upkeep of the house became too much of a financial burden for my grandmother. My parents moved in with their two daughters in 1925 and I was born in 1928. Finally, the grand house was converted into three apartments. The first floor was rented to a semi-retired army officer with his disagreeable wife and obnoxious daughter, Christa. The second floor was made into two apartments. Ours included four spacious rooms as well as two small ones, a kitchen and bath, and a wonderful large balcony out front. My grandmother's apartment with two large rooms and kitchen and bath was also very bright and nice. For Käthe and her son Rudolf, an extra room was built in the large attic. We had a full-time, live-in maid and our Oma had a cleaning lady who came three times a week. Her name was Hertha Pultke and she married a Mr. Basuhn. They named their son Udo and he came to work with his mother.

Käthe, my mother (Lisa Marie) told us, was utterly spoiled, and seemed to hold a grudge that she did not receive a middle name. At sixteen, she was enrolled in an exclusive boarding school in Switzerland which offered, among other things, French and cooking lessons. She returned to Lübeck when WWI began. She was very beautiful, had several suitors, but nothing and nobody was good enough for her. She enjoyed piano lessons, was good at crafts, and waited for the right man to marry. Regrettably, her marriage in 1926 to a Dr. Wilhelm Hagen lasted less than two years. Käthe, who had given birth to her son, Rudolf, was forced to move back to live with her mother. Rudolf was cared for by our grandmother while Käthe had to earn a living as a secretary. Her husband disappeared from their lives. Käthe's "I am better than thou" attitude proved to be detrimental in her vain search for happiness and a satisfied mind set. In later life, Käthe still could not find true happiness despite the fact that her son, who was devoted to her and was most successful in his career, was married to a wonderful woman, Fidele, who gave her three lovely grandchildren.

My mother, Lisa, did not have it easy becoming widowed with four young children, but she always had a bright disposition and I will write more about her.

Our Onkel Hans would study medicine and, after extremely trying times during WWII, would make his way to America and become the guiding force that would eventually bring his sister Lisa and her four children and grandchildren to start a new life in the United States. I will write more about him in another chapter.

Onkel Rolf had envisioned a career as a university professor. However, he was taken out of school at age seventeen. He needed to earn money to support his mother and his sister Käthe as well as his brother Hans who had to complete his medical studies. His sister Lisa had already married Carl Philipp Martens. Rolf was apprenticed at a Swiss coffee firm. My grandfather, Heinrich Martens, asked Rolf to join his company in Lübeck when he realized that Walter Prahl was not able to be a contributing partner. (I overheard my grandfather say, "Er ist ein Sandmann, aber er kann ja nichts dafür." He is not very capable, but he can't do anything about it.) Prahl's name was kept since his wife contributed more money. Rolf proved to be an ingenious businessman. He was highly approved by Heinrich Martens and soon assumed co-ownership of the company. Rolf married Annemarie. Their sons Stephan and Christian both worked for the company and now Stephan's daughter Julie is a partner of the company.

It was wonderful to have our grandmother so close by. The best thing was that she was always home and there for us. Her cookie jar was always filled with the best homemade baked goods. She knitted sweaters, cardigans, socks, and hats for all of us; told us fascinating stories of our seafaring grandfather whom we did not know; and, whenever we were sick, Oma would sit by our bed with her knitting. To make sure that she would come back soon when she wanted to leave for her apartment, we asked her to leave her knitting. Little did we know that Oma always had two different knitting projects going.

My brother and I remember walking to the local tavern in the Hotel Drei Ringen just three houses away. I was about ten years old and Hinni was just five. Oma gave us a glass mug and enough money (about 50 cents) to have it filled with beer to go with her dinner. Oma even let Hinni have some of the foam from the mug when we got back. Can you imagine that happening today?

Once a month, Oma's "Kränzchen" (circle of friends) came to her place for an afternoon of socializing and, of course, wonderful cake and coffee. This group consisted of widows, all former captains' wives. Rudolf and I were allowed to participate, provided we were very quiet. I loved listening to the stories. There was Frau Thoms, whose unfortunate son had been imprisoned after having printed his own money, and Frau Lübke, whose sons had gone to America. They had invited her to stay with them but she had returned after some months, unable to cope with the language. Her verdict was that America was "too noisy for comfort." Frau Behrendt, the only one who did not knit or do any needlework, was hard of hearing and, as a consequence, spoke in a very loud voice. She often did not get the whole conversation and made the wrong comment. Oma looked at us children sternly when we laughed.

Oma was fluent in the North German dialect, "Platt-deutsch." "Platt" means "flat." And North Germany is a low-lying country indeed (just like the Netherlands, "nether" meaning "low.") This ability endeared her to Mr. Schroeder, who came twice weekly with wonderfully smelling fresh bread. The milkman and other service people always stayed a while to chat with my grandmother. One visitor, Miss Schumacher, however, conversed only in the most refined German. She appeared every other week to get some food. At one time, she had been in charge of supervising the children's homework, especially for French and English. Now she was impoverished, unkempt, and unwashed. It was the first time that I ever saw a truly hungry person eat, licking all fingers between bites. Rudolf and I helped to get the things from the kitchen that our Oma had prepared for her to take home. After each such visit, my grandmother's living room had to be aired out.

Elise with sisters Emilie, Marie

My grandmother, Elise Sophie, was the warmest, kindest, and most loving woman.

My Mother's Life, Marriage, and Children

"Don't you think that you should get Karin and Peter out of their pajamas? Surely, they want to get dressed, go outside, and play!" my mother would frequently admonish me. Karin and Peter were my dolls that I had received for Christmas. They wore the same red-and-white checkered pajamas that Mutter had also made for me. I dutifully changed their clothes (which were also made by my mother), sat them down on the floor, and then went on to other projects. Unlike my mother, I was not fond of dolls. My sister, Brigitte, loved dolls and had my mother's old dolls as well as Emmeli's two in her collection. There was also Bob, a handsome negro doll, who sat well protected in a cabinet behind glass. Bob was not to be played with. My mother's father, Captain Rudolf Bartelt, had brought this precious doll from one of his trips to Africa. He was special and most loved. Only his ceramic head survived the war. My mother brought it to America with her and kept it safe in a glass cabinet.

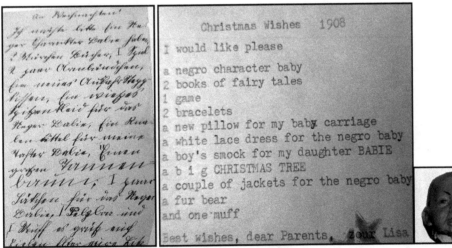

Christmas Wishes   1908

I would like please

a negro character baby
2 books of fairy tales
1 game
2 bracelets
a new pillow for my baby carriage
a white lace dress for the negro baby
a boy's smock for my daughter BABIE
a b i g CHRISTMAS TREE
a couple of jackets for the negro baby
a fur bear
and one muff

Best wishes, dear Parents, your Lisa

Lisa's Christmas Wish List, Age 7, 1908   *Bob*

Mutter often told us stories about her very happy childhood in their spacious home that was filled with love. She enjoyed a privileged time with her constant playmate, Annemarie Martens, from across the street. She would become her sister-in-law. There were tea parties with other children (and their dolls!); spending the summers at the seaside resort, Travemünde; playing with her two younger brothers; ice skating on the river Wakenitz; hiking to the surrounding woods; and the four wonderful years at the private school of Amelie Roquette who taught them French and etiquette. Emma Hagedorn, the "best story-teller ever," was added to the household as a governess. She became my mother's life-long friend.

Lisa and Hans Ice Skating

Ice Skating on the Trave

At age ten, Mutter transferred to a secondary school, a private school for equally privileged girls. Twenty-six young women stayed together for seven years. Some became related to one another but all remained in contact, especially the close friends. Mutter loved poetry, especially those poets whose lyric verses emphasized a highly personal expression of love for home and nature. To mention a few of her favorites: Immanuel Geibel, whose fame did not reach much beyond Lübeck; Joseph von Eichendorff (1788-1857) whose poems were set to music by Schumann, Mendelssohn, Brahms and others; Heinrich Heine (1797-1856) whose poetry inspired Schubert to wonderful melodies; and Friedrich von Schiller whose "An die Freude" ("Ode to Joy") prompted Beethoven to incorporate the memorable text in his Ninth Symphony. Mutter also became an avid reader of short stories (Guy de Maupassant in particular) and novels by Charles Dickens and Leo Tolstoy in translation and, of course, Lübeck's very own Thomas Mann.

Lisa and her siblings on the beach 1912.
Lisa did not want to wash her hand of the sand since she
had been kissed by the Crown Prince

In 1892, sailors from Lübeck, Hamburg, and Kiel established "die Travemünder Woche," involving many regattas and other festive events. Held at the end of July, sailors came from all over to compete in the many races. This event belonged to one of my mother's most favorite childhood memories. In 1912, when she was eleven, the Crown Prince had come to oversee the celebration. Being the daughter of a captain in the Merchant Marine, Lisa was fortunate enough to stand on the bridge onto which the Imperial Family was to embark. She curtsied and the Crown Prince kissed her hand. What an unbelievably fantastic experience! My mother related the story often, embellishing various scenes. Sometimes, the Crown Prince became the kaiser himself.

She was thirteen when the Great War began and learned with dismay that her beloved imperial family was despised by the world. She and her girlfriend, Annemarie, said goodbye to her friend's brother and worried with his family about his welfare. At the end of the war, she and her friend, Erna Heddinga, began working as nurses in a veterans' hospital. Both girls were debating about going back to school for two more years of Science and Latin to make them eligible to enter the university to study medicine. They needed to attend a boys' Gymnasium since these subjects were not offered at a girls' school. Erna went through with this plan. However, Mutter went to the railroad station with the Martens family to welcome home Carl Philipp Robert as he was returning from POW camp in England. She knew then that she was going to marry him. For that reason, she abandoned her plans to study medicine. The Martens family no longer lived across the street. They were a fifteen-minute bike ride away. Since no proper girl could ride alone, she persuaded one of her brothers to go along for the visits. Soon, Carl Philipp began calling on her parents and asked permission for their daughter's hand.

Lisa and Carl Philipp

CARL PHILIPP   LISA MARIE

Lisa Bartelt
Carl Philipp Martens

Derlobte.

Lisa wrote the following poem in 1920 in German for Carl Philipp as an engagement present. I translated it to English in 2016.

An Autumn Picture by Lisa Martens

Oh, how they need peace, the old yet proud trees after the long
stormy days and nights!
They are still standing together, frightened and trembling,
And a sad shudder goes through their stems and branches
Until their children, the golden leaves, feel it and move softly.

So, the mighty fall storm did come after all;
The one who causes their death every year.
Just a few days ago they were still wearing their full and sparkling
dress of late summer.
They had been happy and content.
All branches and all leaves turned toward the sun and were
mumbling,
"Do not move! Do look at the sun just once more!
Listen to the birds singing just once more!
You will have to die soon!"

Hearing that, they became very quiet and watched sadly as one after
another of their siblings
Broke off with a small haunting cry and flew trembling towards the
ground.
Its short life had come to an end.

This is a fall day as I have never seen before.
The air is quiet as if no one was breathing
And yet the most beautiful fruits fall off from every tree.
Oh, do not disturb nature's celebration.
Today is nature's own harvest.
Only the leaves that are ready and touched by the mild sun's rays
come loose and fall.

And then!?
Then comes the storm that inconsiderately interrupted the trees'
farewell party.
The storm bent the trees so that they moaned and groaned.

My Mother's Life, Marriage, and Children

The storm attacked the branches with a whistling wind
So that masses of golden leaves rained down to the ground.

But the tall trees stubbornly defended themselves.
They called to their children, "Stay strong and stay with us!"
Many heard their calls and attempted to cling to the branches
That had held them throughout the spring and summer.

When the storm realized that he was not yet victorious over the
proud leaves,
He continued to blow even harder and howled,
"Auf Wiedersehen! (Goodbye)"

Now the trees have become silent.
They are exhausted and enjoy the peace.
They know that they must die when the storm returns.
But a deep stillness has moved into their soul.
They are still able to smile in their time of loss.
With a final farewell, they stretch their limbs
And release their last beautiful children into the blue sky
Which empathizes with the trees as it envelopes their leaves.

Oh, you put on a most wonderful show
When you make the sky a sparkling heavenly blue
Out of the strong and bold red and golden colors
You remind us of a blue sea
Where happiness has dropped its anchor
So that it may rest in peace.
The last drop of earthly anguish
Will fall from its rudder.

Marriage customs are different in Germany. When a couple gets engaged, the groom buys two golden rings: one for himself and the other for his bride. They both celebrate their engagement by wearing their respective rings on the left hand. When they get married, the ring is moved to the right hand. My father also bought this lovely figurine as a special present. (It is marked Rosenthal which indicates it was made by a very famous porcelain factory.) A lovely party was held in May 1920 to celebrate the engagement of Lisa Marie Bartelt to Carl Philipp Robert Martens.

Engagement Figurine

Instead of pursuing his dream of studying architecture, Carl Philip joined his father's business to enable him to support his future wife. He had to work long hours, allowing just Sundays for leisure time and getting together with his fiancée. Lisa did not like being engaged. Instead of continuing the carefree times she used to enjoy with her friends, she had to monogram her linens and towels, learn to cook (or at least acquire some knowledge about appropriate menus), and how to become an efficient housewife. She looked forward to Sundays. However, her walks with Carl Philipp were always properly chaperoned. She liked it least when her future sisters-in-law came along on these outings since they always stayed within earshot and took over the conversation when they stopped for coffee and cake. Her favorite chaperones were her brothers, who remained at the first bench in the park and began reading their schoolbooks. And when the couple stopped in a café, they elected to find seats as far away as possible. She was certain that she would be a good wife and mother. But waiting seemed very hard.

Finally, the day of the wedding came. It was January 14, 1922, a very cold day. The ceremony took place in the cavernous St. Petri church which was not heated. All invited guests wore winter coats, leaving just her father, who led her down the aisle, the bridal couple, and the pastor in festive garments. Carl Philipp made Lisa laugh during the serious ceremony, when he whispered into her ear, "I wonder how many layers of warm clothing the pastor is wearing underneath." There were no bride's maids or groom's men. A ring bearer was also not necessary since the groom removes the golden band from the bride's left hand (a symbol signifying that the girl is engaged) and places it on the right ring finger. Horse-drawn carriages with heated blankets took the guests to Lübeck's most famous restaurant, the Schiffergesellschaft, which is still renowned today. A "wedding photographer" did not exist at that time. Apart from the marriage certificate, just an attractively designed menu card bears witness to this special event. By all accounts, it was a lovely wedding and a most happy occasion. Mutter remembered that she wore a long-sleeved satin gown and that Carl Philipp looked great in his black tuxedo. While the couple was away on their honeymoon, which they spent in their beloved Travemünde, the Martens family prepared the lovely three-room apartment in her father-in-law's house. It was located on the second floor, had a large balcony and, of course, a kitchen and bath. The furniture, curtains, and pictures had been selected by her mother. It was all beautiful.

Yet, Lisa was homesick. Her husband left for work at 7:30 a.m. after a short breakfast, and Lisa was done with her "housework" within an hour. There was no need to prepare dinner since her father-in-law's housekeeper took care of that. Dinner was served downstairs at 1:30 p.m. sharp together with her two sisters-in-law and at times, also her mother-in-law, who was often indisposed or in a sanatorium. These meals were not happy affairs. The two men were talking about business and a maid brought the food and cleared the table without as much as a word. The only bright moment was when the young couple went to their apartment for a little less than an hour before it was time to go back to work. For the remainder of the day, Lisa persuaded her sister-in-law and former playmate, Annemarie, to visit her parents' house to enjoy warmth, laughter, and genuine happiness. Saturday afternoons the young couple went biking or hiking and in the evening they would enjoy a concert, opera, or a show.

Annemarie loved their visits to the Bartelt house which had become routine. Lisa missed her parents, her sister and brothers, Emma (the governess), the dachshund (Juppi), and her irretrievable childhood.

Things changed dramatically when the midwife informed her that she was pregnant. Both Carl Philipp and Lisa were blissfully happy. The future father began designing a crib, as well as a chest and a table to use for diapering and dressing the baby. All three pieces turned out to be beautiful. After the woodworking was finished, he painted them white. Much to his father's dismay, Carl Philipp did all projects upstairs, either in one of the rooms or on the balcony, while Lisa was knitting booties, hats, jackets, etc. This way they could admire each other's handiwork. Lisa continued to visit her mother at least twice a week and got more directions on intricate knitting patterns, baby care, and mothering.

Emmeli was born on November 25, 1922. Lisa's friend, Liesel Siem,

Lisa with baby Emmeli

was still in training to become a midwife, so she assisted with the birth, which took place at home. The new father thought that his daughter was the most beautiful ever (although the baby's head was a bit out of shape due to the delivery by forceps) and grandfather Martens was said to suppress his disappointment since Emmeli was not a boy. Time and weather permitting, the young couple made frequent trips to the Bartelt house, with the proud father pushing the carriage. He was a "hands-on" father, helping with bathing, diapering, feeding, and playing. It was a happy time. They were expecting again and Carl Philipp began building a little bed for Emmeli, so that she would become used to her new bed by Christmas 1923, the anticipated arrival of baby number two.

*Emmeli and Brigitte
as Toddlers*

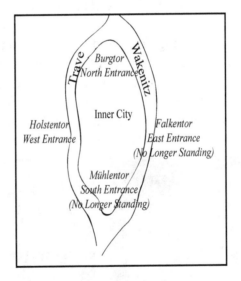

Sketch of Lubeck

On December 12, 1923, the little family walked once again to the Bartelt house. It was cold and the sidewalks had become slippery. They decided that it would be their last visit before Christmas. Once again, Lisa's parents greeted them with open arms and grandfather Rudolf Bartelt took little Emmeli on his lap, allowing her to play with his gold pocket watch. Suddenly, Emmeli fell to the floor. Her grandfather had suffered a stroke and was dead.

A second daughter, Brigitte, was born on December 22, 1923. Liesel Siem was the midwife and Emmchen Benöhr came to take care of the mother and baby for two weeks. Grandfather Martens again swallowed his disappointment. No male heir! However, the young parents were proud, happy, and most content. My sisters Emmeli and Brigitte were born in my grandfather's house, Friedrich Wilhelm Strasse 13. Carl Philipp and Lisa occupied the second floor apartment with the beautiful balcony. However, after my grandfather, Rudolf Bartelt, died suddenly, my grandmother, Elise, needed financial assistance for the upkeep of the large house. For that reason, the little family of Carl Philipp, Lisa, Emmeli, and Brigitte moved to Lisa's family home, Hansestrasse 4. My grandfather's house was located outside the Mühlentor, the entrance gate castle on the south side of the inner city; our house was outside the Holstentor, the castle gate entrance to the west. The house was certainly big enough. Lisa's brothers had left: older brother, Hans, to study medicine in Heidelberg and younger brother, Rolf, was learning to be a businessman in a firm in Zürich, Switzerland. Lisa's oldest sister, Käthe, was still at home, waiting for a suitable husband.

A third daughter, Hedda, was born on February 5, 1928. I am told that the fifth day of February, 1928, was one of the coldest on record. The window panes were frozen over and my father scraped them so that my mother could see a little of the blue sky through them. I was born at 5:00 a.m. with the assistance of Emmchen Benöhr, the midwife. Emmchen was a much sought-after midwife in Lübeck. Reservations had to be made months

Emmchen with Hedda

White Crib Bedding

in advance of the actual due date. Emmchen, called "Tante Emmchen" by the children, stayed for four weeks helping the mother with the children and of course the baby. She came two weeks before the due date. My own room had been prepared for my birth. It was the belief that a baby required total peace, therefore everything was white! Not a spot of color to excite the baby. My parent's bedroom was large so a white divider was placed between them and my "private" room.

Brigitte, Carl Philipp, Emmeli, Lisa, Hedda, 1928

Brigitte, Hedda, Emmeli, 1930

My Mother's Life, Marriage, and Children

The delivery was uneventful and Dr. Grünewald did not need to be called. My father was thrilled that there was yet another girl and called his father, Heinrich Martens, to report the great news. My grandfather was not thrilled. He had hoped for an heir to the family name. He voiced his disappointment in no uncertain terms. I think this rejection prompted my father to make me his most favorite little girl.

I was a ten-pound healthy baby at birth, but became severely jaundiced for a month. However, my first few years of life were happy. I was an easy baby, happy and healthy, reaching the milestones of walking and speaking at the appropriate times. My mother claimed I was the smartest of her children because I was the earliest to be toilet trained. Unfortunately, Emmeli and Brigitte brought germs home from school and I became very sick with diphtheria, whooping cough, and pneumonia as a baby. My father carried me many nights so that I could get a breath. Once recovered, I had to relearn how to walk at age three. I do remember when my father sang to me and also when he told me many wonderful stories before he tucked me into bed in a very special way.

I think I was about five years old when this mysterious large silver ball called the moon provided enough light for me to see my father while he told me wonderful stories.

"Mr. Moon assembled his children and taught them how to polish their white metal coats. Sometimes he required all of them so that the children on earth could see the magnificent silver ball. At other times he needed only a few workers." According to my father, Mr. Moon was a very kind man who always expressed his wishes in a quiet endearing manner. My father had given names to some of the stars so that he could admonish some of the culprits by name. My father described some very eager ones who were in need of special praise. He also talked about those who were trying to do less work but hoping to get away with it. He never forgot to encourage Henry and Peter who had trouble keeping up with the others. My father never ran out of individualized stories about specific stars.I was able to read by the time my father was too sick to tell me stories and he was finally hospitalized, but I really missed my father's voice and his stories.

While the content of the preceding paragraphs is primarily based on stories that were related to me, I will begin with the year of 1934 and rely on my own memory. I had started school early in spring of that year, immediately after Easter at the end of March. Emmeli had taught me to read, which was frowned upon by Frau Hempel, our teacher. (Only teachers can do it the correct way.) However, Frau Hempel followed the directions of the just year-old educational system, and I learned quickly about our Führer, Adolf Hitler. I thought Hitler was great. We were taught immediately how great he was and indoctrinated early when we were six, seven, eight, nine, and ten that the regime was wonderful. In first grade, I learned three big words: Jews, Capitalists, and Democrats. I had no idea what they meant, but I was taught to hate all three. The teacher explained that democracy was a Greek word that meant, "Rule by the people."

I listened enthusiastically to the stories about Hitler and promptly related them at dinner. The reaction to my "reports" from school was not what I had expected. My father responded with "Hmm," while my mother admonished me for speaking with my mouth full and not using my napkin. My parents were not for Hitler and had to be very cautious to never say anything bad about him in the house because we might go to school and say, "But my mom says Hitler is not good." I did not find out until later that my parents were against the movement because it was too dangerous for them to voice their opinions around us.

I also learned that Hitler had been a "hero" in WWI and was awarded the Iron Cross Medal. My father never told us that he too was awarded the Iron Cross Medal after he was wounded in WWI and taken to England as a prisoner of war. My mother saved this medal as well as his WWI participation cross and my brother has them today. Unlike Hitler, I presume my father wanted to keep his war experiences private.

Carl Philipp's WWI Medals
Left: WWI Iron Cross
Center: Miniature Versions to Attach to Uniform
Right: WWI Participation Medal

Emmchen Benöhr arrived on April 20, 1934, indicating that the birth of a baby was imminent. Two years before, a major construction had transformed our one-family home into three apartments. The apartment on the first floor was rented to a retired army officer, von Heimburg and his family, while two separate apartments were built for my grandmother and our family on the second floor. "Tante" Emmchen moved into Emmeli's room, while Emmeli reluctantly shared once again the children's room, which was occupied by Brigitte and me.

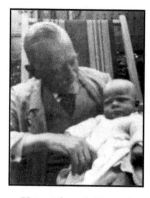

Heinrich with Hinrich

My brother, Hinrich, was born on April 21, 1934. He was not a healthy baby. His skin was delicate and it was advised that he be bathed in a special solution that carried the strong aroma of almonds. I do not know what the concoction was. I remember that he was frequently exposed to the sun by an open window. Several weeks went by before I was allowed to hold him. (It was years later when Emmeli was in medical school that she guessed Hinrich's problems were caused because our mother was Rh negative and our father was Rh positive, affecting the bilirubin level in the amniotic fluid.)

Needless to say, grandfather Martens was elated. I remember being a bit disappointed that my brother was not born on April 20th, Hitler's birthday. A son born on that day would have meant that we would receive a special congratulation from Hitler as well as a signed photograph.

The baby thrived and his baptism was celebrated with a spectacular fest on July 20, 1934. My brother was named Hinrich (not Heinrich, as my grandfather had wanted), Dethlef (after my maternal grandmother's maiden name, Dethlefsen), and Robert, my father's middle name. Today, he is officially known as Hinrich R. However, due to problems with pronunciation, he is called "Hinni." As a toddler, he had used this very name when referring to himself.

My brother was an early walker and talker. My father's health declined, requiring more and more of my mother's time. I was more than happy to play with my brother and show him off to my friends in the neighborhood. No one else could possibly have such an incredibly special little brother. I told him bedtime stories, read fairy tales, and sang lullabies. When he was three, he told me that he preferred stories to my singing.

Hinrich Baptism, July 20, 1934

Hedda, Brigitte, Emmeli, Hinni

It is unfortunate that my brother has no memory of our father who died when Hinrich was some months over two years old. Yet I think that he walks and smiles like our father.

Emmeli, Brigitte, Lisa, Hinrich, Hedda
Enjoy a Meal in their Grandfather's backyard

"Wäsche waschen mit Persil" (Do Your Laundry with Persil)

When I moved to East Aurora in 2007, I splurged by including the tennis channel in my cable. I thoroughly enjoy "traveling" with the players from city to city across the world. While watching a tournament held in Basel, Switzerland, I noticed that the towels given to the players during breaks were considerably smaller than the normal size that is usually used. "Good idea!" I heard myself saying, since these small towels would be exchanged more often. Soon after this little side-trip into the field of hygiene, I concentrated on the phenomenal shots the players were able to execute. As the game grew in intensity, the towel was used after each shot. When I espied the word Persil, printed in large letters on the towels, I was suddenly back to a Sunday in the summer of 1934.

The Martens family was enjoying breakfast in our spacious dining room. Seated at one end of our large oak table was my mother, Lisa (thirty-two years old), my sisters, Emmeli (eleven), Brigitte (ten) on one side, my father, Carl Philipp (thirty-six) opposite my mother, and I (six) sat on the other end next to him. A lovely crib, holding my baby brother, Hinrich (five months) made the family complete. We were all dressed in our Sunday-Best. Every Sunday, a new white cloth was put on the table, as well as new cloth napkins that were held in our personalized napkin rings. The table was set with our best china and fresh rolls, toast, strawberry jam, butter and orange marmalade, soft boiled eggs (eaten from special egg cups), hot chocolate for the children and, of course, coffee for the parents. (I might add here that the children all had a bath on Saturday night and received new underwear for Sunday to last for the coming week.)

I remember waiting for my father to give three "Groschen" (thirty pennies) to Emmeli so that we could go for our Sunday treat after breakfast: going to the cinema to watch wonderful short films, featuring the very successful commercial, "Wäsche waschen mit Persil." I loved it! As my mother would tell us later, our parents enjoyed a very peaceful morning since our outing, including the fifteen-minute walk to and from the movie house, lasted about two hours.

Upon returning home, we always stopped in to visit our very dear grandmother, Elise Bartelt, who had a cozy apartment in our house. As usual, we would find her seated in her comfortable chair by the window, working on yet another knitting project. My grandmother made all of our sweaters, cardigans, hats, mittens, and socks, using the same colors and patterns for her three granddaughters. While listening to our stories, her needles kept going at an incredibly fast speed. As soon as a new row was started, it seemed to be done. Although my mother had told us not to eat a cookie, we were allowed to taste one from her always-full beautiful jar.

Much too soon, my father called us and it was time to depart for my grandfather's house for our Sunday dinner at 2:00 p.m. sharp. My father pushed the baby carriage during our forty-minute walk.

Fraulein Schröder, "Schrödi," would greet us at the door. She was my grandfather's housekeeper at the time, since my grandmother, Emma Martens, was often absent. One of my father's sisters, who were both nurses at hospitals in Hamburg, was often present at these dinners. The cook, Frau Grabow, always produced a masterpiece. Schrödi presided over the table. She had the air of an aristocrat; unfortunate circumstances had forced her to go into service, she claimed. The adults enjoyed an animated conversation; the children, however, were there to be seen but not heard. I remember my father getting angry when his sister reprimanded one of us for poor table manners: "If there is a need for criticism, I'll take care of it. In this case, no admonition was necessary, thank you."

After dinner we enjoyed the lovely garden. The gooseberries were ripe and despite our Sunday outfits, we were allowed to climb the plum tree and harvest the delicious fruit. We also played some games. I always won when I played croquet with my father. At around 6:00, it was time to go home. Bedtime was at 8:00 for me.

It certainly is strange that the name of a detergent can bring back memories from almost eighty years ago. My father died in 1936. "You might not have come to the USA," my daughter says when she sees sadness in my eyes as I think about my father.

Memories of Christmas in Lübeck, 1935

When I visited my grandchildren in 2008, ten-year-old Erika was busy painting on the dining room table. "Mumu," she called out, "do not look!" She was busy designing precious presents for Christmas. I was touched and my thoughts went back to my childhood when I was making my own many presents.

By the middle of November 1935, my mother went out to buy supplies for the various projects we had in mind for our presents. Emmeli, thirteen years old, had requested new blades for her little table saw and different kinds of woods for Christmas tree ornaments; Brigitte, twelve years old, asked for white plain tiles which she would decorate with flowers and then have them burnt and glazed; and I needed lots of yarn for my potholder production. When all homework was done, we would sit on Sundays around the big dining room table and make our presents.

First, I made a list of the people to whom I wanted to give presents: Oma Bartelt, potholder; Grossmutter Martens, potholder; Grossvater Martens, a handwritten paragraph on decorated paper; my godfather Arvid Hasselquist and his wife Hertha, a potholder; my great-aunt Marie and aunt Käthe, potholders; my uncles Hans and Rolf always requested that I sing at least two carols; Frau Hempel, my teacher, a potholder; and last but not least, my parents who always had the same wish for good behavior, good report cards, and a big hug and a kiss.

My mother always crocheted the first two rows of my multicolored potholders and then I was on my own. Often, the edges became crooked, but miracle upon miracle, they somehow got straightened out while I was away at school. Quite often, my potholders had also become a little bigger (several rows were added) during my absence. My mother had no idea how that happened and we left it at that.

Church and state are not separate entities in Germany and therefore we not only had religious education in school but also a Christmas play. Inge Schmidt and I were the stars that enabled the three kings to find their way. Ruth Sachau, Isolde Spelge, and Andrea Mueller portrayed the three kings while Renate Weber and Ruth Zarnow played Maria and Joseph. Inge and I had the only speaking parts: "I am the big star (Inge), I am the little star (Hedda)." Inge was much taller than I. I do not remember whose doll had the part of Jesus.

My cousin Rudolf and I began to plan our Christmas play for our family at home. Rudolf was a year older than I. He was the scriptwriter. Rudolf would be Joseph and I, of course, Maria. My brother, Hinrich, (at that time nineteen months) would be Jesus. My brother behaved quite well during the various practices.

Several days before the first Advent Sunday, fresh branches of fir were delivered and my mother began making a beautiful wreath. We had a black wooden stand for the table. My mother attached the wreath with red ribbons that were held by a nail underneath a golden star. Four candleholders were affixed to the wreath to hold the candles. On the first

Pictured here is the fourth Advent celebration in 1939. Although our father was no longer with us, my mother continued making the beautiful Advent Wreath. Left to right: Brigitte, Hedda, Hinrich, Lisa, Emmeli

Advent, my mother lit one candle when we had our cozy Sunday morning breakfast. The magical season had officially begun.

Sometimes, December 1st and the first Advent Sunday fell on the same day. The night of November 30 to December first, we put our shoes out on the windowsill and found them filled with an Advent calendar, a little chocolate, and an apple. The calendar depicted a Christmas scene, or a Christmas tree, with twenty-four windows and we would open one every day. December 6 always showed Saint Nicholas and December 24 the Nativity Scene. Our Oma began preparing the dough for her special gingerbread cookies (the dough had "to sit" for a couple of days so that all the spices would be effective) and soon her apartment in our house was filled with the wonderful aroma of her

Christmas Stollen, a delicious bread filled with raisons, nuts, and marzipan.

December 6 was a very special day. St. Nicolas would personally come to each house and inquire whether the children had been good. After we had gone to bed, we heard a loud knock on the house door. My mother went to open and we heard her greeting St. Nicolas. And then we heard him asking about us. My mother had only good things to report. The next morning, our shoes were filled with an assortment of goodies. St. Nicolas was and remained invisible. He was the helper to the Weihnachtsmann (Father Christmas). On the second Advent Sunday, we lit the second candle on our wreath and the excitement grew. On the 20th of December, my father went with us to pick out our Christmas tree, which we carried home. The tree then disappeared into the designated Christmas room and the door was locked. My parents decorated the tree and put out our presents. The door remained locked. Even the keyhole was blocked!

On the 23rd, we all had a bath in the evening because early in the morning of the 24th, three carp were delivered to swim in our bathtub. Carp, a delicacy, was only served to the adults. On this special day, my parents hired a cook who slaughtered and prepared the fish and cooked the most festive meal. The children were served a long wiener, which we preferred. Around three in the afternoon, my father went with us to church for carol singing, while my mother stayed behind to do last-minute touches in the Christmas room. My little brother also stayed behind, of course. On the walk home, my father, a baritone, and my sister Emmeli, continued singing in two parts that I remember very well. It was wonderful. Upon arrival at home, we heard the "Christmas Bell" ring for the first time. This was a signal that we could assemble near the door. Then my father also went into the "secret" room. Soon we heard the ringing for the second time. The excitement grew. Rudolf (Joseph), holding Hinrich (Jesus) on his arm, and I (Maria) were the first by the door. Then we heard the key turn and the bell rang for the third time. The door opened and there was our Christmas tree, its many wax candles shining brilliantly. (Behind the tree, my father kept two buckets of water, but we never had a fire.) Rudolf and I sang *Adeste Fideles* (in German) and Baby Jesus was on his best behavior, letting himself be adored through two stanzas. (Hinrich's demeanor was all the more remarkable, since he not only could walk but run and climb *and* talk!) After that we were allowed to look at our presents which were on designated little tables. The presents were not wrapped, one of the reasons for keeping the door locked.

Memories of Christmas in Lübeck, 1935

The adults who had come to celebrate with us were my grandparents, Heinrich and Emma Martens, their two daughters (my father's sisters) Annemarie and Lisa, Oma (my mother's mother), my two uncles, Rolf and Hans (my mother's brothers), and Rudolf's mother Käthe (my mother's sister). It was a splendid evening. All gifts were admired and appreciated. We were allowed to stay up as long as we wanted. In contrast to many other countries, Father Christmas walks from house to house and delivers his gifts by Christmas Eve. On the first day of Christmas, we played with and enjoyed our gifts and on the second day of Christmas (yes, there are two festive days!), we went to visit my grandparents for a festive meal and more presents. It was the only time that we went by taxi, which made the trip most special. I remember being very sad, however, that my dear cousin Rudolf was not invited for this particular outing. "We cannot have tears on Christmas," my father said, and Rudolf was quickly dressed in his festive suit and simply came along. It was the last Christmas with our father.

The untimely death of my father on September 16, 1936, made my mother a young widow. She was just shy of being thirty-five years old. My father's life insurance, RM (Reichsmark) 40,000, was invested in an apartment building. The monthly rent from the eight apartments added to the pension received from the company which my father had co-owned together with my grandfather. My mother took me along on her first, and only, monthly visit to collect the rent from her tenants. She despised that job since several tenants were unable to pay at the time and asked her bank manager to take over instead. Due to the rather significant loss of income, we no longer had full-time help, and my sister, Brigitte, moved into the former maid's room. My brother and I shared the "children's" room. It was a known fact, however, that Hinrich left his bed in the middle of the night, took his little pillow, and crawled into my mother's bed for the remainder of the night.

My mother was a firm disciplinarian and adhered to a strict daily routine. We ate dinner at 2:00 p.m., when everyone had returned from school. With dinner over and the dishes done, my sisters and I did our homework on our large dining room table, while my mother rested with a book, one of her favorites was John Galsworthy's *Forsythe Saga*, and my little brother played quietly with his building blocks. After two hours or so of quiet studies, my mother helped with testing our English or French vocabulary, listened to piano practices, or sent us out to play. Supper consisted of a sandwich, milk, or tea. The daily schedule provided us with a small sense of security.

Carl Philipp Robert Martens, Not Forgotten

I was eight-and-a-half years old when my father died and I am amazed how many things I remember about him. He took me to school on my first day, he carried me on his shoulders when we went on family walks, he never failed to tuck me in at night after telling me one of his wonderful stories, he took me along to hear my first opera, and he was consistently on my side when my sister, Brigitte, and I had a disagreement. I do not think that he was ever angry or stern. He was my protector.

Family Picture on Beach in Travemünde
From Left: Emmeli, Carl Philipp, Brigitte, Lisa, Hedda
All bathing suits were hand-knitted by my mother.

He was in many ways a "modern" father. When he came home from work, he was **home**! He played with us, built sports equipment in our garden for us, helped with homework, and was always available. Unlike other fathers that I knew, he did not have a special room in our house—a room that was **not** for children. He was a family man.

Family Walk in the Woods

My mother was the disciplinarian of the family. Although Emmeli recalled severe punishments at the hand of our father, I only remember one incident where he raised his voice at me, but he never slapped me. Emmeli said I was an easy child, always happy, never rebellious or obstinate.

I remember when our neighbor's house was being painted. We were strictly prohibited from climbing on the scaffolding. Nevertheless, I did, and my father saw me. He stood on the little balcony by the kitchen. A long, fairly steep, wooden stairwell led to our back yard. I was at the bottom of the stairs, having climbed down from the scaffolding and over the stone wall which separated our garden from the neighbor's. "Come up," my father called firmly from the top of the stairs. I clung to each step for as long as possible, certain that a spanking awaited me. When I reached the top, my father merely said, "You go barefoot to bed." He was, in retrospect, obviously relieved that I had not been injured. My father erected a swing set, other sports equipment, and built a sand box. Our yard was **the** playground for our friends and the neighbor children. We also had a huge pear tree as well as a plum tree. My father loved being a family man. It was such a happy time to be with him.

One day I misbehaved at the dinner table and my strict mother instructed me to take my plate and eat in the kitchen. Our kitchen was not a cozy place at all, just a stove and a sink, and definitely no table or chair. No sooner had I arrived at my assigned destination, I was joined by my father who came with his plate, knife, fork, and napkin. He smiled and said, "I was naughty as well." He lifted me onto the counter and I recall that we had a wonderful time together. We almost did not want to rejoin the family when we were allowed to return for our dessert. I am still smiling when I think of the two of us being banished from the dinner table.

My father, Carl Philipp Robert Martens, was born on September 18, 1897. His father had just founded an insurance company and the family lived in well-to-do, middle-class circumstances. My father's childhood was not a happy one. His mother, Emma, suffered from serious depressions and was often sent to a sanatorium for shock treatments. A housekeeper took care of the family. My father made his father proud by doing well in school. He volunteered for the army and went to war immediately after finishing school in 1916. He was soon taken prisoner in France and spent the rest of WWI in a prison camp in England. When he returned in 1919, he was greeted at the railroad station by his sister Annemarie and my mother who were best friends. My mother told us that she knew at

Carl Philipp, 1919

that moment that she would marry Carl Phillipp. My father had dreams of going to the university to study architecture. However, his father would have none of that. My father had to learn the insurance business and, reluctantly, he joined the firm. On the other hand, he was also very anxious to get married and needed to be able to support a wife. Carl Philipp and Lisa Bartelt were married on January 14, 1922, and my sister Emmeli was

Lisa and Carl Philipp in Travemünde

born on November 25, 1922. Brigitte was born on December 22, 1923, and my birthday was February 5, 1928. My mother told us later that my father never liked to be a businessman but he loved his family and was so proud of his three daughters.

Emmeli, Carl Philipp, Brigitte

Emmeli, Lisa, Brigitte, Hedda

My brother was born on April 21, 1934. My grandfather was glad to finally have a grandson who would guarantee the continuation of the family name and, of course, take over the business. It was a happy occasion and our family seemed perfect and complete.

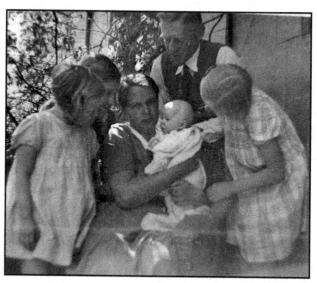

Hedda, Emmeli, Lisa, Carl Philipp, Hinni, Brigitte

Fate would have it otherwise. My father began to suffer from unusual fatigue, frequent dizziness, blurring vision, and headaches. He underwent many examinations, consulted several physicians, was hospitalized for more invasive tests, but no answer could be found. Was it a brain tumor, multiple sclerosis, or an insidious infection? His ailment did not appear to be contagious so my father stayed home. A comfortable lounge chair served as his daybed so that he could always be with us. Being the youngest and without any extracurricular activities as my sisters had, I spent a lot of time with my father. He taught me several card games which we enjoyed for hours on end. Once he sent me to get a glass of water and when I returned I saw him cheating. He was shuffling the cards and then arranging the deck. I pretended not to have noticed but he could not help smiling. My father had arranged the cards in such a way that the game would come to a quick ending so that he could rest a little.

In 1934, it was a Saturday ritual for my cousin Rudolf and me to be sent to the neighborhood bar, Three Rings, to get beer for my parents. Equipped with two large glass mugs (my mother did not think that the bar owner really cleaned his glasses), we walked to the bar at the end of our street, maybe three houses down. On our way home, we sipped the white foam. Although we didn't like it, the "forbidden" drink was very good.

The month of September 1936 was very difficult for us all. My father had to be hospitalized and my mother spent most of the time at his bedside. Our maternal grandmother and friends took care of our household. Exploratory brain surgery left my father with his head shaven and my mother felt that I would be the least likely to be upset by his appearance, so she took me along for a visit. To this day, I remember his pale, gaunt face, trembling hands, and his inability to give me a hug.

My father greeted me with a smile and said that he would be home for his birthday on September 18. Never one to keep a secret for long, I had brought my early birthday present, a potholder that I had crocheted myself. He held it in his hands and told me that he would put it to good use very soon.

My father died two days before his birthday, on September 16, 1936. Mourners in black dresses filled our house and the smell of lilies reminds me to this day of the many wreaths that were delivered to our very sad home.

When my little granddaughter, Erika, was ten years old and we were playing a card game, I told her about my father's "cheating." I saw my father in her "guilt-ridden" smile when she tried to "organize" her cards to her liking.

I was always happy when I overheard visitors say, "Hedda looks just like her father." I could write long stories about my father yet I cannot find any words to properly describe him…except perhaps **love!**

My father is not forgotten.

My School Experiences (1934 to 1946)

The German school system was different from the American educational system.

1. There was no kindergarten.
2. All children entered first grade at age six. Boys and girls were in separate schools.
3. All children took a comprehensive test at the end of fourth grade (arithmetic, social studies, German essay).

Based on the outcome of this examination, the children were divided as follows:

1. Stay in the elementary school until age fifteen, followed by a three-year apprenticeship in a trade.
2. Enter middle school; concentrate on business subjects and at least two foreign languages. Graduate at age seventeen. (The largest group entered middle school.)
3. Be admitted to the secondary school (also called Gymnasium). Here the student studied for nine years, then had to pass the Abitur which immediately qualified him or her to enter any university. (This comprises about fifteen percent of the entire student population.) At that time, there was a fee to enter the secondary schools (in our case, my oldest sister was charged full tuition, the second one half, and I would have been free.) All tuition for secondary school, as well as universities, was later declared invalid. Apart from lab fees and other incidentals, there was no charge to attend the university. However, the students had to pay for room and board.

I remember my first day of school very well. It was right after Easter. Our seamstress had made me a beautiful dress, my mother had knitted a lovely red sweater with white and green stripes, and my father had gone with me to a shoe store to buy light brown leather shoes and white socks. My father took me to school since my mother was about to give birth to my brother, Hinrich.

My School Experiences (1934 to 1946)

We were seated in alphabetical order on four rows of wooden benches on either side of the classroom with room for five children on each bench. Yes, we were forty girls. The parents said goodbye at the door and Frau Hempel, clad in a long black dress, was now in charge.

"Take out your slate and show me that your sponge is wet in the container. Now take out your chalk and copy the numbers from one to ten that you see on the blackboard." When that was done, she called our names. We had to stand up and curtsy and say, "Good morning, Frau Hempel." Whenever a girl did not speak up, she was admonished. Frau Hempel was strict and all business.

Rudolf and Hedda
Ready for School

After one hour of writing the numbers, we opened our primers (we all had to provide our own school supplies and books). My sister, Emmeli, had already taught me to read which was actually frowned upon since only teachers could teach the correct way. Frau Hempel read three words and we had to repeat them. The third class (there was no break) was using our slate again to learn to write the letters A, a, B, b, and C, c. For homework, we had to finish two rows each of numbers and letters. School was over at 11:00 a.m. My father was once again at the door with a huge school bag and a colorful cardboard cone filled with all sorts of goodies.

School was six days a week. On Saturdays, we had gymnastics and music. Second grade was four hours a day, from 8:00 to 12:00. Some children had failed the first grade, but girls who had to repeat the second grade were taking their place. We were still forty. It was 1935. The Hitler regime had dictated that all children had to take a bath once a week. Our day was Wednesday. Six huge bathtubs had been installed in the basement of the school. Four girls sat in each tub. When Frau Hempel whistled, we had to get in and scrub each other's back and wash our hair with soap. Then we rinsed off with cold water and were glad to use a towel. My mother hated this routine more than I and she wrote an excuse for me stating that I had a bath at home. I only participated twice. Many girls in my class did not have a bathtub at home and liked to get clean at least once a week.

Frau Hempel succeeded in helping me overcome my lisp. I had to repeat "Lisa sitzt zwischen zwei Stühlen" (Lisa sits between two chairs) until the lisp was gone. Now I had to struggle with the English "th" sound. There was the "soft" sound found in the word "the" and the "harsh" sound in the words "three" and "theft." In German, there are no "silent" vowels as in "house" or consonants, as in "eight." It is interesting that the English language has become in many ways the language of transportation, business, politics, and science in the world when you consider the erratic pattern in pronunciation (ought, through, enough, drought, etc).

While rummaging through a box filled with photos, post cards, letters, and other miscellaneous things, I came across a letter that I had written to my mother while my cousin Rudolf and I were visiting with "Tante" Emma in Hamburg. Emma Schneider was the former governess for the Bartelt children. She remained a member of the family. It was summer vacation 1936 and I was eight years old. My father was a patient at the University Hospital in Hamburg while undergoing exploratory surgery on his head. My mother stayed with him. She had many helping hands to take care of her infant Hinrich and the general household. My cousin, Rudolf, and I were invited to visit "Tante" Emma in Hamburg for three days. While I was visiting, I wrote this letter to my mother:

Dear Mother,
The day before yesterday, we took a tour around Hamburg. Then we visited Mrs. Jordan who has a large apartment. Several men lived there as well. Then we visited Frau Grimm passing the towns of Flottbeck and Altona and also passing the house where Rudolf once lived. At Frau Grimm's house we had cake and coffee which was very good. We then traveled back to Tante Emma where we had some more delicious cake. Happy Regards,
Your Hedda

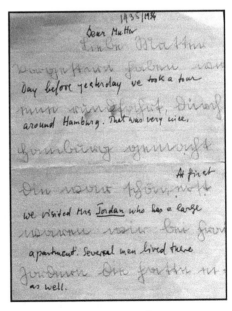

Actual Letter Written by me as an
Eight-Year-Old

My School Experiences (1934 to 1946)

Why is a letter written by an eight-year-old worthy of mentioning? One reason is that the letter was written in the old Gothic script which I learned only in the first grade. The school system switched to the Latin alphabet in 1937 as per proclamation by Dr. Joseph Goebbels.

Drawing of Rummelpot by Wilhelm Grimm a good friend of my Onkel Hans.

The other point of interest is the names Frau Jordan and Frau Grimm. They were two well-to-do women who both exhibited kindness toward homosexuals by protecting them. Frau Jordan had a large house and estate that enabled her to help those men. Frau Grimm's son, Wilhelm, an artist, also lived with Frau Jordan. He became one of my uncle's good friends. A drawing by Wilhelm Grimm currently hangs in my room. It depicts a young boy, dressed up for the yearly "Rummelpot" festival (the German version of Halloween) where boys go through the streets and make noise on their drums.

This letter evoked many memories. I am grateful that I was taught the art of letter-writing which I have practiced and loved throughout my life. Also, the instructions I received from my first-grade teacher, Frau Hempel, enabled me to earn quite a bit of money in Rochester, NY, years later when I translated old German documents written in this script.

Third grade still stressed reading, writing, and arithmetic. However, social studies, geography, and of course, learning about Hitler's life were added. We had a fifteen-minute break around 10:00 a.m. where we ate our sandwich from home. The school provided milk for children who looked pale. This included me. I detested the warm milk and was fortunate that my friend Inge Schmidt took mine. At the end of the third grade, we all took a comprehensive test and I, Inge Schmidt, Gisela Ambrosius, and Isolde Spelge were selected to skip the fourth grade in the elementary school and enter the secondary school. Oddly enough, we all lived on the same street: Hansestrasse. The four of us met every morning and walked together through the city to our new school. It took exactly thirty-five minutes.

Life in my family had changed dramatically during that year. I was eight years old when my father died in September 1936, my uncle was no longer visiting, and my little brother had taken center stage. My grandfather, grief stricken over his son's premature death, hovered over the little boy, showered him with attention and presents, and I felt somewhat left out. It was good that I had accomplished something special at school. I was a good student.

After performing in the All County Music Festival at Kleinhans Music Hall in Buffalo in 2007, my then nine-year-old granddaughter said to me, "It was a dream come true—well, one of them." This happy comment caused me to reflect about dreams that I had when I was nine years old. It was a time of disorder, discontent, disappointment, and the realization that I could not fulfill many of my dreams. I loved to sing and had definite visions of becoming an opera singer. Alas, when I sang Brahms' *Lullaby* to my three-year-old brother, he commented, "Stop singing, Hedda, tell me a story." And my musically gifted cousin, Rudolf, who was around my age, ruined my dream with the unforgettable comment, "You sing like a crow." Recognizing that I could hold a tune and had a loud voice, Herr Fey made me lead singer for the German anthem, *Deutschland, Deutschland, Über Alles,* and the Horst Wessel Lied, *Die Fahne hoch, die Reihen fest geschlossen.* Every morning at school there was a brief assembly and we belted out these songs.

My other dream was to become a ballerina. My next-door girlfriend, Erika, was long legged and had ballet lessons. She taught me the beginning and I pleaded with my mother to be allowed to take classes. I "auditioned" for my mother and grandmother. Then I made the mistake of listening behind the door while the two were deliberating. I heard my grandmother say, "A sweet little girl, but not a future ballerina." My dreams of being an opera singer or ballet dancer were not meant to come true.

The doctor decided I had to have my appendix removed as a matter of convenience in 1937. I spent five days in Saint Marien Hospital. The doctor visited me after a few days and asked, "How is your stuhl (stool)?" I was most puzzled because I knew only one meaning of the word stuhl and it was chair. Saint Marien is still in use as a private clinic today.

Secondary school consisted of the following grades: Sexta, Quinta, Quarta, followed by Untertertia, Obertertia, Untersekunda, and finally Obersekunda, Unterprima, and Oberprima, for a total of nine years. We always stayed together and got to know one another very well. Teachers came to our classrooms for most subjects, but we went to different classrooms for music, science, art, and gym. French and biology were added to the curriculum in the fourth year, physics and chemistry in the sixth year, and Latin (which was an elective as well as Spanish) followed thereafter. If a pupil failed two subjects, she was dropped from the class to repeat the year.

Hedda's High School (Photo taken in 2011 from top of St. Peter's Church)

I entered high school in April 1937 when I was nine. Gifted children were selected in Lübeck—thirty-six girls—to form a special class. After the achievement tests at the end of the third grade, it was recommended that we skip the fourth year of elementary school. This action was based on Nazi ideology to further the gifted. Seven months after my father's death, my mother received a notice from the government that our family no longer qualified for government subsidies which stipulated that families with four or more children would pay reduced fees for the high school tuition. I, being the third child in high school, would have been free. This was no longer the case and I still remember that I had to use an old song book in religion class because my mother could not buy me a new one. The page numbers were different, causing me embarrassment. It was hard to swallow that the lack of money was an issue. Fortunately, my grandfather came forward and paid for our tuition, but our proud mother felt that using old school books was perfectly okay.

Fräulein von Knobelsdorff, my favorite teacher, taught German, history, and English. Herr Kehler was our unforgettable math teacher; Frau Lütge taught religion (all thirty-six of us girls were Lutherans); Herr Fey made music a most interesting and wonderful experience; Frau Tralow tried her best to teach me how to draw; Herr Kunze taught geography; and twice a week, "Gushy" Hargus, who had won a Bronze medal for running and hurdling at the Olympic Games in 1936, allowed no weaknesses in her attempt to make us fit and successful in all sport activities.

Another teacher, Frau Dr. Kühl, who taught in the upper grades, was not mentioned at school anymore. She had admonished my friend Inge Schmidt and me when she saw us kicking the shoes that were strewn all over the sidewalk. That was the morning after the "Kristallnacht," or "Night of the Broken Glass," November 9, 1938, when stores owned by Jews had been smashed and plundered. Somebody reported her and she had to leave her position. She lived on the same street as my grandfather and was supported by her neighbors throughout the war. One of her punishments was that she was not issued any ration cards for food or supplies. Years later after the war, she was reinstated to teaching.

As a little girl, I never questioned my teachers and believed everything they taught. Nothing could ever be wrong with our lessons. Now I'm sure that many of the teachers knew what they were teaching us was horrible. With twenty-six girls in our class, there could always be one who would report the teacher if he or she said anything negative about the war or Hitler and then that teacher would be gone the very next day.

Some examples of the propaganda we were subjected to appeared in the Marburger newspaper in 1939. They write about the dangers of the Jews and the Soviets.

"Alle Kriegsgefahren wurden von den Soviets und der jüdischen Weltpresse herbeigeführt. So ist es den verständtlich wenn immer mehr Menschen die Gefährlichkeit des Judentums erkennen." Loosely translated: "All the dangers of war that were mentioned were introduced by the Soviets and the Jewish world press. Therefore it is understandable that more and more people recognize the dangers of the Jewish people."

Here is a quote from Hitler: "Wenn mich jemand fragt, Welche Aufgaben stellen Sie den deutschen Stämmen? So antworte ich: Es gibt nur eine Aufgabe. Erzieht eure Angehörigen zu den besten Deutschen dann tretet euch ein für unser ganzes Volk." Loosely Translated: "When someone asks me what the German people should be doing, I tell them that their only job is to educate their offspring in the best German manner possible and then to work for the good of the German people.

My School Experiences (1934 to 1946)

I brought a multi-grade literature textbook with me when I immigrated to America. Some quotes from Adolf Hitler within include: "Loving your father and mother is most important. That is politics! Heil Hitler!" Also, "Always think of God and your duty to the country." This book is a treasure, because it is unreal. In second or third grade you are seven or eight years old and your teacher is god. What he or she says to do you do. Teachers are very influential and important to get the machine of politics going. It was very clever. People who went to church heard the same messages because church and state were one in Germany. The priests and pastors were paid by the government. As a consequence, if you heard Hitler was great in school, then you heard the same thing in church. You were indoctrinated around the clock with the idea that the Nazi regime was fantastic.

Our teachers also informed us that it was Napoleon who allowed the Jews to gain citizenship. In 1808 Napoleon decreed that all Jews acquire a fixed family name to help the government and consistories supervise the Jews' movements. They were restricted in their choice of names and weren't allowed to pick names from the Hebrew Bible or any town names. Until that time, Jews had not been entitled to own any land. (They were artists, teachers, merchants, jewelers, art dealers, etc.). The Jews were given surnames. One location where this took place was in Frankfurt am Main. The people were given a choice from various books carrying the names of minerals, gemstones, colors, plants, flowers, etc. Thus, the following names were created: Wasser (water), Stein (stone), Gold (gold), Diamant (diamond), Silber (silver), Schwarz (black), Weiss (white), Blau (blue), Grün (green), Baum (tree), Berg (mountain), Blume (flower, bloom), Rose (rose), Tal=Thal (valley), Löwe (lion). Then there were combinations: Blaustein, Goldstein, Goldberg, Blumenberg, etc. These names made the persecution of Jews in Germany easier for the National Socialist regime.

One day my mother asked me to help her tidy up the bottom shelf of her beloved bookcase. "I want to put all the books from the front row into the back row," she said. I did as I was told but asked my older sister whether she knew the reason for this change. "Yes, the books that are now somewhat hidden were written by either Jewish authors or, as was the case with Thomas Mann, by 'undesirable' authors." My sister declined to give any further explanations. Nevertheless, another courageous teacher taught us poems by Heinrich Heine but mentioned that the poet was "unknown."

The war started on September 1, 1939, with the German invasion of

Poland. England and France declared war two days later. The German army was victorious on all fronts. We defeated Poland in the so-called "Blitzkrieg," and occupied Belgium, Holland, France, Denmark, and Norway. Many men from my hometown were killed. Our Math teacher and our principal had been killed on the Russian front or, as it was said, "had proudly given their blood for the fatherland." December 7, 1941, brought the United States into the war. Hitler declared war on the United States on December 9, 1941. Germany incurred horrible losses in Russia. The battle of Stalingrad comes to mind, which showed that Germany was not invincible. While England had already endured serious bombings, civilian death, and destruction, Germany had as yet to suffer that fate.

In school we learned from our History teacher, Dr. Bülow, that the Polish people were mistreating the Germans in the Polish Corridor (the region between Germany and East Prussia). This gave us the right to invade Poland to protect our "brothers." I was eleven at the time and very proud to have the job at school during geography class to place markers on the European map indicating the countries that our army had occupied. The "Luftwaffe" (air force) was making successful bombing raids over England causing serious destruction and civilian death. Our geography teacher, Herr Kunze, who proudly told us that he had been standing near the Niagara Falls, had seen the skyscrapers, as well as the Grand Canyon said, "Children, there is no need to go into details about the geography of England. It will soon be erased from the world. Instead we will focus on America so that you will be prepared when we invade them."

The German troops were advancing at lightning speed on both the eastern and western fronts. The war that had seemed so far away did come closer when the first death notices of fallen soldiers appeared in the newspaper with the headings, "These heroes have proudly given their blood for the fatherland." One day we had an assembly in school to honor the father of my friend and classmate, Wendla Lüders. Mr. Lüders had suffered a "hero's" death in Poland. I was angry that Wendla's father was celebrated while the school did not even mention my father's death three years earlier. I have disliked the words "hero" and "hero worship" ever since.

We were ordered to greet our teachers with, "Heil Hitler," and also use that greeting when buying delicious bread at the bakery instead of simply saying, "Good Morning, Frau Wemmel." All teachers were instructed to tell us about the great things that Hitler was accomplishing.

My School Experiences (1934 to 1946)

It must have been around 1941 when school was totally normal, that is, not interrupted by air raids. We had chorus twice a week with Herr Dr. Hermann Fey, a no-nonsense choir director who was also involved in all opera productions produced at the theater in Lübeck. It was one of my favorite classes, although I was Herr Dr. Fey's least favorite pupil. Why? I loved to sing, but the choir sounded better without me.

Before every class, Frau Fey appeared and put something under the lid of the Steinway piano. We were all curious about this secret item and held a meeting to determine which one of us girls would have the courage to find out what it was. The first choices were Renate Bruhn or Annemarie Hirsh since they were the teacher's pets and had beautiful voices. When they adamantly declined, we asked Hilke Juhl, the accompanist on the piano. However, her twin sister, Frauke, declined for her. Courageous, eager-to-please Hedda volunteered. I found a piece of delicious chocolate, a precious commodity available only to soldiers on the front and definitely not for ordinary citizens.

Soon after I did the deed, Herr Dr. Fey appeared and, as was his custom, lifted the lid of the piano. The irate Dr. Fey looked around the class. It did not take him long to find the culprit. I blushed too much. The precious candy had melted in my sweaty hand which proved to be clear evidence when we had to show our hands. I suppose Herr Dr. Fey did not want it known where he got the chocolate, so the punishment I received was an F in chorus. This really wasn't quite fair, since I continued to be the lead singer for the National Anthem which I sang correctly and loudly, just not beautifully.

School attendance requirements were very strict under Hitler. For example, in 1943, my brother went with my mother to visit my sisters, Brigitte and Emmeli, who were both studying medicine in Freiburg. They were gone for three or four weeks. During that time, Hinrich had to report to a school in Freiburg every day. My brother hated the school. He could hardly understand the southern German dialect and was very homesick for his own school. However, had he missed three weeks of school, my mother would have been in trouble with the government which kept strict track of all school attendance. I remained in Travemünde and remember eating dinner with the Hinrichsen family but stayed alone in our apartment.

Hinrich celebrated his tenth birthday on April 21, 1944, one day after Hitler's birthday. This milestone meant that he had to join the Hitler Youth. So that he would not get into any trouble, my mother gave him money to buy the required uniform. "They were sold out," he said when he returned home. He said that he left the money at the store. My mother asked me to inquire about the uniforms and I learned that my brother had never been to the store and that there were plenty of uniforms. I was puzzled. Was it possible that my brother had lied to our mother? What did he do with the money? He bought an album filled with beautiful stamps. In 2017, I confronted my eighty-two year old brother, and he "confessed" that there were other occasions when he opted not to tell the truth to our mother.

Now thinking back to high school, I have good memories of reading Shakespeare. *The Merchant of Venice* was very popular during the Hitler years since it deals with the Jewish money lender, Shylock, who demanded "a pound of flesh" when a merchant was unable to repay the loan of 3,000 ducats. What could be better fodder for instilling blind hatred than having a greatly honored poet write about an evil Jew? (Jews were the victims of prejudice in the sixteenth century and Shakespeare merely gave a true account of historical facts at the time.)

And then there was *A Midsummer Night's Dream*. I regret so very much that our performance, in English, was not taped. There were not even many parents in the audience that night in June 1944. Constant air raids caused people to stay home or go to the shelter. But our class performed. At least we got almost halfway through it before the sirens signaled incoming enemy airplanes. I had hoped to play the part of Puck; however, that was given to Renate Buchwald. My second choice was the role of Oberon. That too went to another girl. What was my part? Lacking any kind of technical devices for the stage, my task was to announce to the audience things like, "This is a tree," "This is a castle (pointing to the ever-present piano)," etc. At least I wore lots of makeup and some kind of costume. (This situation would be unthinkable for an American high school performance today.)

When the sirens stopped wailing and one was allowed outside, I ran to the railroad station (twenty-five minutes) in hope of catching the last train to Travemünde. It was 10:50 p.m. and a nice summer evening. There was a complete black-out, of course, and I could barely detect an empty spot in the compartment when I boarded the train. Once the train had left the station, one passenger lit a cigarette and he held his lighter in front of me. The other seats were taken by five dashing ensigns. They were curious about my appearance and we enjoyed a good time during the thirty-minute ride. I was certain that my glamorous appearance intrigued them. Once we arrived at our destination, they asked me if I would like to see their ship, *Hugo Zeye*, that was out in the bay, since no ships were allowed in the harbor at night. I accepted and was shown a little of the ship and also met the captain who told Dirk, the most handsome of the soldiers, to take me home.

We passed my house and took a romantic walk on the beach before he needed to take the boat back to his ship. My frantic mother had been searching for me and was outside our home. My dear mother greeted me with a hard slap on my face, putting a rather abrupt end my wonderful night. The next day the captain came with Dirk to apologize. My mother befriended the captain. I was madly in love with Dirk. It lasted but a few weeks until *Hugo Zeye* went to the Mediterranean Sea. We learned later that the ship had been sunk.

By the end of nine years of high school, only seventeen of us took the final examination, called the Abitur, which would entitle us to attend the university.

It was 1946. The war was over. Germany was in ruins, divided into four zones: Russian, American, French, and British. We lived in the British Zone but could see the Russian Zone from our window. The hotels were filled to capacity with maimed soldiers who screamed for pain medication. They were filled with sadness and despair.

Children's Voices and Their Remarkable Orchestras and Bands

On December 4, 10, and 18, 2008, I had the great privilege of attending lovely concerts given by the East Aurora Middle and Elementary Schools. The children, the music teachers, and the many invisible helpers deserve tremendous praise and a thank you for bringing not only enjoyment, but also successfully instilling happiness and putting the audience in the right frame of mind for the festive holidays before us.

All concerts were very well attended. Especially noticeable was the presence of many very proud grandparents. I now belong to the latter group. Just looking at those bright-eyed, lovely children filled me with warmth and hope, wiping away feelings of nostalgia.

My grandson, Carl, sang in the chorus and played the trumpet in the middle school band. My granddaughter, Erika, danced in the "Loco Cocoa Dance Troup" while the choir sang *Hot Chocolate*, and joined the band with her French horn. Both children had little solo parts that were wonderful, despite little hiccups. Every child in grades four through eight participated in these lovely concerts.

This brought to mind a Christmas concert at my school when I was twelve. It was in 1940. Our music teacher, Herr Dr. Herman Fey, had selected only the gifted singers for the performance. I was not one of them. However, I was intent on being on the stage somehow. I borrowed my sister Emmeli's flute and appeared with the orchestra. Or course, I only pretended to play, since I did not know how to use the flute. Dr. Fey noticed me, but it was too late to get me off the stage.

I was called to the principal's office afterwards and ordered to write a five-page essay about my "unforgivable" behavior. Fortunately, my mother had been unable to attend the concert. Was my daring exploit worth it? Yes.

Dr. Fey had divided our class into the "A" and "B" chorus groups. I was in the latter group. Since I could sing correctly and had a loud voice, I was the lead singer at the assembly which took place every morning before classes began. My place was in the first row and I did not have the luxury of resting my arm on anyone's shoulder. We sang one stanza of the German national anthem and two of the *Horst Wessel Lied*.

The text for the German anthem was written by August Heinrich von Fallersleben in 1871. He was a professor of philology (the study of linguistics) at the University of Breslau (now Baleslawiec in Poland) Silesia. He was dreaming of a united Germany and became very unpopular when he called for the dissolution of the many principalities and dukedoms within Germany and lost his position. This poem (using a melody from Franz Joseph Haydn) was not used as the anthem until 1922. The first stanza was particularly suitable to the Hitler regime due to its geographic delineations:

Das Lied der Deutschen (The Song of the Germans)

Deutschland, Deutschland über alles, über alles in der Welt,
Wenn es stets zu Schutz und Trutze brüderlich zusammen hält!
Von der Maas bis an die Memel,
Von der Etsch bis an den Belt:
Deutschland, Deutschland über alles, über alles in der Welt.

Germany above all, above all in the world
When she is united in brotherhood in defense and offense
From the Meuse (a river in Belgium) to the Njemen (East Prussia)
From the Adigo (a river in Northern Italy, to the Belt (North of
        Denmark)
Germany, Germany above all in the world.

The first stanza was prohibited in 1945. In 1952, thousands of new texts were submitted, but the new West German government opted to retain the lovely Haydn melody using the third stanza of von Fallersleben's poem. That was on May 6, 1952.

Einigkeit und Recht und Freiheit für das deutsche Vaterland!
Danach lasst uns alle streben, brüderlich mit Herz und Hand.
Einigkeit und Recht und Freiheit sind des Glückes Unterpfand;
Blüh im Glanze dieses Glückes, blühe, deutsches Vaterland!

Unity and law and freedom for the German fatherland!
Let us all strive toward that in brotherly love and deed!
Unity and law and freedom are the basis for happiness
Prosper in the glory of this fortune, prosper German fatherland!

This anthem has been much maligned. It really represents just the dream of a romantic soul.

It should be noted that Otto von Bismarck had just founded the "Second German Empire" in 1870 under the rule of a Prussian Kaiser.

The *Horst Wessel Lied* is quite a different story. It was written for the Nazi propaganda.

Die Fahne hoch, die Reihen fest geschlossen
S.A. marschiert, mit ruhig festem Schritt.
Kam'raden, die Rotfront und Reaktion erschossen,
Marschier'n im Geist in unsern Reihen mit.

Zum letzten Mal wird Sturmalarm geblasen
Zum Kampfe steh'n wir alle schon bereit;
Bald flattern Hitlerfahnen über allen Straßen-
Die Knechtschaft dauert nur noch kurze Zeit.

Raise the flag, close the rows
The storm troops are marching and determined.
The comrades who have been murdered by communists and
         reactionaries
March with us in spirit.

For the last time, the bugler is calling
We are all prepared to fight;
The Hitler-banners are already flying in all the streets.
The servitude will not last much longer. (a reference to the Treaty of
         Versailles after WWI)

Horst Wessel was killed by communists in 1929 and Nazi propaganda made him a hero. I do not know who is responsible for the lyrics or who wrote the music.

I regret to say that I remember the text only too well, having sung it so many times. It is apparent that Hitler planned the war all along; England, France, the USA, and others were in denial.

We all know that music plays an important role in church services and political rallies. Chanting refrains is powerful. As a consequence of my school experience during the Hitler times, I am against repetitive rituals to which we subject our children today. I am thinking of the Pledge of Allegiance. I am not sure whether the schoolchildren give much thought to the powerful text and realize that in our country, church and state are separate entities. Hence, God should be omitted from the pledge. I also feel that the Bible should not be used as an instrument in court proceedings or when swearing in public officials. During my formative years, we were told of a god who protected **only** the Germans, not all of mankind.

My Classmates

Class photo from 6th grade in 1939
1: Inge Schmidt, 2: Fraulein von Knobelsdorf (our teacher), 3: Dina Dummar,
4: Rosemarie Woch, 5: Frauke Juhl, 6: Hilke Juhl (twins), 7: Ilse Magnus,
8: Ingrid Bülow, 9: Hedda Martens

As I have mentioned before, we were together in the same classes throughout the years in secondary school. I would like to talk about some of my classmates: Inge Schmidt and I had been close friends since primary school; even before that. Inge's parents owned a big transportation company consisting of six enormous horses and many wagons that were located just one block from my house. We played in the hayloft, were allowed to ride the horses back to their stalls after they completed their day's work, and watched the blacksmith shoeing them. Inge also liked to play with dolls. I did not care for that so I brought my little brother to our pretend tea parties. He was real and considerably more fun for us all. Inge was a most conscientious student and frequently briefed me on oral assignments on our way to school.

My Classmates

When I was twelve or thirteen, my mother made the mistake of cautioning us in a stern voice: "Never, ever go to Clementine Street!" The street was a bit out of the way, not on the direct route to our school. My friend Inge and I had heard rumors about "that" street and became more and more curious. Should we dare go there? We needn't tell anybody. However, it would be great to share our daring trip through the forbidden street with our classmates. We debated for many weeks. Finally, we made the excursion. The street, located near the harbor, was lined with small houses that had large display windows. There was no merchandise on display. Instead, window after window displayed an array of either half-naked or almost-naked women who were sitting, standing, or reclining on ottomans. We were horrified. Suddenly, a door opened and a lady screamed: "Get out of here!" Totally ashamed and stupefied, Inge and I ran downhill and out of "that" street.

We were puzzled. What was going on there? Naive as we were, we now had to find out what "that" street was all about. But whom should we ask? We did not have the courage to approach anybody who could still our curiosity. Two years later, we learned about the "evil" of prostitution in school. The very blond Miss Bauer, blushed (to our delight) when she told us that this "profession" was legal and that it was "healthier that way." When pressed to tell us details about the services rendered by these "ladies," Miss Bauer blushed even more but refused to go into details. I was determined to ask my older sisters. "You do not need to know that," was their response. The temptation to "open the forbidden thirteen's door," as we learned from fairy tales, was too enticing. Years later I talked to my mother about this unpleasant experience. She smiled and confessed that she had done the same thing when she was young but had wanted to spare me the undignified experience.

After our house was destroyed in 1942 and we had moved to Travemünde, my close friendship with Inge was limited to our time in school. I had become a commuter and had to adhere to the strict train schedule.

Ilse-Maria Sierig had been a commuter all along, coming from nearby Schwartau, where the train made one of its five stops. Ilse was the best essay writer in the class and an accomplished pianist. We had a strange relationship, always seeking each other's company, yet I despised her, and suspected the feeling was mutual. She was very beautiful, had a great figure, and was always immaculately dressed in foreign clothes. Her family had connections, no doubt. By contrast, I wore hand-me-downs and dark black saggy pants that were fashioned from fabric that had been used for blackout curtains during the war. You couldn't buy a thing outside of groceries which were sparse and rationed. Ilse's father owned a huge candy and jam factory that was in operation again for the British army. In fact, that factory had been producing jam, vitamins, and candy for the armed forces throughout the war. Now it was doing the same thing—but for the former enemy.

Ilse needed me for help with math and I sought her advice in German literature. We were reading *Faust*, the required text for our class and material sanctioned by the British. Ilse had a knack for literary interpretation and her answers always pleased Dr. Bülow, our teacher. Dr. Bülow had rejoined the faculty just a few weeks before. His past had been questionable. We never did find out why he had not been allowed to teach for some months. He revealed nothing and we were left to guesswork and rumors. I had not known him during the Hitler times. He had always just taught the upper-class men. His classes were fascinating, although I could not please him. He frequently dismissed my essays with the criticism of "immature mumbo jumbo" though he appeared to favor me when it came to oral recitations or discussions.

Ilse had a winning way when it came time to expressing her thoughts in writing. It seemed as if she had read *Faust* before. She understood the theme, the protagonist, and all the secondary players in the drama. She shared her thoughts on the assigned chapter with me. The train came to a stop. We had reached our final destination and now had twenty-five minutes of walking ahead of us. We were totally engrossed in Margarete's tragic pregnancy and her impending imprisonment and death. We wondered how Dr. Bülow would present Margarete's predicament. Would he condemn Margarete and side with Faust? Would he view Margarete's action as sin? Ilse and I agreed that she had in fact done wrong by accepting jewelry from the stranger and by deceiving her mother. On the other hand, we felt that Margarete loved Faust which in our estimation somewhat justified her action. We sided with Mephistopheles who suggested that the jewelry be given to the parish priest. What marvelous irony. We both loathed the church and everything it stood for. It was pure hypocrisy to greedily collect money and goods, and very selectively dole them out. We left the subject of Faust for a while.

Ilse and I always sat together on the train and walked to school, but one day Ilse made the following comment: "You will not be able to succeed in Lübeck without a father." I was devastated by this cruel remark. Our friendship was no more.

My Classmates

When I was in sixth grade, Jutta Fischer disappeared from our lives overnight. We never heard from her or her family again. Her disappearance was never explained to us.

Lovely Andrea Müller sat next to me in art class. She could draw and paint and frequently helped me with my artwork. I confess that I had no qualms presenting what was essentially her work as mine to the teacher. Andrea was not healthy. She was excused from all exercise. Andrea died of tuberculosis when she was thirteen. The entire class attended her funeral service. I remember it well. It was so very sad. It was the first funeral service that I attended. My mother had not taken me to my father's service. She thought it would be too hard for me. I think that my mother was right.

Annemarie Hirsch, Ilse Magnus, and Ingrid Bülow (Dr. Bülow's daughter) were an inseparable trio. They had known one another since first grade. I was proud to finally be accepted into their group. They were gifted, fun loving, and wonderful to be with. Ilse and I both became teachers and were the only ones to obtain graduate degrees, Ilse at the University of Kiel, and I at the University of Rochester.

There were the twins, Hilke and Frauke Juhl, daughters of an obstetrician. Hilke was studious and later became a well-known organist, while Frauke loved sports, disliked academics, and left school at sixteen to get married.

Wendla Lüders was the niece of Germany's most prominent actor, Guenther Lüders, whom I was privileged to see in a performance of Goethe's *Faust* in New York in the early 1960s. I took my high school students from Pittsford to this wonderful performance. Wendla's father was killed at the very beginning of WWII in Poland. There was a huge assembly at school, honoring the hero. I remember being resentful. Nobody at school honored my father. He did not have a celebrated hero's death.

Thione Wessel was every teacher's pet and a true tattletale. She kept a record of all admonishments and misdeeds such as "was not prepared," "talked in class," and "forgot the assignment." She seemed to love her job, although the rest of us disliked her throughout all of our years together since she applied for the same job each year that nobody else wanted.

Maike Drechsler was the daughter of a prominent dentist who opted for a political career and quickly rose in the ranks of the Nazi regime. He was appointed as Governor of Latvia after the Baltic country was occupied by the Germans, and the entire family left Lübeck to "rule" in Latvia. Accused of war crimes in 1945, he committed suicide just before his upcoming trial. Despondent over her father's death, Maike, age seventeen, threw herself before an oncoming train. Her death was just one more tragic event that occurred in the years of 1945 to 1946. Confusion, hunger, the horrible photos from the concentration camps, the disillusionment, the uncertain future, all contributed to the fact that my friends and I thought that school was totally ridiculous and out of place. Fortunately, however, the educational system continued to function under the strict supervision of the Allies.

Elke Lorenzen was also a commuter. She came from Rheinfeld, a small town located about twenty miles away from Lübeck. Elke did not have to participate in our religious instruction class. Religion was a regular subject in school for all children under the age of fourteen. This was not a big deal in our city since ninety-four percent of the citizens were Protestant. Nevertheless, we all envied Elke having a free hour. Elke's family was "Deutsch Gottgläubig," meaning that they believed in a German god only, disregarding any story about Jesus who was Jewish. I think their religion was short lived.

Many teachers had to be "de-nazified," while others, who had been dismissed by the Nazi regime, returned to our schools. History was taught by an English officer who was totally casual. No longer did we have to stand up when he entered the class or if we wanted to answer a question. He smoked and put his feet on the desk. German and world history stopped with the year 1918. It was unclear at the time how the rise of Hitler would be taught. Tests were considerably easier this way. He gave his classes in English, which was not always easy for us to comprehend.

I remember one of our biology classes about mammals. The professor, Dr. Abshagen, was an old man. He had been brought back from retirement because the other biology teachers had been killed or not yet de-nazified. We had a bonafide skeleton in the classroom and memorized some Latin words for all the bones that seemed miraculously connected to one another. These bones were surrounded by muscles which in turn were covered by various layers of skin. Human organs consisted of the heart, which acted like a pump; the lungs, necessary for breathing oxygen; and the liver, which acted like a policeman for white and red blood cells. The function of the kidneys was never quite clear. We suspected that Dr. Abshagen could not bring himself to say the word "urine" out loud.

We had a class reunion in 1962 and I met ten of my friends again. Only one, Ingrid Bülow, was happily married and talked glowingly about her children. The others were divorced, widowed, or never married at all. Times had not been easy for all of us after graduation and many boys whom we might have married had died in the war or had to struggle themselves to forge out an existence.

Mutterkreuz: Unwanted Honors

Bronze Mutterkreutz Awarded to my
Mother and Grandmother

In 1937, when I was nine years old, party officials came to our house to present my mother with a bronze Mutterkreuz. The Hitler regime awarded the Mutterkreuz to mothers who had multiple children: bronze to a mother who bore four children, silver to a mother with six, and gold when there were eight children. As I said, my mother had given birth to four: my sisters, Emmeli and Brigitte, me, and my brother, Hinrich. My grandmother, Elise Bartelt, widowed and residing in her own apartment in our house, was "honored" as well with the bronze edition. Neither woman wanted to have anything to do with this award. I was present when the officials came and remember feeling special and honored when the uniformed officers arrived and upset that my mother did not appreciate the honor. My mother put the medal into an old carton in the basement. Ironically, it survived the war. Much later I would learn the reasons these "awards" were not appreciated.

What was the reason for my mother's albeit silent disapproval of the Hitler regime? My father had died of an undiagnosed disease in September

1936. There was suspicion of a brain tumor, of multiple sclerosis, and other problems, but the actual cause of death remained unsolved. Thus, shortly before that Awards Committee came to see my mother, somebody from the finance office came, informing her that she would surely understand that the German government could not sponsor the education of four children that were not likely to become healthy contributors to the Reich. So instead of paying full tuition for Emmeli, half tuition for Brigitte, and free tuition for me and my brother Hinrich, my mother would now have to pay full tuition for all of us. Luckily, my grandfather was able to pay for us to continue our schooling.

Going back to my mother's visit by the "Mutterkreuz" Committee, it is most understandable that my mother was hurt, and probably livid.

Lübeck: My Hometown and Place of Birth

Lübeck enjoys a rich and illustrious history. The name Lubice appears for the first time around 1066 in connection with the founding of cloisters and abbeys. It was ruled by the sovereign Gottschalk, who was assassinated in a rebellion. All cloisters were subsequently burned. His son, Heinrich, avenged his father's murder, and Heinrich's rule remained uncontested.

The hill between the two rivers, Wakenitz and Trave, seemed an ideal location to found a city. The goal was to fortify the city and build a harbor with access to the Baltic Sea for mercantile trade, as well as to create a center for the Christian religion. The six churches: St. Marien, St. Jakobi, St. Petri, St. Aegidien, St. Katharinen, and the Dom, as well as the castle gates, Holstentor and Burgtor, bear witness that their plan succeeded. The Mühlentor to the west and the Hüxtertor castle gates to the south did not survive WWII. The majestic steeples that tower over the city gave Lübeck the nickname of "The City with Seven Golden Steeples." (St. Marien has two, St. Jakobi has one, St. Petri has one, St. Aegidian has one, and the Dom has two.) Five steeples were rebuilt after the bombing in 1942.

Lübeck with its seven Steeples: View looking East across the Wakenitz River

In June 1216, the Hohenstaufen emperor, Friedrich II, authorized that Lübeck would become a "free city" within the empire. The deed is still in the

Lübeck: My Hometown and Place of Birth

Lübeck-Rathaus

Rathaus in Lübeck. During the thirteenth century, Lübeck became the only port of transit for finished goods from the west in exchange for raw materials, grains, and cattle from the east. There was, however, no transit to East Prussia and Lithuania, since the German merchant ships usually brought unwanted Christian missionaries along.

Pirates plagued the merchant ships. In the Baltic Sea, there were the "Ranen" from the island Rügen, who succeeded with their bloody attacks. In the Atlantic Ocean (sailing from Hamburg), the ships were attacked by the Moors who had been expelled from Spain. The Moors subsequently began the lucrative business of piracy by capturing ships and enslaving the seamen who awaited a terrible fate unless they converted to Islam. The pirates demanded money for the captured men. The exact amount of money they charged was 4000 taler for a captain, 2000 for the pilot, and 800 for a sailor. These tragic events forced the participating merchants to start a "Sklavenkasse," requiring the merchants to pay into the "slave bank."

The founding of the Hanseatic League was very important. Many cities: Lübeck, Hamburg, Bremen, Köln, Stockholm, London, Antwerpen, Venice, and others joined and paid their dues. The league provided extra ships to provide protection for the merchant ships. It was a kind of insurance company. Lübeck became the "Queen" of the "Hanse" and, to this day, it is called Hansestadt.

I clearly remember my mother's protest to hanging the Swastika flag from the house on Hitler's birthday, April 20. Our house was one of the very few on our street which flew only the red and white flag that represented the Hanseatic League of which Lübeck was a founding member.

The most important painter and sculptor in northern Europe during the fifteenth century was Bernt Notke who died in Lübeck in 1508. He painted the *Totentanz*, (*Dance Macabre*) for St. Marien church. This masterpiece was regrettably destroyed during the bombing raid in March 1942.

The reformer and friend of Martin Luther, Johannes Bugenhagen, came to Lübeck in 1530. He started schools and saw to it that all schools and churches adopted the Lutheran doctrine and preached Protestantism. For many years, Lübeck had only one Catholic church and one Synagogue, serving very small congregations.

Music played a major role in Lübeck. There was the highly regarded organist, Dietrich Buxtehude (1617-1707), a composer of choral and organ music, who was the organist of St. Marien. Johann Sebastian Bach (1685-1750) traveled 300 kilometers to Lübeck to hear Buxtehude. The latter is said to have offered Bach to succeed him in St. Marien, provided he would marry Buxtehude's elderly daughter. Bach declined the offer but learned a lot from the master.

In more recent years the Music Directors, Wilhelm Furtwängler and Erich Leinsdorf began their careers as conductors in Lübeck. Leinsdorf came to Rochester, NY, before he became the Music Director in Boston. I heard him in Rochester. The Music School of Lübeck is highly regarded worldwide. I had two students at the Eastman School of Music in Rochester who went to study organ music in Lübeck and play the famous organ of St. Jakobi, which was not destroyed during the war.

Barlach Figurines

Last but not least, the graphic artist and sculptor, Ernst Barlach (1870-1938), deserves to be mentioned. He created beautiful figures for the outside wall of the St. Katharinen church. When the Hitler regime prohibited Barlach's "undesirable" sculptures, several Lübeck citizens labored one night to remove the figures and hide them in their basements. Thus, the sculptures were not destroyed and stand proudly today in their original location.

St. Marien Kirche, Holstentor, St. Petri Kirche

The inscription of the Holstentor castle gate reads in gold letters:

CONCORDIA DOMI FORES PAX
(Harmony within the house, peace outside the walls)

I had the opportunity to show my grandchildren, Carl and Erika, my hometown in 2011. It was truly wonderful to share some of my memories with them firsthand. When our train from Hamburg approached Lübeck, I could hardly contain my excitement and joy of being back in my beloved city with "seven golden steeples."

My Neighbors on Hansestrasse and How WWII Affected Us (1933-1942)

In 1933 I was five and my world revolved around four rather big houses, separated by large front yards and iron gates, and nearly two-meter-tall brick walls in the backyards. The Franzes lived in Nr. 2, my family in Nr. 4, the Blumenbergs in Nr. 6, and the Ebmeiers in Nr. 8.

Dr. Franz and his wife resided in Nr. 2 and had two children: Ursula, who was about my age, and Michael, who was a few years younger. Ursula and Michael often came to play. Dr. Franz was the owner of a pharmacy. One day in 1936, the family disappeared. I was sad because Ursula was a good friend.

Michael Franz, Hinrich, Ursula Franz

My family, including my parents, Carl Philipp and Lisa, and my three siblings: Emmeli (born 1922), Brigitte (born 1923), Hinrich (born 1934), and I (born 1928) lived with my grandmother, Elise Bartelt, my cousin Rudolf (born 1927) with his mother Käthe (my mother's sister) in Hansestrasse Nr. 4. Rudolf, almost a year older than I, was my constant playmate and dearest friend. My father was a partner in his father's insurance business, Martens & Prahl.

Herr and Frau Blumenberg lived with their son Hans (born 1920) in Nr. 6. Hans Blumenberg, who was a few years older than Emmeli, did not participate in our sports activities. Instead, he often invited us to his shed in the garden where he told us wonderful, mostly scary stories. Hans was great fun. Herr Blumenberg was an art dealer, specializing in religious paintings. Interestingly, the family was Catholic. They had converted to Catholicism in an effort to remain safe. Hans was removed from the Jewish school and sent instead to a Catholic elementary school and then a regular high school which was predominantly Protestant. The practice of Jews converting to Catholicism was commonplace, an attempt to thwart the negative response to being Jews. It did not help them. Sadly, they were labeled as Jews when the time came.

The Ebmeier family lived in Nr. 8. They had four children: Carl (born 1920), Clementine (born 1921), Alfred (born 1922), and Clara Paula (born 1923) who was nicknamed "Uschi," and became my sister Brigitte's best friend. The Ebmeier children were frequently in our backyard, where my father had constructed a sandbox, a huge swing set, parallel bars and a horizontal bar, which also served to hold rugs for beating since there was no vacuum cleaner. Their mother was Greek and all the children had beautiful black hair. Brigitte and her friend Uschi were an interesting pair, one blond and the other dark. Both were pretty and happy children.

My brother Hinrich was born in 1934. There was great excitement in the street and all the children were anxious to wheel his carriage around the block. Younger children from across the street, Maria and Christian Attikes, joined Hinrich in the fun of our backyard play. Occasionally, a truck, which had begun to replace the horse-drawn carriage, would pass on our street. A horrible accident happened one day. Our maid, who had done some shopping with Rudolf and me, was holding our hands very tightly. Rudolf suddenly let go of her protection, ran into the street, and was hit. My mother watched from the balcony. Rudolf's mother was at work. My mother ran with the bleeding and unconscious child to the nearest doctor's office and an ambulance took them to a hospital. Rudolf recovered but lost his hearing in one ear. I learned to always be on his right side when we talked.

In 1936 Emmeli was up early one morning studying for a test and saw a huge truck in front of the Franz house. Some furniture was loaded up along with many suitcases and finally Dr. Franz, his wife, and the two children got into the truck as well. I overheard my parents talking about the Franz family and hoped that they would find a safe haven in Australia. I didn't understand until years later that Dr. Franz had lost his pharmacy and thus his livelihood because he was Jewish. Dr. Franz's pharmacy began to operate under new ownership. It was located on the Lindenplatz which would soon be renamed "Danziger Freiheit" (freedom for Danzig which is now Gdansk, Poland).

Things also changed for the Blumenbergs. Although they had converted to Catholicism, the German government was classifying Jews as a race in addition to a religion. As such, the Blumenbergs were forced to comply with the orders that had been set forth against the Jews. Hans Blumenberg no longer played with us. Mrs. Blumenberg and my mother conversed through open windows and it was agreed that Mrs. Blumenberg would throw her shopping list into our backyard. Nearly a two-meter-high-brick wall separated our yards. I was sent on my scooter to get the requested groceries. When my mother told me it was a good time, I would go over and knock on her door. Mrs. Blumenberg opened her door just wide enough to take the bags and give me the grocery money and a piece of candy which had been on the list. When I asked my mother why Mrs. Blumenberg did not take care of her own shopping I was told that she was simply too sad to leave the house following the death of her second son.

I did not learn the real reason until much later. Being Jewish, they were only allowed to shop on Saturdays, the Jewish Sabbath, in stores that were outside the city, and they were not allowed to use public transportation. For Jewish people, getting food was difficult. (The Jewish intelligencia, people who were teachers, scientists, actors, etc., were all fired. Many went to America, but it was hard for them to comprehend and accept what was happening because they loved Germany, their own country.) Mrs. Blumenberg never left the house. Her husband, a prominent art dealer, had to wear the Star of David on his coat. He usually had some pictures wrapped in brown paper under his arm. He also visited my grandmother who purchased two pieces of art from him that she intended to give my sisters for their upcoming confirmation.

After my father's death in 1936, our family's living arrangements needed to change. The ground floor of our house was renovated and a high-ranking, retired Army officer moved in with his most unpleasant wife and older daughter, Christa. We no longer had access to our front yard. My mother needed the income from the apartment. Our backyard was no longer the center of activities. Just Rudolf and I used the equipment. Rudolf began to raise rabbits. He built their stalls himself and we were busy gathering food for them. He named them Käthe and Lisa, after our mothers. They had many babies which had to be given away for lack of room.

In 1937, Mr. Ebmeier was promoted to Minister of Finance and the family moved to the city of Kiel, a harbor north of Lübeck. Brigitte visited her friend and reported that the Ebmeiers now resided in a most exclusive neighborhood and that their immediate neighbor was Admiral Dönitz, a highly celebrated officer in the German Navy.

A Friend, Maike, as well as Hinrich and Hedda, look into the Blumenberg Shed

My cousin Rudolf and I rekindled our friendship with Hans Blumenberg. We would climb the wall when we were invited by Hans to participate in his special sessions in the garden shed. He called them "trips to heaven and hell." Accompanied by gruesome noises, he would put us into a "pretend" elevator. I think I can still hear the utterly frightening noises made by him grinding chains in the "basement" aka "hell." During the adventure, Hans would describe in detail heaven, hell, and the stages in between in the most colorful and frightening words. It was horrifying yet wonderful at the same time. I am guessing that he based his pretend elevator on a real grain elevator that had no doors but that people had to jump onto and off from at the appropriate times. We were strictly forbidden to go on it which of course meant that we did. Getting on was as challenging as getting off and we called it the "Pater Noster" since it was deemed wise to say a prayer before daring the courageous jump. Hans had a wonderful imagination! Equally fascinating were his renditions of Greek and Roman sagas. I remember that Rudolf and I were always sad when his mother called him back inside and we had to climb back into our own yard.

Hans Blumenberg graduated from secondary school. He had been the best student ever in the region but was denied the honor of giving the graduation speech. He was also denied admission to a university since a new policy had been put into place that prospective students had to present an "Ahnenpass" (proof of ancestry) proving that they had no Jewish ancestors for at least four generations. Thanks to the excellent bookkeeping of the church and public registers, my mother was able to go back to the 1700s to establish all maternal and paternal ancestors were Aryan for each of her children.

The Hinrichsen family moved into the vacant house of Nr. 2 in 1937.

Mr. Hinrichsen was in charge of the canal systems. They had six daughters: Annemarie, Hilda, Erika (my age), Inge, Karin, and Margarete. Erika would become my best friend throughout my life. I shall write about her and the family a little later. My cousin Rudolf had befriended Herman Rohrbach, a neighbor across the street. Herr Rohrbach, recognizing Rudolf's musicality and beautiful voice, arranged for Rudolf to participate in several operas that were performed. Rudolf could sing all parts in *Carmen*. Erich Leinsdorf was the conductor at the time. He too lost his position because he was Jewish. I later saw him conduct in Rochester, NY, before he became the Music Director in Boston.

In 1938, I was obligated to join the Hitler Youth at ten years old. The program was run by the school so no one could opt out. You were expected to buy your own uniforms and meet twice a week. Wednesdays was a so-called political meeting and the Saturday meeting included sports activities. We were required to go to a weekend camp once a month. At the time, I liked being in Hitler Youth a lot and became a leader, in charge of eleven other children whom I then indoctinated with the Hitler story, teaching them about where Hitler lived, when he was born, and how wonderful he was.

On November 9, 1940, there was a huge assembly of the Hitler Youth in Lübeck. I was very certain that I would be promoted to "Schaftführerin." The position also included a white and red cord for my blouse. However, my name was skipped and I was devastated. Then my friend Erika said, "Hedda, forget about this nonsense." That day was essentially the end of my enthusiasm for the Hitler regime.

My cousin, Rudolf, was also in the Hitler Youth. The boys had stricter rules. A rough translation of their rules says, "The Hitler Youth boys are tough, keep silent, and they are faithful." They have to show their stamina and strength. Once they learned to fight and win, they were allowed to carry a knife. They would carry the knife all the time, even when they went to school.

I practiced my love for teaching on my little brother who was a most eager student. His birthday was April 21. This date was quite a mouthful to pronounce, so I taught him to say "One day after Hitler." Neither one of us has forgotten that date. On March 12, 1938, German troops marched into Austria to annex the German-speaking nation. Bunkers were built and sandbags were delivered to all the houses to store in the attic together with many buckets of water in case of a firebomb attack. The streets were filled with marching soldiers who would be sent to the front and soon the newspapers reported the death of "fallen heros." Carl Ebmeier and two teachers were among the first fatalities in Poland. Travel outside of our country was no longer allowed and imports from Denmark and other Scandinavian countries were stopped. Ration cards were introduced for meat and dairy products. Did I make a significant contribution to the war effort? Well, Inge Schmidt (you may remember her from November 9, 1938, "The Kristallnacht," when we kicked shoes along the street that had been strewn from the stores after all the windows had been shattered) and I went with a wheelbarrow from home to home and collected used paper goods. Once the wagon was full, we took it to our school. Depending on the weight, we received some kind of reward. I remember feeling very proud.

Meanwhile I continued to go shopping for Frau Blumenberg while learning at the same time that Jews were dangerous and evil. When I asked whether being Jewish was not simply a different religion, I was told by teachers that Jews belonged to a most undesirable race and that they would be wise to leave our country.

In 1940, Russian prisoners of war began working as our garbage men. Mrs. Hinrichsen took pity on the starving prisoners and put hot potatoes on top of her garbage cans. A neighbor reported her. She was arrested but, since she was a mother of six and a wife of an army officer (Mr. Hinrichsen had been drafted and had served in WWI as an officer), Mrs. Hinrichsen was let go after hours of interrogation. I remember my mother, who had comforted the Hinrichsen children, being outraged. Not knowing who had turned in our neighbor made everyone more cautious and afraid.

Meanwhile, the daily routine in the Hansestrasse neighborhood remained much the same. Herr Schröder brought bread with his horse and buggy, the milkman delivered every other day. He brought whole milk for my brother and me since we were under fourteen and skim milk for the rest. Buttermilk became a favorite. Emmeli graduated from high school with high honors in 1941 and had to work on a farm before she would be allowed to start her medical studies. I was allowed to visit her on the farm one weekend.

In 1940, my dearly beloved grandmother died. She had suffered from diabetes and had been hospitalized for a long time. One leg was amputated and Rudolf and I had made plans to push her wheelchair and build a ramp to get our grandmother upstairs. Our dear "Oma" died in the hospital. Her death was an enormous loss for all of us and her many friends. It was particularly hard for my cousin, Rudolf, since Oma had taken care of him all his life while his mother worked. Rudolf's father had deserted his family soon after Rudolf was born.

One evening in October 1941 my mother was awakened by the doorbell. Hans Blumenberg had come. My two older sisters rushed to the door as well. I heard voices and was curious, but my sisters told me to go back to bed at once. Hans was asking for shelter. He had been drafted to work with Wernher von Braun in Peenemünde where missiles were developed. Hans was very bright and thus could be useful to the war machine. Someone informed him that he was about to be arrested and he escaped. My mother put him into a small room in our basement. We kept our potatoes there. It was customary and more economical to take in potatoes for the winter. Emmeli brought Hans blankets and some food. My mother informed me that Emmeli would be getting the potatoes for dinner. This was normally my job, but I didn't mind since I very much disliked this assignment. I knew nothing about the actual reason until much later. Hans stayed there for two days until one of Emmeli's friends, Ursula Heinsohn, convinced her father that their house could be a safe hiding place. Mr. Heinsohn repaired our shoes and had a spacious basement. Actions like this were extremely dangerous since there were many miserable informers. Hans remained safe throughout the war and married the shoemaker's daughter after the war. Hans Blumenberg later studied Philosophy, became the youngest full professor in Germany, and wrote many books. He died in 1996. The city of Lübeck honored him and his work. Regrettably, it all came too late.

Christmas 1941 was different. The German soldiers were suffering in the snow and cold in Russia. The German population was requested to contribute woolen hats, gloves, socks, and skis. I had received skis from my grandfather who planned to take me on a vacation in Bavaria. However, since skis were not allowed on trains, I turned my new present in. I wrote my name and address on them, but I never got a response from a soldier.

My other present was a pen that could write in four colors if one pushed a little lever. I was unable to push the lever. My fingers were swollen and I had no strength. That night I became very ill with scarlet fever. The doctor advised that I should be hospitalized so that my family would not be infected. I remember my painfully swollen fingers due to fever and my swollen throat which made breathing difficult and swallowing impossible. I did not return to my home and neighborhood until almost the end of March 1942, when I promptly infected my brother Hinrich and sister Brigitte.

The British air raid bombing of our city on the night of 28/29 March, 1942, brought an end to the Hansestrasse neighborhood and my childhood. Thanks to my courageous mother as well as my then fourteen-year-old cousin, Rudolf, who went up to the attic to throw as many of the "fire sticks" out of the window, our house appeared to escape some of the raging fires for a while, but was eventually destroyed along with the neighbors' homes. They had all sought refuge in our basement. When we were ordered out of the house due to intense smoke, all families went in different directions hoping to find friends or relatives who had escaped the bombing. Our neighborhood was no more. I was fourteen years old.

In November of that year, we moved to an apartment right by the river in Travemünde, a seaside resort town located sixteen km northwest of Lübeck. In December, the Hinrichsen family took up residence in a most beautiful villa, just three minutes away. My friendship with that family became stronger and stronger. Erika and I were always together. We did not attend the same schools (there were two secondary schools for girls), but we took the train together and enjoyed endless walks discussing the world's problems, books that we were reading, and of course, our dreams for the future.

A Girl Comes to Dinner in Lübeck

It was in the fall of 1938 when the Hitler regime dictated that upper-class and middle-class families had to serve dinner to a less privileged child at least once a week. My mother was instructed to serve a simple stew, nothing fancy. A thirteen-year-old girl from a poor family came to have dinner with us every Thursday. My mother had decided that Thursday would be the best day of the week. Mondays and Tuesdays were usually busy with lots of homework. Wednesdays we were required to attend the meetings of the Hitler Youth and/or BDM (Bund Deutscher Mädchen). On Thursdays, we usually just studied for tests and/or oral presentations to be given on Fridays. On Saturday, we took a sandwich for lunch, since we went straight from school to have several hours of sports activities with the youth movement.

Another reason for selecting Thursday was that Erna Schacht, our maid, had the day off. We had to say goodbye to Agathe who had been our full-time help since 1933. After my father's death in 1936, my grandfather took control of my mother's finances. He decided that the money being spent on Agathe was an extravagance and thus Agathe lost her job with us. Erna Schacht came three times a week from 8:00 to 3:00. In contrast to Agathe, she never shared our dinner table. Erna cleaned the house and left after having done the dinner dishes. My sisters and I shared that job on her days off.

The girl was supposed to show her gratitude and do the dishes when she was with us. However, my mother thought that it would be better for her to sit with my brother and me and "do homework." I remember asking her to join in my "teaching" geography, as we were studying the countries of Europe, the capital cities, rivers, mountains, etc. She watched with interest as my little brother pointed to the cities on the map (he had been trained by me) and even asked whether she could find the places as well. I was a proud teacher. She was not a good student and had not been selected to attend middle school. Therefore, she would stay in the elementary school until she was fourteen. If the parents could afford it, she might have been selected for an apprenticeship, such as seamstress, hairdresser, baker, etc. But in her case, it was necessary that she would contribute financially to the family and she was destined to become a maid.

My mother cautioned us to never make a comment regarding the girl's table manners. She made noises when chewing, held the fork and spoon incorrectly like babies when they are learning, had her elbow on the table, and the list goes on. However, my mother corrected her incorrect grammar. Unfortunately, I have to admit that I felt superior to her. That poor girl! She must have dreaded Thursday dinners at the Martens residence.

My mother would take me aside and admonish me if I ever acted snobbish or thought I was better than someone else. In my defense, I have to say that I was one of thirty-six girls from Lübeck selected to skip the fourth grade and enter the secondary school. It was an experimental program to advance "gifted" girls, but the experiment was not repeated. It was found that facts and figures could be taught to children so they did well on exams; however, an individual's maturity could not be rushed.

Tante Annemarie and Onkel Rolf

I am going back to the year of 1941. It had been five years since my father's death and my mother's youngest brother, Rudolf Bartelt, had taken my father's place in the insurance company owned by my paternal grandfather, Heinrich Martens. We were all fond of our Onkel "Rolle." He was a most handsome bachelor and very kind and loving to us. It was great that he joined us for dinner at least three times a week and participated in many of our activities. He was our protector. I remember that he told me he would go to my school to complain about my grade in the sewing class, which was only "satisfactory." He felt that I deserved better. (Of course, at that time no parent ever complained to the school about grades or any other matter involving a child. The teachers were always right.) Every once in a while, he took me with him to his bachelor apartment to help him clean and tidy up, which made me feel proud and special.

One Friday in late April, my uncle came accompanied by a woman who looked so totally different from all the other women in our town. Dyed hair, red fingernails, artificial eyelashes, high-heeled shoes, runs in her nylon stockings, and a skirt just above her knees. Her blouse was not buttoned to the top and she smoked a cigarette! My dear uncle informed us that the two were planning to attend a party that night and that his friend needed to go to a hairdresser. Could I be so kind to take her there, since she did not know the town? I was stunned and so jealous and angry. How could my uncle bring this intruder?

So we went to our hairdresser. I was embarrassed to be seen with this lady. If asked, I would say that she was a famous actress but certainly no friend of ours. At the hairdresser, she decided to have her hair color changed to ash blonde from her current brunette. This procedure required some time and we started talking. She must have sensed my disapproval but she engaged me in a rather humorous and enjoyable conversation. I had to concede that she had beautiful eyes and even told her so. When she was finally done, the hairdresser combed her hair neatly and was proud of her work. She took both hands and ruffled her beautifully combed coiffure which upset the hairdresser. However, she left a substantial tip. Our outing must have taken just under three hours and once again it took all my courage to walk home with her. By the way, I learned that her name was Mrs. Annemarie Heinz. I stress "Mrs." since it made me feel secure in thinking that she was probably the wife of a business man.

Upon our return home, I found my mother and uncle in an unfamiliar serious mood. Of course, I had no idea why they were so somber. My uncle and Mrs. Heinz had a cup of coffee and left soon thereafter. Mrs. Heinz said to my mother that she was going to stay in Lübeck and visit us again the following week. My mother did not seem to be overjoyed but said that it would be nice.

Mrs. Heinz moved into my uncle's bachelor apartment. My cleaning services were no longer required and my uncle no longer joined us for dinner. Instead, Mrs. Heinz visited my mother fairly regularly. The two obviously enjoyed each other's companionship and were soon addressing each other by their first names. I learned that Annemarie and my uncle planned to get married in June of 1941. My rather old-fashioned grandfather insisted that the wedding take place as soon as possible. I had overheard rumors that Annemarie was pregnant. My mother confirmed the latter and told me that the

Annemarie

baby was due in November. Despite my strong feelings of animosity, I could not help beginning to like her and enjoy her most entertaining visits. The wedding reception took place in our house after a quick civil ceremony. So this lady became our "Tante" (aunt) Annemarie.

Stephan, called "Mucky," was born in November 1941 and my mother was very busy helping with the baby and teaching my aunt how to care for him. I loved the little boy and visited often. Six years later in 1947, the couple had a second son named Christian. It was not a happy time for my aunt and uncle and the two boys spent many weeks with us in Travemünde so that my mother could take care of them.

My uncle was drafted in 1944. Since he was over six-feet tall, he was ordered to serve with the SS. He despised the army and his duties. I think that the horror of his war experiences and a tumultuous marriage caused his alcoholism later on. A very successful and respected businessman in Lübeck, he was unfortunately not able to have a happy family life. My aunt Annemarie tried her best by giving lavish parties and keeping my uncle's disease a secret. Sadly, my uncle committed suicide in 1986.

Onkel Rolf in Italy

My aunt lived to be one-hundred years old. She died May 19, 2010.

There is a touching incident to relate. My uncle and aunt visited us in Rochester in 1958. In expectation of their visit, I painted several rooms in the house and my nephews had been constantly told "DO NOT TOUCH." Nevertheless, they did touch the walls and woodwork and I had to use turpentine frequently, especially to remove paint from their clothes. Tante Annemarie had bright red hair on this visit. This prompted my little five-year-old nephew, Christian, to put his hand on her shoulder and say with loving compassion, "Don't worry, Tante Annemarie, Hedda has turKentine and can get rid of the red." From that time, we always called that paint remover "turKentine."

Annemarie, Rolf, Lisa, Hans, 1979

Tante Annemarie and Onkel Rolf visited us several times in America. My mother and Onkel Hans were always happy to have visitors. Rolf, Annemarie, and Hans enjoyed playing bridge and my mother would willingly be the "4th" player, although she was never really good and was always happy when she became the "dummy" hand.

Onkel Hans, Lisa, Tante Annemarie in 1979

Thirteen-year-old Girls Discussing World Affairs

I have attempted here to remember my conversation with a classmate, Renate Bruhn, that took place in December, 1941.

Hedda, did you hear the latest? The Japanese bombed a harbor and destroyed hundreds of American battleships.

Aren't the Japanese our friends? I did not know that the Americans were our enemies. What harbor was it?

I think it's called Pearl Harbor in Hawaii. The Japanese outwitted the Americans with a surprise attack.

Aren't the Japanese the inferior yellow race?

No, I think you are referring to the Chinese. Remember, Herr Kunze (the geography teacher) told us that the Chinese were just good enough to work on the American railroad. Well, maybe, the Japanese also have a yellow skin.

And now America is joining England, Russia, and France in the war against us. Herr Kunze said that the Americans would not want to kill Germans since over forty percent of the American population is of German descent.

Yes, that's true, but remember in *Gone with the Wind*, we learned that the northern states destroyed the people in the south to free the slaves. So they killed each other.

Well, whatever. No harm will come to us. We are strong and very powerful. We have the best soldiers in the world and unbeatable weapons.

I heard someone say that the war will be long and terrible.

Don't be silly. England will be erased from the map in no time. Herr Kunze said so. And the French soldiers aren't any good and the Russians are just wild disorganized hordes.

They say that thousands of American soldiers were killed during the bombing of the harbor.

Oh.

Chocolate Fell From the Sky

The Nobel Laureate novelist, Thomas Mann, was born in Lübeck. In the 1880s, he used to spend the summers during his childhood and adolescent years in Travemünde. This lovely place is located at the mouth of the river Trave that empties into the Baltic Sea. Thomas Mann referred to it as an "Idyllic Paradise."

This small town has undergone many transformations. Already in the nineteenth century, Travemünde had attracted many well-known people. Thanks to its location on the Baltic Sea, shipping lines had opened to Denmark and St. Petersburg. They did not come to swim but they came to play in the casino where the game roulette fascinated the clients. Among the notables were Nicolay Gogol (1809 -1852) and Fyodor Dostoyevski (1821-1881) who frequented the casino and popularized Travemünde. The year 1872 brought about the beginning of Otto von Bismarck's new empire and casinos were prohibited under the new regime of the Kaiser. Thus, Travemünde lost its appeal and became a fishing village once again, an "idyllic paradise."

Travemünde became a harbor for the German navy during the war years of 1939 to 1945. The town then witnessed the endless lines of refugees crossing the river to escape the advancing Russian soldiers. That sorrowful scene was followed by the Iron Curtain, when a painful border separated the Baltic Sea and stopped us from venturing less than two miles to the east of the river Trave. Today, Travemünde is a very busy place. There are still some fishing boats and many sailboats in the harbor, but huge cruise ships sailing to Skandinavia, Lithuania, and Russia now dominate the scene.

For me, Travemünde was my summer paradise.

During my childhood, the same ritual took place every year. The first day of our vacation from school we put away our schoolbooks, tidied up, packed our bags for Travemünde and last, but not least, visited our grandfather to show him our report cards. He awarded good grades most generously, and

Emmeli, Brigitte, and I, as well as my little brother, Hinrich, would come home with quite a bit of money that we could use for "special" things during the vacation. Ice cream, soda, a five-penny ride on one of the donkeys that grazed in the adjacent park counted as my top priorities.

For many years we rented a cottage for the entire vacation; however, after my father's death in 1936, it was necessary to reduce our expenses. Instead, we rode the train each day for thirty-five minutes to our beloved destination. We left the house at 8:00 a.m., got the train at 8:25 and arrived at our destination, Travemünde Beach Station, at exactly 9:12. We could see the Baltic Sea from the station and we eagerly raced to the beach. My mother rented a beach basket reasonably close to the water. Right away we started building a big wall out of sand around our basket with room enough for all of us. We decorated it with shells and placed "flags" (one for each child hand-stitched by our grandmother) on the top. Our castle remained undisturbed throughout the summer. All visitors to the beach respected the area. Nobody trampled it down. It was safe.

In 1939 my mother, three siblings, and my cousin, Rudolf, took the train from Lübeck to Travemünde as usual. The weather was glorious and the Baltic Sea most inviting. As we had done for the past few days, we anxiously awaited the "Trumpf" plane that advertised the company's wonderful chocolate.

The plane flew over the beach at 11:00 a.m. and dropped delicious chocolates. Unfortunately, the plane did not come again. (We learned much later that it had actually been a British spy plane photographing the harbor.) Our life remained carefree as we swam, dove, and even took a short ride on a sailboat. When we returned home each evening we were sun burned, full of sand from the beach, happy, and tired. Our grandmother was often waiting for us with her famous Rote Grütze, a dessert made from several fruits and served with milk. We usually finished the day playing a game of Monopoly or reading a book before going to bed early. We needed Nivea cream over our faces and backs to soothe the burning skin from the day's exposure to the very powerful sunrays.

At the end of August 1939, there was talk of war among the adults, but whenever children came within earshot they changed the subject.

What did I know about war as an eleven year old? My father had been taken prisoner in WWI and all he told us was that he learned English during his two years as a POW in England. He never spoke about the horrors of the slaughter in the trenches in France. In any case, I was convinced that Germany was safe and secure. I was taught in school about the infamous "A-B-C-D" meeting, in which England decided not to oppose the German invasion of Czechoslovakia. (A= Adolf Hitler, [1889-1945], B= Benito Mussolini [1883-1945], C= A. Neville Chamberlain [1869-1940], and D= Édouard Daladier [1889-1950]).

The newspapers and our teachers proclaimed that Hitler wanted peace. He merely wanted German-speaking countries and territories returned to the Reich. World War II began on September 1, 1939, with the invasion of Poland. We were told by the regime that the Polish people mistreated Germans who lived there. However, many of the soldiers who fought in Poland came from Lübeck and died. There were tremendous losses and the people of Lübeck began to turn against the war. But, it was 1939 and no one could express their concerns. England and France declared war two days later and the U.S. joined them on December 7, 1941. Then Germany started a war against Russia and lost the Battle of Stalingrad in 1942. By that time, my family and I were completely convinced that the Nazi regime was terrible and Hitler was awful.

The war that had seemed so far away did come closer when the first death notices of fallen soldiers appeared in the newspaper with the headings: "These heroes have proudly given their blood for the fatherland." Included in these deaths were our math teacher and our Principal. Yet at our weekly meetings with the Hitler Youth we sang, "We are dropping our bombs on 'Engeland', trali, trali, trala" to a rather catching melody. December 7, 1941, brought the United States into the war and Germany incurred horrible losses in Russia.

Chocolate Fell From the Sky

No chocolate fell from the sky during the evening hours of the eve of Palm Sunday, March 28, 1942. Bombs fell instead. My neighborhood was hit hard. Our house was destroyed and the city was on fire. Soldiers came and ordered everybody out. My fourteen-year-old cousin elected to stay behind to rescue his rabbits (to no avail) and also to salvage what he could. My oldest sister was not at home. She had to work on a farm for six months (Reichsarbeitsdienst) before being permitted to begin her medical studies. My other sister and little brother were sick with scarlet fever and I thought of my birthday presents, which I had just received two days before. To this day, I see my presents before me: a tennis racket, two books, slippers, and yes, some chocolate. We found refuge at my grandfather's house. His neighborhood was not destroyed.

Lübeck was the first city to be bombed by the British Air Force. Köln was to follow two weeks later. The attack on these old, beautiful cities was designed to undermine the morale of the Germans. No military installations or factories were hit. War had become a cruel reality. Germany was not invincible.

Not chocolate, but bombs fell from the sky. I was fourteen and I had grown up.

The Air Raid on Lübeck

I had just come back from a six-week stay in the hospital due to scarlet fever. I was actually sick for about three weeks, but I was then quarantined for the additional time so that I would not infect my family. These precautionary measures did not help and this highly contagious disease got hold of my brother, Hinrich, and my sister, Brigitte. Both were very sick with high fevers. There was, of course, no penicillin yet.

I remember sitting with my mother on our dining room sofa, enjoying my belated birthday presents which I had not been allowed to receive in the hospital. I can still see the gifts before me: three books, a pretty blouse, a dark blue skirt, and a pair of cozy slippers. It was an exceptionally cold night and my mother mentioned that the six buckets of water we were required to have in the attic in case of fire bombs were probably frozen. At about 9:25 p.m., March 28, 1942, the wailing noise of the sirens announced enemy planes. My mother ran to get my brother from his bed and carry him with his warm bedding to our basement. I went to help Brigitte. I wrapped her bedding around her and, thanks to my slippers, her feet were warm. Her room was brightly lit, not from our lamps but from "Christmas trees" that lit the sky, fired by the British planes. My cousin, Rudolf, and his mother joined us in the basement. They were still dressed in their street clothes. The ensuing noise was horrible. The FLAK (an acronym for the German Flugzeugabwehrkanone, meaning "aircraft-defense cannon") tried valiantly to defend the city and shoot down the planes, but all attempts were unsuccessful.

Lübeck was the first city in Germany to be bombed. Thousands of incendiary bombs were dropped. They were a little bigger than hand grenades and filled with combustible material that ignited on impact. While our basement was soon filled with our neighbors on either side because their houses were burning, my mother and Rudolf ran to the attic to try to throw the bombs out of the window. (While waiting, my mother took down the laundry that was hung up to dry and was stiff from the cold.) Mutter and Rudolf's courageous deed appeared to have been successful and my mother went up once again to get our photos, some pictures from the wall, her jewelry, and some treasures from the china cabinet. By 9:45 p.m., the raid appeared to be over. It was quiet.

Our basement was filled with frightened, stunned, and sobbing people. Frau Hinrichsen with five of her daughters (the eldest, just like my sister, Emmeli, away from home), Herr und Frau Jenkel who resided on the third floor of the Hinrichsen house, and Herr und Frau Blumenberg were all there. Frau Jenkel was hysterical. "My furs, my furs," she sobbed. Herr and Frau Blumenberg wore beige coats with the Jewish star attached to the front. My mother ran upstairs once again to fetch a pair of scissors and those ugly yellow patches were carefully removed. Nobody said anything. By 10:00 p.m., soldiers came to order us out since the entire street was filled with smoke. My brother was put on a makeshift stretcher but my sister, wrapped in her comforter, had to walk.

Aegidienkirche Night of Bombing

As we were leaving our house, the roof caught fire and flames were coming out of our living and dining room windows. In spite of my mother's and Rudolf's efforts to throw the bombs out of the attic, a major fire had broken out in a warehouse nearby and spread to our house.

I was glad to have my winter coat. It was cold and the wind had picked up. Some of our neighbors were led to a nearby bunker; we heard that the Blumenbergs found a new place somewhere near Bargteheide, about 40 km west of Lübeck. Rudolf and his mother moved to my uncle Rolf's apartment, the Hinrichsen children were distributed among friends, and we hoped to find refuge in my grandfather's house, located on the other side of the city.

Church Destruction

As we walked around the city, we saw our beloved Lübeck, "The City of the Seven Golden Steeples," succumbing to a most spectacular fire. The flames were literally licking up the steeples which then crashed to the ground, destroying what had not yet been devastated. It was a most gruesome, unforgettable sight. My grandfather's house was not damaged and we stayed with him for the next six months. Not a single school was damaged and school started a week later, with Hinrich being transferred to a different elementary school. For me, it was the end of my piano lessons and my tennis racket was gone. The walk through the cold night did not hurt my sister and brother. On the contrary, their fevers were gone.

Lubeck After the Bombing

The bombing of Köln (Cologne) followed a week after the bombing of Lübeck. I remember heated discussions and articles in the newspaper arguing which city was more precious, historically more important, where more lives were lost, or houses destroyed. We listened to the strictly forbidden British news and learned that the raids had been "successful in undermining the morale."

My cousin, Rudolf, and my sister, Emmeli, who was allowed to come home, returned the next day to our bombed house in hope of finding things they could rescue. As is always the case, when destruction like this occurs, looters are not far away. They found the bicycles in the basement and loaded them up with some precious belongings. Many of our belongings had been stored in a heavy oak chest. It was so heavy it fell through the floor and into the basement when the floorboards collapsed. Among other things, all of the family's silverware and some special decorations were in the chest. The heat of the fire was very intense because the forks, spoons, knives, a complete service for twelve, melted into an unrecognizable lump. My mother later consulted a silversmith who advised her to make one ladle to always remind her of the fact that we all had been so fortunate to escape unharmed.

I have disliked fireworks ever since that night.

Hedda's house after bombing 1942
and the ladle that was forged from all the melted silver.

After the Bombing of Lübeck in 1942

We were very fortunate that my grandfather's house had not been damaged and we could move in with him. My mother was back in the same house where she had given birth to her first two children, my sisters Emmeli and Brigitte. It was different now though, very different. The lovely upstairs apartment which she had occupied as a young bride was rented to Mr. Castelli, his wife, and her mother. He was a well-known photographer whose specialty was images of Lübeck which are still being printed today.

We shared my grandfather's living quarters on the first floor. His faithful housekeeper, Fräulein Schröder, called "Schrödi," offered to move to a small room on the third floor so my mother and brother could move into her room. The back verandah was transformed into a bedroom and study for me. The large, oak-paneled dining room, as well as the living room, was shared by all of us, while leaving my grandfather with his bedroom and adjoining study. The guest room was reserved for his daughters when they visited. There was enough room, but it was difficult at times. My grandfather had also lost his beautiful business building and had to rebuild his insurance company in make-shift, cramped quarters. He displayed amazing energy, considering that he was seventy-three years old.

My mother missed her home. She did her best to hide her unhappiness. Both of my sisters were away now "serving the fatherland" in the Kriegshilfsdienst (mandatory war service). I had the good fortune that three of my classmates and good friends all lived in the same neighborhood; two of them, Ingrid Bülow and Annemarie Hirsch, even lived on the same street, Friedrich Wilhelmstrasse, and we walked together to school. The Hirsch family was my grandfather's neighbor. Ilse Magnus joined us on the way to school. Ilse was an outstanding athlete. Annemarie was a gifted musician, and there actually wasn't anything that Ingrid could not do. We were all good students and I thoroughly enjoyed getting to know them better.

One Friday in October 1942, the four of us returned from school and were looking forward to cake and hot chocolate at Ingrid's house to celebrate her fourteenth birthday. (At this point, the reader should take time to remember the dreadful sound of sirens you might have heard in movies such as *The Diary of Anne Frank*, as well as other films depicting the Nazi regime.) Just as I was parting from my friends, three cars displaying swastika flags pulled up in front of my grandfather's house. Four men, clad in black, jumped out, pushed us aside, and entered the house. We waited in Annemarie's front yard. Soon we heard horrible screaming and then saw a sobbing Mrs. Castelli clinging to her mother. I had never seen Mrs. Castelli's mother before that time. She was Jewish. The entire incident did not take more than a few minutes. The four of us stood frozen and frightened. We were told by the men to "move on" as they carted Mrs. Castelli's mother away. Needless to say, we never celebrated Ingrid's birthday. My distraught mother hugged me and said, "Hedda, I am sure that Mrs. Castelli's mother will come back soon. You witnessed a dreadful scene. I am so very sorry. You are too young to comprehend." Mrs. Castelli's mother never came back.

House in Travemuende, Vorderreihe 63

In October we were offered an apartment in nearby Travemünde and moved there on November 1. Our new address was Vorderreihe (front row) 63. It was located directly on the River Trave. We were elated and especially happy when we learned that our former neighbors in Lübeck, the Hinrichsen family, had also found a house just one block away. So, we were united again. Erika Hinrichsen and I did not attend the same school, but we were best friends and continued our friendship throughout our lives. We left the house at

6:45 a.m. to catch the 7:35 train to Lübeck and then, after a thirty-minute ride, ran to our respective schools.

Erika and I were fourteen years old. Our world revolved around school, friends, and family. Our teachers assured us that Germany would emerge victorious from the war. Our mothers could only utter, "Ach Gott!", when, as fourteen-year-old girls we were obligated to join the BDM (Bund Deutscher Mädchen Confederation of German Girls). Erika and I soon found out, however, that no attendance reports were submitted to our respective schools so we simply stopped going to the Wednesday meetings. Antje Ahmels, our leader, gave up reprimanding us when she happened to run into us on the street.

Travemünde from the Air Showing the Vorderreihe

My mother was happy in her new home. She had been able to obtain furniture from an antique dealer: a lovely bookcase that would soon be filled again, a beautiful glass display case, an attractive chest of drawers, three beds, and more. All was made of her beloved mahogany. We settled quickly into this beautiful town by the Baltic Sea which had been the destination for our wonderful vacations for so many years. One could almost forget the war. That is, until August 1943, when Hamburg, Germany's second largest city and an important harbor, was bombed. The destruction was colossal. And it was close by. Two weeks later, Kiel, a harbor at the Baltic Sea and about 60 km north of Lübeck, was in ruins after repeated air raids. The newspaper reported more and more "heroic deaths" of soldiers at both the eastern and western fronts. Some parents signed the death notice "in proud honor." Sirens cautioned us at least twice a week to seek refuge in the bomb shelter.

After the Bombing of Lübeck in 1942

When my mother and brother followed me and immigrated to the USA in December 1952, they moved into my uncle's home at the Tuberculosis Hospital compound in Mt. Morris, NY. The residence contained state-issued sturdy maple furniture, not as elegant as the pieces that my mother had left behind. "Forget about the mahogany furniture you received after the air raid in 1942," my sister Emmeli said, "It had most likely been confiscated from families who were either expelled from Germany or sent to concentration camps." That blunt statement stunned us all. Regrettably, it was probably true.

Wartime in Travemünde (1943 - 1945)

Note: The English word "refugee" denotes that a person has left his native country in hope of finding a safe haven or a refuge. In German, the word used is "Flüchtling," meaning someone who is escaping or fleeing, not someone who has found a safe place to live.

It was 1943 and Travemünde had changed. The cities of Hamburg and Kiel had been severely bombed and destroyed and Kiel could no longer serve as a harbor with access to the Baltic Sea. The Navy began to bring ships to our harbor which had been used exclusively for fishing and small sailing boats. The big ships went out into the bay every night so that civilians would not be at risk during possible attacks from the British Air Force. But during the day, our small town was filled with sailors and handsome Navy lieutenants who looked very sharp in their uniforms.

Emmeli and Brigitte were away studying medicine in Freiburg in the Black Forest, not too far from the Swiss border. Certain things seemed normal there, which is amazing in light of the horrors of war. Mutter and Hinrich visited my sisters for two weeks and I visited Freiburg during my summer vacation. It was a twelve-hour train ride.

My sisters returned home with me in August 1943 to visit with family during a break from school. We had left peaceful Freiburg and met with horror. Our train stopped sixty miles south of Hamburg in the small town of Lüneburg. Red Cross workers were busy helping bombed-out refugees from Hamburg. The city was an inferno after a massive bombing raid. We were transferred to a train to Lübeck along with many stunned refugees. I remember one woman who was clutching a suitcase. When someone tried to help her put the suitcase on the baggage rack, she screamed. Her dead child was inside. It was a memorable train trip and a true picture of what war is really like.

My Onkel Rolf Bartelt was drafted in 1943 at the age of thirty four. He was assigned to the SS (Schutzstaffel or Protection Squadron) and tatooed on his arm, as was the custom for SS members. He would not talk about his dreadful experiences when he had to obey the orders of lieutenants who were in their twenties. He only told me that his most horrible experience took place in Greece when he was ordered to destroy books in a monastery. By the end of the war, he was in East Prussia where he was able to catch a boat which brought him to safety in North Germany. When the Allied Forces were looking for war criminals, my uncle escaped imprisonment with the help of medical students who removed his SS tattoo and added scars on his arm to hide the branding. He rejoined my grandfather's company in 1946.

I had discovered boys. Helmut Bremer, two years older than I, became my good friend. He was also a commuter to school in Lübeck. We never sat together on the train because the boys played skat, a popular, three-player, trick-taking card game invented in nineteenth-century Germany. Helmut and I did walk together on the way home and he would take Erika's place for longer strolls to the beach.

It was always pitch dark at night now. All windows were covered with dark blankets. Almost every night the sirens howled and my mother was anxious for us to seek safety in the nearby bunker. It was fruitless to get changed for bed. We heard the planes and occasionally some bombs fell at random without doing any major damage except for some windows. Only my brother and I were living at home. My cousin Rudolf had found a room with his mother in Lübeck, where his mother was working.

The American and British forces landed in Normandy on June 6, 1944. The Russians were driving the German army out of Russia and Field Marshal Hermann Göring, who was in charge of Germany's weakening air force, proclaimed, "We will fight until the last drop of German blood is shed!" The Allies had defeated Rommel in Africa and were approaching Rome and Il Duce. The leader Bernito Mussolini, who had been dismissed and imprisoned by Italy's King Victor Emmanuel III, was successfully freed by the Germans. In late March of 1945, Mussolini and his mistress were killed by Italians. Their bodies were hanged upside down in a public square in Milan, depicting a grotesque scene.

On July 15, 1944, I received notification from the school that I, together with my sixteen other classmates, would be dismissed from school and granted the Abitur without the completion of another year and the final examination since we were needed in the defense of our country. The boys would be building walls and bunkers along the west coast of North Germany facing the North Sea while the girls were supposed to prepare the food and take care of the laundry. Erna Biehler, our pediatrician and my mother's friend, conducted my physical and, much to my mother's happiness, declared me unfit for this job. Instead, I was placed as a telephone operator in a small, almost defunct airplane factory on the Priwall, located across the river Trave, very close to our house. I had to report at 7:00 a.m. and stay at my job until 5:00 p.m. There was nothing to do. One day I brought a book which was taken away by my bosses who still believed in the German victory.

My cousin, Rudolf, was on call every other night to help out with the FLAK. He and I walked to school together and parted in the city to go to our different schools. Boys went to one school and girls to another. We usually met again after school, but one day Rudolf did not show up. When I returned home, my aunt asked where he was and I told her I had no idea. When she inquired about him at the school, she was told that he had been drafted. A bus had come to the school and taken all boys age sixteen and older. We learned later that he was sent for two weeks of training and had to learn to shoot during that time. He was deaf in one ear and had poor eyesight, but it didn't matter. He was shipped off to fight at the Russian front.

My friend, Helmut, was also in the Army now. My brother entered the Katharineum, a secondary school for boys. My father had attended the same school. So Hinrich too had become a commuter.

On July 20, we celebrated my grandfather's seventy-fifth birthday. It was a most somber occasion. My grandfather had lost his beautiful office building during the air raid on Lübeck in 1942. However, he had been able to relocate his insurance company and moved into three modest rooms. His office staff was reduced to six women. The male employees had been drafted as was my grandfather's partner, my Onkel Rolf Bartelt. The last news from him had come from Prague. My cousin, Rudolf, was believed to be in Silesia (in central Europe). I remember the excellent cakes provided by my grandfather's housekeeper; however, they did not raise the spirits of the guests. A late arrival to the party came with the news that there had been an assassination attempt on Hitler. Everybody rushed to the radio only to hear Hitler's voice stating that he had survived the attack of "cowardly traitors." For a brief moment (all too brief!) we had hoped that the war would come to an end.

The failed attempt to kill Hitler had taken place in Hitler's lair in East Prussia, a heavily guarded compound. An officer, von Stauffenberg, who had worked his way into Hitler's inner circle, had placed his attaché case under the conference table. Faking an unexpected phone call, he immediately left the room and managed to escape from the compound to a waiting plane which took him to Berlin. He had heard the explosion and announced the death of the Führer. The officers involved in this long-planned attack were quickly rounded up and on October 17, 1944, they were hanged. One officer was Field Marshal Erwin Rommel, known also as the Desert Fox for his brilliant warfare techniques in Africa. Rommel was a much-loved hero to all Germans and it was decided to ask Rommel to kill himself instead of standing trial. He was given a full-dress state funeral befitting one of Germany's greatest heroes, including sympathy cards from Hitler, Goebbels, and Ribbentrop cynically lamenting his untimely death. The Germans differed in their opinions of the attempted assasination. Out loud people joined with the regime and called these men "traitors." Behind closed doors, some might have lamented, "What a pity it did not succeed."

The North German cities of Bremen, Hamburg, Kiel, and Lübeck were no longer bombed. The enemy planes flew directly to Berlin and Peenemünde where Wernherr von Braun had built the underground factory for the infamous V-2 Rockets. The FLAK had become ineffective and the German air force had suffered severe losses in the air and on the ground. While we no longer had to fear air attacks, we became very worried and afraid of horrible warfare on the ground.

The sirens now also went off during the day. Schools closed. Streetcars and trains stopped running and, if we did not go into a bunker in Lübeck, we walked home the twenty kilometers. There was no FLAK anymore and the enemy planes flew low. We could see the pilots at times. Occasionally, a shot came from the planes, but no bombs were dropped on the ships or on the town. The planes were all headed for Berlin to destroy that city, most likely targeting Hitler and the high-ranking officials. One night, a huge bomb landed in the backyard of the bank that was next to our house. The impact shattered several windows but fortunately, the bomb was a dud. The explosive device was removed and the bomb stayed in the yard until after the war.

School started again in August—without me. My girlfriend, Erika, was a class below me and thus fortunate enough to be able to go to school instead of watching a telephone which never rang. Erika shared her homework in

English and French with me so that I could keep up. By the end of August, I had enough of the work at the factory and decided to stay home. By 9:00 a.m., my mother saw two men approaching our house. She sent me to bed. My two Nazi bosses told my mother that I could be sent to prison if I did not report to work. My mother's physician friend came once again to the rescue and certified that I had a severe intestinal infection. I stayed put for about two weeks. By that time, the ground war had intensified and my former job was no longer classified as "important to the national security." I was sent to work in one of the veteran's hospitals in Travemünde. Four of the big hotels had been transformed into hospitals.

My "hotel" primarily took care of wounded Rumanians and Hungarians who, although they had fought on the German side, were not treated as well as the German soldiers. Their linen and bandages were not changed as often as they should have been. Most of them spoke a little German (their ancestors having settled on the Danube under the Austrian Empress Maria Theresia). It was my job to feed those whose hands were either amputated or bandaged, to read to those whose eyes were bandaged, to hold their cigarettes, take care of their bed pans, and often just sit with these homesick young men. The stench in the wards was unbearable, the screams of the amputees horrendous and, since there were not enough nurses, I was taught how to give morphine shots and change bandages. The wounds of the amputees were frequently filled with maggots which was a horrific sight. I was told that maggots helped the healing process. I do not remember if I was wearing gloves; however, I was given some gauze to put over my nose. Many a morning when I reported for work several mattresses were rolled up and I was told to scrub the beds. No new soldiers would occupy these beds. The new wounded would no longer be transported to Germany. The Russian onslaught was fast. The Rumanians and Hungarians were either killed or the fortunate ones disbanded and sent home.

I missed being able to go to school, although I felt almost too grown up to be called to the front of the class to recite my homework or be told that my chemistry assignment was late. At the end of March 1945, approaching the final days of fighting, I received a notice from the School Board, that I was awarded the Abitur (final examination from secondary school). My report card was enclosed. However, a month later, I was notified that this certificate was no longer valid and that I and my former classmates had to report back to school in October to complete the last year and take the examination in March 1946. It was amazing that the bureaucracy in the educational system was intact in those tumultuous times.

I no longer asked if there was any news about my uncle or cousin. It was too painful for my mother. I knew I would be told if there was something good to report.

The newspaper still wrote about battles on either the eastern or western front from which the Germans emerged as victors. However, Reuters, the British radio to which we listened under blankets, reported otherwise. We were afraid of street fighting in our city. No English boats had landed on the coast of the North Sea in Northern Germany. The building of the bunkers was stopped. My former classmates who had participated in this futile enterprise were not assigned other duties, but they could not go to school.

The Russian Army had already occupied the Baltic countries (Lithuania, Latvia, and Estonia) and much of Poland. Refugees began coming to Travemünde. Some came by boat, others by train, and many just walked. Endless lines of desperate, hungry, homeless people streamed into the seaport. Mothers pulled their small children and meager belongings on wooden wagons, former landowners had their horses and larger wagons packed full with some furniture and, of course, children and old people, and many just simply walked alone. Then, one evening in December 1944, our doorbell rang. There were two young women with a two-year-old child. Would we have room for them for the night and some food? My mother told me to get blankets and bedding ready for the two small attic rooms which belonged to our apartment. Twenty-one-year-old Gerda Helm; her son, Bernd; and sister, Edith, moved in "for the night." They stayed until 1952. Gerda said she hoped that her husband, who was in the Navy, would find them and help.

On New Year's Eve, December 31, 1944, the Hinrichsens decided to give a party called "Enjoy the war, the peace will be dreadful." They had a big house and could invite several girls, including me, and ten young officers from the navy ship *Hugo Zeye* which was in our harbor. My sister Brigitte, on leave for two days from a Navy hospital where she was working as a future medical student, also came to the party. We danced (an old record player supplied the music), talked, laughed, and generally had a good time until the sirens went off and we all ended up in the bunker. We renamed the short evening "The dance on the volcano."

Brigitte met Werner Moller at this dance. He pursued her for many years, even after she was married and had a son. I "fell in love" with Hubert Höke, who died in February of 1945 when his ship was destroyed. My friend Erika met Albrecht Löper, a dashing young lieutenant. They got engaged soon after, but Albrecht broke off the engagement when he decided to escape with his pro-Hitler family to South America shortly before the end of the war. Erika later admitted to me that when she was kissed by Albrecht, she counted the flower pattern on the wallpaper. Obviously, the kiss was not a romantic one for her. The party let us flirt and pretend to be oblivious to the world outside for a while. We were all totally confused and looking for some normalcy in life, such as marriage. But instead the sirens went off and we all ended up in the bunker.

The winter months were filled with fear, speculation, and anxiety. The bombing of Berlin continued day and night. We no longer paid any attention to the sirens. Nobody went to the bunkers. Schools were closed. The military ships were gone from our harbor.

In 1945 the lines of refugees from the east grew longer and longer. The American Army was still fighting strongholds of German resistance. There were fierce battles in France with staggering losses of soldiers on either side. The Germans were driven out of France, Belgium, Luxemburg, and Holland and soon the American Army crossed the river Rhine. Air raids continued daily and, if you have read Kurt Vonnegut's novel *Slaughterhouse Five*, you know about the totally senseless bombing and destruction of the city of Dresden.

The British and American Armies were coming from the west, while the Russians, aided by the American Air Force, were fighting to conquer Berlin where Hitler was known to be hiding out in a bunker. The Americans appeared to be more interested in getting to Peenemünde to conquer the V-2 production installations and the big prize: Wernher von Braun (von Braun was captured in early April and was flown to the US with five-hundred coworkers. By 1950 he was director of the development operations division of the Army Ballistic Missiles Agency, developing rockets for the manned lunar program. He lived from 1912 to 1977.)

We had hoped that the British soldiers would be the first to come to Lübeck and Travemünde. Dreadful rumors preceded the Russian soldiers. "They rape all women and act like animals" was heard everywhere. So Mrs. Hinrichsen and my mother decided to sew towels together to make sacks to fill with some of our belongings. The two mothers were determined to send their daughters up north to Denmark to escape the cruel Russians. Fortunately, this drastic measure did not have to happen.

On May 1, 1945, the English Army arrived in Travemünde. We had been instructed to hang white sheets from our windows. We saw the army coming. Led by bag pipers and not in disciplined formation, looking haggard and tired, the soldiers stopped in front of every house. Two soldiers entered and looked around for weapons. They were satisfied when we told them that we had none and left. However, when my grandfather opened his door during one such search, a soldier saw his beautiful gold watch and chain and confiscated both with a wry smile. My grandfather was very upset because the watch that was stolen from him had been my father's. After his death, my mother had given Carl Philipp's watch to his father. He in turn gave his watch to my mother. Fortunately, my mother was able to keep my grandfather's pocket watch safely hidden behind the tea kettle and was able to return it to my grandfather. My brother, Hinrich, now has the watch. Peace was formally declared on May 8 when the Allies accepted Germany's surrender to end the war. The war was over. The retributions began.

Heinrich Martens' Watch

Many bigger houses were declared out of bounds and English officers moved in. This included the Hinrichsen house. They had twenty-four hours to evacuate. This measure left not only the Hinrichsen family, but also five refugee families, suddenly homeless. The three oldest Hinrichsen girls moved in with us, while Frau Hinrichsen moved with the three younger daughters to relatives in nearby Bargteheide. It was summer so nobody was cold. Despite these difficult circumstances, we made the best of this time and laughed a lot. Gas and electricity were only available from 6:00 to 8:00 in the morning and 5:00 to 8:00 at night. Since gas was available on a limited basis, we also cooked on our wood stove, called "Hexe" (witch), and I remember the oldest Hinrichsen sister, Annemarie, wearing a gasmask because the wood was too fresh, and she was enveloped in smoke. We had gathered it in the park which was, of course, strictly prohibited. The stores were empty. Whatever had been in storage went to the occupation army. Long lines formed from midnight on in hope of getting bread when the baker opened at 7:00 a.m. My sisters and I took turns waiting for bread. Our butcher, Herr Knoop, who lived on the ground floor in our house, often gave us a bucket filled with water in which he had boiled sausages for the occupation. That was delicious! There was no radio. An English Jeep drove through the streets with a megaphone, giving instructions for the following day.

Refugees kept coming. The stores were empty. Everybody hoped that the end of the war would come soon, regardless of the consequences.

Newly chosen German quartermasters looked at homes and apartments to find lodgings for refugees. Our second-floor apartment on Vorderreihe 63 had two large rooms, each with a personal verandah with glass windows facing the river Trave. There were also two medium-sized bedrooms toward the back of the house with a hallway leading to the bathroom and kitchen. Stairs led to the attic where we had two small bedrooms and another staircase led to the downstairs. The main level of the house served as the office and waiting room for a dentist, Dr. Gerdes, as well as the living quarters for Mr. Knoop, a butcher, his wife, and son Kurti. Half-way up the main stairs, there were two toilets, but they were reserved for the Dr. Gerdes' patients. However, those toilets came in handy when our apartment was packed full of refugees during the latter part of the war. My mother became incredibly protective of "her" bathroom as more and more refugees stayed in our apartment.

It was determined by the quartermaster that my eleven-year-old brother did not need a separate bedroom. Our living room also served as my mother's bedroom and my sisters and I shared a room. This measure freed up two rooms and refugees were ordered to move in.

By May of 1945, our apartment was occupied by many refugees. Gerda, Bernd, and Edith were the first to move in in December 1944. Ursula ("Usch") Haberkorn and her husband were the second family to move in with us a few weeks later. They moved into my mother's former bedroom. The owner of the apartment building, Frau Paeprer, had to move her belongings out of two rooms and consolidate into one room to make enough space for all the refugees. The Thomas family was next to move in. Mr. Thomas claimed to have been incarcerated by the Nazis and therefore was entitled to preferred treatment. They came from Belgium. The family included his wife, one severely retarded son, and their daughter-in-law. Extra beds were brought in. A few days after their arrival, Mr. Thomas began to make demands. He dictated when he wanted to use the kitchen, when he wanted to take a bath, and more. He got a job as a cook in one of the English officer's houses and brought home delicious leftovers that made us both envious and angry.

Night after night, my sister Emmeli and I held our ears to the wall to listen to what the Thomas family was plotting. They spoke French, but fortunately raised their voices so that we could understand most of it. There were rumors that Mr. Thomas was a true criminal. Many prisons were destroyed in the war and real criminals simply reported that they came from concentration or forced labor camps. One night, we heard the family leaving rather abruptly. We saw them walking toward the ferry and assumed they were headed for the Russian Zone. It was in early August of 1945. By that time, the military police came to investigate. It turned out that Mr. Thomas was a wanted murderer. "Good riddance," said the Englishman. If you committed a crime, the best thing to do was to disappear in the Russian Zone.

With the Thomas family gone, a new family joined us. Hermann Hinz, his wife, Selma, their longtime young apprentice, Dorothea Döring, and their dog Nellie. Apart from very few clothes, they had fled with their sewing machine. Herr Hinz was a skilled tailor and haberdasher. Selma Hinz died in 1947. Hermann and Dorothea lived happily together for several years in our house. Herr Hinz died in 1951 and Dorothea later became a very successful hat maker.

My mother fought hard and somewhat successfully for our bathroom and kitchen privileges. The refugees had to use the bathroom belonging to the dentist except for one day a week when they would use ours to bathe. The kitchen was available to the refugees between the hours of 10:00 a.m. and 2:00 p.m., provided the gas was on.

It was almost at the end of the war when we met two sisters: Wilfried (eighteen) and Gerlinde (sixteen). They had come from Berlin. Their mother had sent them away to escape the advancing Russian troops because it was widely rumored that they assaulted German girls. The girls crossed the River Trave on the ferry and marched in a long, silent line along the Vorderreihe.

They rang the doorbell at our apartment in Travemünde and asked us for a bath and some food. Since Emmeli and Brigitte were working as nurses in the veteran's hospital, we had two extra empty beds, so my mother took them in and they were very grateful. After a bath, some food, and a little sleep, they told us that they hoped to rejoin their mother and siblings who had found refuge with some relatives outside of Berlin. They stayed with us for about two weeks until they were able to rejoin their family and later sent us this photo.

Wilfried and Gerlinde with Their Siblings 1946

Hitler's birthday, April 20, was no longer celebrated. Käthe Wittekind, the Bank Director's wife, renamed her husband, B-dolf (pronounce "bay"), since she no longer could bring herself to say Adolf.

Photographs documented unimaginable horror when the concentration camps of Treblinka and Auschwitz were liberated by the Russians in Poland. Prisoners in Buchenwald, Dachau, and Bergen-Belsen, located in Germany, were freed by the Americans. With these tragic discoveries began the seemingly never-ending collective guilt. How could the Germans not have known about these monstrous happenings?! We were, of course, all aware of prisons and penitentiaries. We also knew that the government had been building "special prisons" called concentration camps for so-called "political prisoners." These were the "undesirables": Jews, Communists, gypsies, and homosexuals. One could also be detained for not using the Hitler salute in public, such as when entering a grocery store or the neighborhood bakery. My mother and many others preferred to say, "Guten Morgen, Frau Straubing," or "Guten Tag, Frau Karnatz," and "Aufwiedersehen, Frau Wemmel" when leaving the store. Contemptible informants sprung up everywhere; even "friendly" neighbors did not hesitate to denounce you. However, one could not fathom the unimaginable. Even my uncle, who had spent eight to nine months in Dachau in 1937 and 1938, did not tell us until shortly before his death in 1986 about the abominable circumstances he had to endure during his incarceration. This shame has stayed with me throughout my life.

On May 3, 1945, something horrible occurred. Daylight comes early in the north. We were awakened by the noise from the engines of pilot boats. We rushed to the window and saw pilot boats guiding three large ships (the *Cap Arcona*, the *SS Deutschland*, and the *Thielbek*) out of the harbor. Since we lived directly by the river we could see the "cargo." People in striped prison clothes stood shoulder to shoulder, packed like sardines. We watched the ships in disbelief. "They will probably go to Sweden," my mother said. However, soon after the pilot boats returned, we heard horrendous explosions. We ran outside and looked into the bay and could see that the ships had been destroyed and were sinking. I can still hear my mother today saying, "Not again. Ach Gott, did we not kill enough? Now we did this." Approximately 7,000 prisoners died in this tragedy. Days later, debris was swept ashore and town officials closed access to the beach. One of the instructions given by loudspeaker was that able-bodied girls over age seventeen had to report to the beach to clear away the debris from the sunken ships and, horror upon horror, the bodies and body parts from the murdered concentration camp victims. There were big trucks and men to load the corpses and body parts onto the trucks after we gathered them. That memory of my wartime activity has stayed with me to this day and I can only hope that this will never happen to any sweet, innocent seventeen-year-old girls in the future.

In 2015, the British government declassified sealed records from World War II. It was revealed that the RAF (Royal Air Force) was responsible for the bombing of the three ships in Travemünde Bay, and that they were unaware that the ships were filled with Jewish and other prisoners. In 2016, the Holocaust Research Center in Buffalo interviewed me about my experiences during the war. The resulting videos have been used in classrooms around Western New York. You can watch them by visiting ***http://www. hrcbuffalo.org/hedda-martens.***

Many disillusioned soldiers who returned to find their families gone and homes destroyed, killed themselves. Nazi sympathizers were imprisoned and anyone who had been a member of the Nazi party since 1933 lost his or her job. This measure affected many teachers who had been required to join the Nazi party in order to keep their jobs. It took some time for them to be exonerated. It also caused one of my aunts to lose her job. She had never been involved in politics and had only signed up for the party for fear she might not be allowed to work as a nurse. We also learned that Mrs. Blumenberg killed herself. Nobody who knew the Blumenbergs could understand that.

My sisters, Emmeli and Brigitte, continued to work in the veterans' hospitals (three hotels had been transformed into hospitals). My mother and I also volunteered with the Red Cross.

One day in June 1945, we learned that my grandfather was sick. I packed some food and rode my bicycle from Travemünde to Lübeck, a twenty kilometer trip. I was the only traveler on the county road. Suddenly, three men came out of the woods lining the road. They took my bike and, of course, the basket with the food, but did not harm me. A British Jeep with soldiers passed by and waved to me calling, "Hello Blondie," and then went on their merry way. I continued on foot to my grandfather's house. I found him well taken care of. The housekeeper had called a doctor who determined that he must have eaten the wrong things. I stayed overnight in Lübeck and found somebody who would give me a ride on his motorcycle the next day, but we were minus our precious bicycle.

A few weeks after the war ended, we saw a troop-carrying ship enter the harbor. As it approached the Kaiser Bridge in front of our house, it slowed down and moored. Hinrich and his friends looked on with growing curiosity but nothing happened. As they got closer to the ship they began to recognize a huge number of german soldiers packed close together standing on the deck. They looked sad and were very quiet. British soldiers came and shouted at my brother and his friends to go away. Walk ramps were set up and, one by one, the German soldiers disembarked. As the numbers grew they were ordered by the British to stand in formation. A growing number of German soldiers slowly began to fill the street in front of our house. They formed a long column, guarded by the British. They looked tired, forlorn, and unhappy.

Many people from our neighborhood gathered and stood on the sidewalk. By now word had gotten around to explain what was going on. The men were German prisoners of war, returning from Norway where they had been stationed.

Slowly the entire column was ordered to walk on. They were being moved to a POW camp many miles away. It was going to be a long walk. Many of the prisoners were carrying bundles. By some magic, they began to throw the bundles over to the sidewalk. Hinrich and his friends began to run to grab the bundles and the German soldiers told them to keep them. Inside we found personal items, military clothing, and some food. The clothing turned out to be of great benefit since it included winter clothes; of particular value were the gray leather pants and jackets.

There had been several forced labor camps between Lübeck and Travemünde. These camps were for all the prisoners of the jails that had been bombed during the war like our refugee tenant, Mr. Thomas. The camps were dissolved in late June. The freed men were out for revenge. Malnourished and mistreated for a long time, they acted like outlaws. I am sure that the three men who stole my bicycle and food for my grandfather were from these camps. There was no police force and civilians were not protected. We longed for law and order.

By July it had become clear that Germany would be divided into four zones. We were in the British Zone and we were relieved. The French and Russian Zones endured severe hardships and at times despicable treatment. However, the French and the Russians had suffered terribly under the German occupation. The British soldiers did not bring their own food supplies. They took our farm and dairy products and left the Germans with little food.

The destruction of Hiroshima and Nagasaki in early August and the subsequent surrender of Japan on August 14, 1945, as well as the formal armistice signed on the battleship *Missouri* on September 2, was really not of earthshaking interest to me. Our own struggles for survival were so overwhelming that there was no interest in the Pacific war and Japan. It was much later that we learned about the many tragic events that the American forces endured when imprisoned by the Japanese. WWII was finally over with Germany's most powerful ally now also defeated. The Japanese Emperor had to disclaim his divinity and many high officials were accused of war crimes as was the case in Germany. Japan assumed full sovereignty in 1952.

Konrad Adenauer, who had been appointed Chancellor of the German Federal Republic (West Germany) in 1949, also achieved full sovereignty for West Germany in 1952. Adenauer is credited with having been the political architect of the astounding recovery of West Germany. Adenauer had been the mayor of Cologne, but he was dismissed by the Nazis and imprisoned twice (1933 and 1944). Adenauer was reelected chancellor and served until 1963. Adenauer, a Catholic, met with JF Kennedy (America's first Catholic president) in Frankfurt after Kennedy's memorable speech at the Berlin Wall. The Wall was erected by the Russians in 1961 and separated East and West Germany for the next twenty-eight years. The Wall was taken down on October 3, 1989, and Germany was once again ONE country.

Recovery After the War

After the war, Germany was divided into four zones and occupied by the allied powers who defeated them (the Soviet Union, United Kingdom, United States, and France). We considered ourselves lucky to be in the British Zone in the north. They were not exactly gracious, but not vindictive, considering how much damage we had done to England. The American Zone was the largest and wealthiest, and included Bavaria, Frankfurt, and the middle of the south and southeast. It seemed like the American soldiers had everything, including chocolate, chewing gum, and nylon stockings, but they could be a wild bunch.

The French Zone was in the Black Forest in the southwest. The French people had suffered enormously under German occupation, so they spit on Germans and mistreated them.

People in the Russian Zone suffered unbelievable horrors because the Russians had also suffered greatly under the Germans. The Russians lost countless thousands of people and had been mistreated by the Germans who occupied their land and destroyed much Russian property. Now that the Russians were in control in the east, they retaliated against the people in some of the worst ways imaginable. They divided East and West Germany with a wall, which brought about the blockade of West Berlin. No food or coal, nothing could go to West Berlin for over a year. The Russian blockade propelled the American, British, and French to form one unit. Together they conducted over 200,000 air-lift flights to deliver goods, rescuing West Berlin from starvation. The Russians did not disrupt the airlift for fear it might lead to open conflict.

In mid-August 1945, Brigitte and I suddenly became very sick. I had injured myself with a pitchfork while adding horse manure to some tomato plants in Hinrichsen's garden. An incorrect dosage of tetanus antidote caused severe swelling and breathing problems. Brigitte had suffered from high fever caused by an acute blood infection which she got as a nurse in the hospital. Brigitte had to be hospitalized. She was taken to one of the veterans' hospitals together with the soldiers she had taken care of. Her illness was most worrisome. Delirious for many days, we alternated sitting by her bed. Penicillin was not readily available. It took Brigitte three weeks to convalesce.

The British occupation force was reduced and the Hinrichsens were able to return to their house together with several refugee families. Gerda Helm and her sister Edith earned extra money and food by slightly different means. Edith began a successful career as a prostitute, while Gerda, the mother of the little boy, Bernd, had befriended Rudy, a handsome, polite young man with good connections to the black market. There had been no news from Gerda's husband, Fred.

In the fall of 1945, I began going to school again. As much as I had looked forward to school, I now experienced a very difficult time trying to sit in a classroom again. Teachers had to come out of retirement. Some were probably in their eighties. French and English were taught by Miss Walsemann, math and physics by Dr. Joens who had been asked to come back from retirement, German by Dr. Bülow who had been known to have been a great admirer of Adolf Hitler but had somehow managed to slip through the de-Nazification process, and history classes were taught in English by an English officer so we learned a lot of English in his class. There were no text books available for this class because the Allies had burned all NAZI textbooks. It had not yet been decided what and how to teach Bismarck, WWI, and the Hitler regime; therefore, the teacher only discussed material leading up to 1870. For lack of lab equipment, chemistry was not part of our curriculum. Art history and music appreciation were the most enjoyable, together with Latin with my favorite teacher, Frau Dr. Binder.

My cousin, Rudolf, had been fighting somewhere east of Berlin. He was put on a train, along with many other soldiers, to a prisoner-of-war (POW) camp in Dannau. As luck would have it, the train passed through Lübeck. While he was not permitted to disembark, he was able to give someone a letter to be delivered to his mother. After spending about two months at the POW camp he decided to leave and nobody stopped him. He walked about twenty-five km to the town of Bad Seegeberg where he was able to obtain official discharge papers and then return to Lübeck by train. He went back to school for a short time. My uncle, Rolf, returned safely as well and resumed his work with my grandfather in the insurance company.

The winter of 1945-46 was difficult. The occupation could be harsh. The clothing stores were empty. Food was strictly rationed and we often had none. Children under fourteen received one mug full of milk per day and a slightly bigger ration of butter. Beetroots, cabbage, and occasionally carrots were the only available vegetables. Coffee and tea were highly prized commodities which one could only obtain through the thriving black market. There were long lines in front of the bakeries. Emmeli and I would often get up at 3:00 a.m. to line up at the bakery to see if we could get some bread. Many times, we stood in line in vain and returned home empty-handed. When we did get bread, it was made from corn meal and rather yellow. We took our bucket to the butcher who cooked sausages and meat for the soldiers and he filled it with the cooking water to flavor our soup. We were hungry, but we survived. At least we were together.

My mother, brother Hinrich, and I had grown very fond of my little cousin, Stephan Bartelt. He was the son of my mother's brother, Rolf, and his wife Annemarie. During the last months of the war, the winter months of 1945, my uncle was away as he had been drafted as a thirty-eight-year-old in November 1944. During that time, Stephan and his mother spent a lot of time with us. My aunt was terrified of the nightly air raids when eerie sirens sounded to announce the fact that British and American bombers were on their way to drop their bombs on Berlin. When the war was over and Stephan's father was back in Lübeck, little Stephan continued to visit us often in Travemünde.

In 1946 the stores were empty, the Black Market was thriving, and coffee was totally out of reach for the ordinary person. There was a small field near our house that we crossed in order to go to the beach. Owners of sheep looked for green fields for their animals to graze on. That field was a good location and it was tolerated since the sheep served as lawn mowers, keeping the field reasonably neat. One day, five-year-old Stephan came running home to my mother holding precious cargo in his hands. "Tante Lisa, Tante Lisa, I have a present for you! I have some coffee beans for you so that you can make coffee." What was the little boy really clutching? In his hands, he held beautifully shaped little brown kernels of sheep poop that to him so clearly resembled coffee beans, even though some of them had already begun to get soft in his little warm hands. My mother was moved to tears by this act of kindness.

Gas and electricity continued to be restricted. I remember being cold in the house as well as at school. The Swedish Red Cross supplied hot soup at school. We had to bring our own bowl and spoon. We made warm pants from the dark curtains we had used for the required blackouts for our windows. My friend, Erika, and I laughed about our outfits. Although the mood was gloomy, we at least had a roof over our heads, which was not the case for many refugees. POWs from England and the USA were returning slowly, but loved ones waited and waited in vain for soldiers to come home from the Eastern front.

For entertainment, we went to the movies at least twice a week, seeing the same movie over and over. The cinema only offered British movies. They were not synchronized and did not have subtitles, so it was quite a challenge to understand them. The same movie played for two weeks and we saw films with James Mason, Ann Todd, Margaret Lockwood, and Steward Granger many times. I remember in particular *Man in Grey* with James Mason. This entertainment proved to be an excellent language teacher. All girls, including me, were infatuated with James Mason. Money was worthless. We each brought a piece of coal instead. They used it to heat the theater.

The written examination for the Abitur took place at the end of February. If your test score differed from the teacher's evaluation, you would be called up to take the oral examination. I remember having a better score in the written test in my English essay and was required to take the oral examination in the middle of March. Mrs. Selma Hinz sewed my examination outfit, which had to be black and sedate so that I could appear in front of the committee in proper attire. I was asked about the usage of adverbs, placement of adjectives, and then had to analyze the sentence: "The doctor was being sent for." I stumbled and stuttered and my final grade would be the one the teacher had given. (I shall never forget that sentence.) We were informed of the results a week later. There was no formal graduation. The certificates arrived via mail. My grades were good. However, the remark, "Miss Hedda Martens tried her best; she has decided to pursue a career as a teacher," was most demeaning. Sort of reminiscent of the old adage, "If you can, DO, if you can't TEACH." Needless to say, when the University of Rochester later translated and evaluated my transcripts, a kind professor decided to eliminate the remark, "She tried her best."

My sisters had returned to the Universities of Hamburg and Kiel respectively to resume their medical studies. One of the prerequisites for me to get into the university was to spend time as an assistant teacher. I was placed with a fifth grade teacher in the Travemünde School. I loved this job very much. The ending of my time at the school was regrettably very sad. Toward the end of the school year in July, a special outing was planned for the class. We were to take the ferry across the Trave and visit the border to the Russian Zone. It was a sunny summer day. All the children were very excited when we got onto the ferry. Suddenly one little boy fell overboard. He got entangled underneath the ropes of the ferry and drowned since no one was able to help him. All the children screamed and sobbed. I cannot forget the teacher's comment to me: "Well, he was just a refugee."

My "little" brother Hinrich was busy with his friends just across the river Trave, on the Priwall Peninsula, dismantling three German planes that had not yet been destroyed at a small airstrip. This was, of course, strictly prohibited. However, the twelve-year-old boys were able to "work" undisturbed because there was really no organized law and order. They referred to their adventure as "we are organizing" rather than stealing. They were able to go there for several months before security finally ended these exploits. Hinrich brought home true treasures. He found clocks, parachutes and, best of all, batteries. The thriving black market was interested in the

clocks, my mother and I made nightgowns and blouses from the parachutes and my brother used the batteries to give us light when the electricity shut off. When Hilda, the second Hinrichsen daughter, got married, my brother used batteries to light the church. Frau Hinrichsen had connections to farmers and thus was able to serve delicious cakes for the wedding party. I remember wearing a blouse made from the parachutes. I was uncomfortably hot in that material.

Map of Lübeck and Travemünde

It was August 1946. We were all following our daily routine: going to the baker in hope of getting bread and getting the daily milk from the dairy. Gerda Helm had left for the dairy. She was eight months pregnant (Rudy was the father) and thus entitled to more milk rations. We were watching her son, Bernd. Then the doorbell rang. My mother went to answer. "Hello, my name is Fred Helm." My mother asked the man in but sent me quickly to find Gerda so that she could be forewarned. Gerda was devastated and so shaken that she spilled the precious milk. We returned home together. Instead of a happy homecoming, a horrible scene ensued. When Fred Helm saw his wife, he grabbed her and threw her down the stairs. Thank goodness, she was not badly hurt. It took my mother and me a long time to stop his violent behavior and Fred Helm was finally able to hug his little son, Bernd, whom he had not seen in several years. The little boy was scared to be held by the strange man.

Fred Helm joined his family in the attic room and life went on. My mother played midwife when Gerda's baby was born and she was asked to be the godmother to the very handsome little boy, Rudi. Fred got a job as a driver for the occupation force. He drove the truck that supplied the gasoline. He was caught stealing some fuel and selling it on the black market and was arrested and imprisoned. We never saw him again. Rudy, the baby's father, also disappeared from Gerda's life. We all helped her to manage. She was quite an amazing woman. One day, my mother had sent me to the pastor's house to see about some clothing for Gerda and her children. The pastor quite regularly received CARE packages from Sweden and the United States. Never shall I forget the scene I encountered at the pastor's house. His wife answered the door and seemed reluctant to let me enter the living room where the pastor, assisted by his three children, was busy opening and sorting CARE packages. He was visibly disturbed that I had arrived.

I glanced around and saw his daughters dressed in new sweaters, skirts, and shoes. One was sorting baby clothes; just the things I needed. I went toward her saying I was pleased that they had some available for me to take home. The pastor got up. He strode toward me ordering me to leave immediately. He and only he would determine who would receive what and that Gerda Helm (our refugee) was not even a member of the parish church. I became angry and accused him and his family of taking things for themselves. I played the courageous hero, grabbed some clothes, and left the house. It felt great. Later the pastor complained to my mother about my irate behavior. I declined to apologize and I have never set foot in a church since, except for concerts or to view the architecture.

I visited Gerda in 1966. She had married a croupier from the casino. They had opened a small "hotel" in Travemünde. The rooms were rented on an hourly basis and Gerda's business was most lucrative. Edith had died. Her son Bernd had left home some time ago and "Little Rudi" was studying to be a croupier.

We were surprised and concerned one morning in September 1946 when we saw a small boat with a Russian flag anchored right in front of our house. What was this all about? We had felt fairly secure to be in the British Zone. We saw some sailors on the boat but they did not seem to leave their ship. Rumors flew around. Surely the boat was infested with roaches and we quickly had a name for this mysterious intruder: Kakalatsche. That sounded sort of Russian to us. It was said that they had gone swimming in the nude; however, there were no eyewitnesses. At about the same time, American soldiers had been sighted. They shared a house with British officers. Among the Americans was one super handsome, stunning Negro. We had never seen a Negro before and everybody hoped to see him. I caught a glimpse and agreed with my girlfriend that he was indeed sharp looking. There were some twenty Americans and they became extremely popular. Fraternizing was strictly prohibited but many girls could not resist the nylons, cigarettes, chocolate, coffee, and other amenities that the Americans offered freely. In contrast to the British soldiers, the Americans had enticing lures.

Nobody figured out what the purpose of this strange visit was. The Russians left without much fanfare after about two weeks, while the Americans stayed about a month. We were relieved that the Russians had gone and felt safe in the British Zone.

I applied for admission to the Universities of Hamburg and Kiel with little success. The universities gave preference to war veterans, war widows, the best male students, and a few top female students. In fact, only one girl was admitted to Kiel. I started a six-month course to become a foreign correspondent instead. It was offered in Hamburg. My grandfather paid for my room and the tuition. He was reluctant, since my sisters were already students and he felt that I should see about getting married. This course provided me with enormous tools. I learned to type; take shorthand in German, English, and French; and survive rigorous practice. To this day, I am grateful to Miss Schmatolla. She was a formidable drill sergeant. My knowledge of shorthand and typing was put to great use much later when I worked for Mr. Yakoubian in Rochester.

After having completed that course, I returned to Travemünde and was glad to be home for a while. I continued to apply for admission to the universities. While waiting, I began to volunteer at the veteran's hospitals in our town where help was urgently needed.

Christmas 1946 remains the only Christmas without a tree and any kind of presents. There was no special food that we could prepare. Since it was very cold, we stayed inside. Neighbors came over for some carol singing and everybody tried to tell a funny story of sorts to lift spirits. A neighbor brought a bottle of red wine. We heated some water and concocted a warm grog for the crowd.

January 1947. There was no change in the monthly ration cards: 125 grams butter per person, six eggs, 250 grams sugar, 500 grams flour, milk (skim for people over age fourteen), and I do not remember how much meat was allotted. Vegetables (cabbage, carrots, and beetroots) were not rationed. However, a remarkable event took place, women over age twenty-one received twenty cigarettes per month and men were granted forty. Since neither my mother nor my two sisters smoked, we had sixty cigarettes per month to purchase items on the Black Market. Cigarettes were a precious commodity. I remember that we traded for coffee, shoes, and pants for my growing brother, more meat and butter, among other things. Occasionally, we even obtained a skinny chicken.

My brother, Hinrich, remembers taking his ice skates to a "scary old man" for sharpening. He had brought five Deutschmark with him to pay. However, when the man was done sharpening his skates, he asked for cigarettes for payment. Hinrich was frightened because he didn't have any. He offered the man the money he had, which the man reluctantly took, but told him to have cigarettes the next time.

Bookstores opened up, selling mostly paperback editions by English authors (some in translation). We were able to buy the books since there was nothing else available to spend money on. We became well read and loved all the novels and stories by Charles Dickens. Tolstoy's *War and Peace* fascinated me. (The latter was translated into German. Several years later, I reread it in English and found that the German translation was superior.) Best of all, Thomas Mann's novels were available as well as his novellas and short stories!

A few German authors, who called themselves "Group 47," began

to meet monthly in makeshift quarters in Munich to start anew the once
highly acclaimed German literature. They read their stories and novels to
one another and, once they were approved by the Allies, their works were
published. Heinrich Böll *Group Portrait with Lady* would later be awarded the
Nobel Prize, Siegfried Lenz *The German Lesson*, Wolfgang Borchert *Outside
the Door*, as well as Günther Grass who related his own war experiences,
the anguish of his time as a prisoner of war, joined them later. Grass's best
known work is the *Tin Drum*, which also earned him the Nobel Prize. All the
aforementioned authors focused on the collective guilt and the horrors of war.

My sister, Emmeli, completed her medical studies in Kiel and received
her doctorate. My sister, Brigitte, was in her last semesters in medical school
in Hamburg. She had met her future husband, Ewald Boettrich, a fellow
student. Ewald was severely wounded on the Russian front. His left arm was
amputated which prompted him to pursue the specialty of psychiatry instead
of general medicine. My brother, Hinrich, studied Latin and Greek in school
and took up playing bass in the school orchestra. (He continued to play the
bass when he later moved to America.) My mother volunteered with the Red
Cross in the veterans' hospitals and I worked with an import-export company
in Hamburg for two months. I stayed with a family in Hamburg who supplied
room and board in exchange for babysitting. I did not like this experience at
all and returned home to resume work as a nurse in a hospital in Travemünde.
I was still waiting to be admitted to the university. While I received no salary,
I did get food which saved extra rations for the family.

My life as a nurse was mind boggling. An extreme shortage of
nurses led to the fact that I was soon given tasks which would ordinarily be
handled only by qualified nurses. I gave injections, changed catheters for
cancer patients, and at times, the head nurse would tie a baby suffering from
pneumonia on my back to facilitate its breathing. Washing and feeding the
patients, as well as cleaning the rooms, was also part of the job. I remember
the bathroom, which served as a temporary morgue. Fortunately, there was
always another nurse assigned to help when we had to enter that dreadful
room.

Spring brought the recovering soldiers out to the street. Those who had
lost a leg were on crutches since they had not received artificial limbs. It was
a sad sight. However, they were glad to be alive. The double amputees were
pushed in "strollers" by volunteers. We were not sure if they were glad to be
alive.

Meanwhile, the senators of Lübeck decided to rebuild the churches rather than finding better accommodations for the refugees as well as those families who had lost their homes. At the time, we were all angry and upset over that plan. Today, Lübeck's residents are most grateful that the seven steeples of the majestic Gothic churches are the trademark of this proud Hanseatic city. Due to lack of funds and materials, five of the steeples are not "golden" anymore as they had been when covered with copper.

1951:Some Roofs have been Temporarily Repaired, The Dom in the Background

Spring and warmer weather lifted the mood and spirits. We had acquired two old bicycles which enabled us to ride to farmers in the surrounding areas to get extra vegetables and possibly a chicken or two. We also helped harvest early potatoes, earning some fifty pounds of potatoes for our labor. (To this day, I have the greatest respect for migrant workers who do this back-breaking job).

My sister Brigitte and Ewald Boettrich decided to get married in June 1947. Ilse, my new brother-in-law's sister, had come from Wismar, located in the Russian Zone. At that time one could still get permission to go back and forth between the zones for a short visit. Ilse had brought bread and eel. A few relatives from Lübeck arrived in the morning as did the groom, who came from Hamburg. Brigitte had come the night before. The couple went to the registrar's office later in the morning to sign the necessary papers and Ewald thought one could dispense with the church ritual, but everyone else disagreed. We had a pretty bouquet for Brigitte that was kept fresh in the bathroom sink. Shortly before noon, the wedding party started the fifteen-minute walk to the church. Halfway there, we realized that the flowers were left in the sink, but it was too late to retrieve them. The church bells rang, the organist played, Brigitte's friend, Rosemarie Woch, sang Beethoven's *Ich Liebe Dich, so Wie du Mich* (I love you as much as you love me), and the couple stood at the altar. The closest family members were also seated at the altar. Brigitte wore a wedding dress borrowed from Annemarie Hinrichsen. All was festive and good until Pastor Vorwerg, with great pathos, cautioned the couple to be faithful to one another. At that time, I regret that I started laughing, since the good pastor was rumored to be having an affair with a girl my age. My brother admonished me, "Hedda, behave yourself, this is a serious affair!" And the pastor seemed to drone on and on. Eventually the ceremony ended and we returned home. Our friends had prepared the food and set the tables in our living room. We were not used to the fat eel and I remember getting violently ill. In spite of that, a good time was had by all.

My mother's friend, Anita Chords, had offered her modest apartment to the newlyweds for the night. To our surprise, Brigitte and Ewald returned early the next day. They had been up all night struggling with swarms of mosquitoes.

The relatives in Wismar had connections to farmers and, several weeks following the wedding, it was decided that my brother and I would go for a quick visit to get some bread and sausages. At that time, there was still an exchange of cattle between the two zones. Calves were taken from the British Zone to the Russian Zone. They were traded for fully grown cattle to be slaughtered in Lübeck. Hinrich knew our butcher's son who arranged that we could ride on a truck with the calves to Wismar. The thirty-kilometer trip went well, albeit we arrived at our destination filthy and stinking like cattle. We were warmly received by Ilse's parents, washed up, ate wonderful bread, saw some of the sites in Wismar and planned to meet up with the cattle transport the following day at 11:00 a.m.

Much to our dismay, there was no cattle truck in the morning. The Russians had decided to stop the exchange. There was no time to lose. For all we knew, the Russians might decide to close the border. So we filled our rucksack with the precious food and set out on foot. A farmer gave us a ride for a while but when it became dark, we were on our own. It was scary; every little noise, such as a falling twig, was frightening. My brother was my emotional protector. We reached the border around 2:30 in the morning. There was a lot of action. Russian and English soldiers were cavorting with several girls. Hinrich decided that he would go first with all the food. We were correct in our assumption that nobody would pay attention to the boy. Hinrich whistled once he was on the other side and I approached the border. The guards were "busy" and I encountered no difficulties. There was an additional fifteen-minute walk to the ferry. We had to wait until 5:00 a.m. for the ferry to start. While waiting, I took my shoes off (leather shoes, no socks!) and I think that it took me a week or more before I could fit into a shoe again. Our mother had been frantic all day. She would never forgive herself for allowing us to go on this trip.

My girlfriend came running to welcome us back. She could hardly keep from laughing, "Hedda, do you want to hear the latest news? You won't believe it!" She was not really interested in details about our dangerous adventure. We had to go the hospital (a make-shift guest house) to see the "chocolate babies." There were sixteen, YES, SIXTEEN sweet little babies. One super handsome American soldier had been very busy indeed. The mothers could not keep the babies and they were advised that it would be best if these children would be sent to the American Zone and then hopefully adopted. One mother did keep her little girl. I heard that she grew up to be a beauty and had become a successful lawyer in Hamburg.

April 1948: A Fateful Meeting in Hamburg

Brigitte stayed with us in Travemünde after giving birth to her son, Hans, in early February. She was still a medical student and had scheduled her oral examination with her professor of hygiene. However, she was very sick with a breast infection and high fever and penicillin was not yet available for general use in Germany. Mutter thought it inappropriate to call the professor's office with an apology. We did not have a phone so it was decided that I would take the train to Hamburg and be there at the time of Brigitte's scheduled examination. I took the 7:00 a.m. train and arrived at the institute on time. The secretary saw me but gave me no time to explain. Instead, she showed me into the professor's office where three men in white coats had assembled. Not one of the men looked up. Not one of the men greeted me. The examination began. In answer to the first question I replied, "I don't know which one of you is Professor Harmsen, but I have come to apologize for my sister, Brigitte." I briefly explained Brigitte's predicament and then expressed my thorough dislike for their ice-cold behavior and unfriendliness.

At that moment, Professor Harmsen excused the other two professors and I was alone with him. I got up, admonished him once more, and told him I would get a new appointment from his secretary. He too got up and asked me to stay. "I like you," he said, "Stay, and I will show you my favorite places in Hamburg." He informed his secretary that he would be gone the rest of the day and the two of us went to the Barlach Museum, not too far from the Institute. I was bedazzled and enjoyed my first of many lessons in art. We then went by car to the river Elbe to have lunch. I couldn't believe what was happening. What did he see in me, a naïve twenty-year old? We talked and talked and, yes, kissed until it was time for me to catch the last train home to Travemünde with a new appointment for Brigitte in hand.

The very next day, I made plans to go to school in Hamburg. The universities did not yet admit single girls. Preference was given to returning soldiers, wounded veterans, and war widows. I convinced my dear friend Erika to join me in registering for a foreign correspondence school. We found a room with two beds—no kitchen use—and started our courses. Those six months of intensive study would be valuable to my earning money in the future. Best of all was the possibility to meet weekly with Hans Harmsen. On Saturdays school finished at 5:00 p.m. and Erika and I took the train home to Travemünde. On Sundays we took a bath, since we couldn't use the bathtub in Hamburg, washed our hair, and packed new clothing for the week. Our mothers did our laundry during the week. It took several days to do the laundry since we neither had a fancy washing machine nor a dryer and drying depended on good weather. We completed the tough course with good grades, with the exception of shorthand. I immediately got a job in Hamburg with an export firm using my newly acquired skills.

Meanwhile, Brigitte was successful in passing several interim examinations and was well on the road to becoming a physician. She too lived in Hamburg with her husband, Ewald. Their living quarters were dismal; a room in a closed ward for the criminally insane, which one could only reach by ringing for guards who would open several doors. Brigitte usually went home to Travemünde on Fridays to be with her son, Hans (Hänschen), who was completely in Mutter's care. In November 1948, Brigitte decided to stay in Travemünde and commute to Hamburg. I was assigned the task of picking up her belongings from her husband. A guard opened the room and I found him in bed with Elisabeth, a physician. He never moved from the bed. Once I finished gathering Brigitte's things, I approached the bed and saw him smiling ironically which provoked me into slapping him hard. After all these years, I can still see that face and hear him laugh at me! That was the last time I saw my brother-in-law.

Germany was not a happy place. Daily conversation dealt with missing POWs, deaths, refugees, and more death. My own life was in disarray: in love with a married man I couldn't possibly marry and pondering a proposal that my long-time boyfriend, Helmuth Bremer, had made. He was two years older than I and studying chemistry. His doctorate was three years away and he wanted to become engaged. I could not give my promise, and we left it that we would wait two years.

My Life in London

I had made several unsuccessful efforts to get admitted to the University of Hamburg. However, at that time the returning soldiers had first choice, followed by war widows, and finally the very top students. (Many buildings at the university were destroyed, textbooks were not available, and professors had to be de-nazified). My job in Hamburg was not exactly my dream so I kept looking at the university bulletin board for possibilities of becoming a student. In January 1949, I saw the following notice: "Mother's helper needed by physicians. Will have time to take classes at the university. All expenses paid plus £2 weekly. London, England." I responded at once. Alan and Erica Jones had placed the ad and they also responded at once from England. They made some inquiries about my family and character. They wrote to our pastor in Travemünde who was kind enough to praise my character, despite the fact that I was at odds with him. Rather quickly, my papers were in order and permission was granted for me to leave the country. At that time, just three years after WWII, Germans could only be employed with a family or a hospital that provided room and board so that supervision was guaranteed.

I left for London in May 1949. My luggage consisted of one suitcase filled with meager belongings. I owned one pair of shoes, two dresses, one skirt, one blouse, one cardigan, and one light summer coat. At the time, Germans who were planning to leave the country had to go to a camp-like facility in Hannover, 100 km south of Hamburg. It was a two-day stay that included a physical examination, delousing, and interviews concerning our political beliefs. We slept in large dormitories and were all looking forward to breakfast. I was hungry and very much in the mood for coffee. However, upon entering the cafeteria, the intense smell of porridge greeted me. Well, at least there will be coffee, I thought. No, there was no coffee; tea premixed with milk and sugar was on the menu. I was no longer hungry or thirsty. "Why on earth did I leave Travemünde," I asked myself. However, there was no turning back. I stayed on. The group went by train to Hoek van Holland and from there we took the eight-hour ferry trip to Dover. I had befriended a priest who advised me to stay up on deck in the fresh air to avoid sea-sickness which had befallen the majority of the passengers. The stench below almost did me in when I had to make a necessary visit to the restroom. I practiced my English on the train from Dover to Liverpool Street Station in London and was satisfied that I could speak well. I was met at the station by Dr. Alan Jones, my new employer.

Alan Jones was a tiny man of slender build who was carrying a sign with my name on it. "How do you do?" I said in perfect English. Alan originated from Wales and I could barely understand a word he was saying. His wife, Erica, had just given birth to a son, Gareth, and I was to stay with their friend, Anne, also a medical student, for two days. Thankfully, Anne served coffee and toast, to my great relief.

Gareth

Hedda with Gareth, 1951

Erica Jones with Gareth

Erica came home with Gareth three days after my arrival. Alan had already completed his medical studies, while Erica was in her last semester and busy studying for her final examinations. Despite their medical background, I was surprised how little they knew about taking care of a baby. They purchased the supplies that I requested and were glad to leave the baby's care to me. I had a wonderful life with Alan and Erica. They encouraged me to enroll in night classes since one or the other would be home to take care of baby Gareth. I loved my work.

One morning when Gareth was about four months old, the little boy did not smile at me and his beautiful brown eyes were hidden behind a frightening veil. I rushed to the phone, and reached Alan who instructed me to come immediately to the hospital. "Our car is outside, hurry!" When I told him I did not know how to handle a car, he exclaimed, "For God's sake, any idiot can drive, you saw us do that many times over." He muttered a few instructions and then hung up. There was no mention of calling an ambulance. I grabbed the baby, bundled him up on the floor of the passenger side to prevent him from falling, got the car started, and proceeded, stalling many times, hoping that the police might stop me and help. I reached the destination after about forty minutes, handed the baby to the waiting parents, left the car in a "No Parking" zone, and was led to a waiting room. Hours later, Gareth's mother, Erica, came to tell me that Gareth had an inoperable brain tumor and would not survive. Gareth died after a few days in the hospital.

It was determined that I would stay on to take care of the distraught mother. Actually, Erica's parents hired me. My pay was increased to four pounds a week to enable me to explore London and attend classes at the university. Erica had two sets of parents. Mrs. Littlejohn, her mother, was now married to an engineer for Rolls Royce. The Littlejohns were very well to do and most generous to me. They invited me to sail with them, took me to the Ascot Races, and bought me clothes. Mrs. Littlejohn asked me to select one of her many hats so that I would be appropriately attired for the races.

Mr. Axelrad, Erica's father, was a businessman, now married to a "dud," as Erica called her. I never said more than hello to her. Mr. Axelrad, however, was kind and helpful to me. I remember when he picked me up with his car and told me that it was time to get to know London. We stopped in front of his office on Tottenham Court Road. He handed me a map and some money, made sure that I knew their names and addresses, and pointed to a "Bobby" (a policeman), saying that I should not ask anyone else but a Bobby if I needed help. Then he reached over, opened my car door, reminded me that the tube (subway) stopped running after 11:00 p.m. and, wishing me a wonderful day, he drove off. It took a little time to get my courage up. I studied the map and found that the university was within walking distance. The personnel at the university proved to be most helpful. They recommended two English literature courses for me and even asked me whether I might be interested in teaching a German course. Of course, I was most happy to do that. They also directed me to the Student Movement House on nearby Gower Street where I soon became a member of the Club Committee and met

Steering the Littelohn Boat

Boating with Littlejohns

students from all over the world. My sightseeing of London was done for the day; Buckingham Palace, the Tower of London, St. Paul's Cathedral, etc., had to wait for another day. Mr. Axelrad was satisfied with my accomplishments.

My duties at the flat were now limited. I made breakfast and cleaned up after Alan and Erica left. I went shopping for groceries and, if Alan and Erica came home for dinner, I had to be there around 6:00 p.m. to cook for them. We spent the evenings studying, reading, conversing or their friends came over which was always most enjoyable. When Alan was on call at the hospital, Erica needed me the most. We talked a lot about Gareth. His brief life had brought so much joy, but his untimely death such incredible sorrow.

With the help of the Student Movement House, I had found an additional part-time job at the Inns of Court. I worked for a barrister who served as student advisor to incoming law students from Africa, India, Pakistan, and Ceylon. (Ceylon became Sri Lanka in 1972.) I assisted in finding apartments for them. It was much easier to find apartments for students from India than those from Africa. Indians were treated with more respect and Africans faced more discrimination. As part of a welcome package, free tickets to concerts and shows were made available and I was encouraged to take the students to the theatre, opera, and variety shows. I attended with them when my time allowed. I took advantage of this perk often. Another "job" was to take care of the wig that my boss wore when going to court sessions. I can still see that ridiculous wig in front of me.

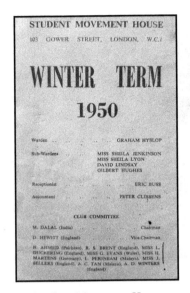

*Student Movement House
Program*

While attending a party with some students from Ceylon, I learned of the hatred between the Tamils who are Muslim and the Sinhalese who are Buddhist. At the party, I was having a good time playing table tennis with one of the students. Another student stepped up to my opponent and whispered something in his ear. Suddenly he stopped the game. He had thought I was Danish but, upon learning that I was German, he made some rude remarks and left. I was heartbroken and found myself close to tears. Then one student reached out to me and said he would take me to my home. He was soft spoken and had a kind smile. I took his hand. He was not a law student but an artist. His name was Stanley Abeyesinghe, a painter and artist from Ceylon, who had won a scholarship to London's most prestigious Art Institute. We became best friends and enjoyed countless hours at museums admiring the art. I fell in love.

Just as my thoughts about Hans Harmsen began to fade, he wrote me that he would be visiting London in two weeks. Ironically, he told his students in Hamburg that he would be in London and Brigitte, who was one of his students, asked a favor of him: "Would you possibly look up my little sister?" My family believed me to be very homesick. Hans dutifully took my address and assured Brigitte that he would look me up. No one in my family knew that he had written to me nearly every day. I had shared my friendship with Hans Harmsen only with my best friend Erika Hinrichsen.

Hans came and I told Stanley that I would be very busy for two weeks but, as luck would have it, Stanley was scheduled to go to Edinburough for ten days during Hans' visit. Hans and I visited Windsor, Oxford, Cambridge, and the famous Tate Gallery which was already very familiar to me due to my frequent visits there with Stanley.

It was with Hans that I attended the most memorable concert of my entire life: Beethoven's *Ninth Symphony* at the Royal Albert Hall conducted by Wilhelm Furtwängler of the Berlin Philharmonic Orchestra. Furtwängler had enjoyed special privileges and honors bestowed upon him personally by Hitler. Because of that, Furtwängler had been heavily criticized by the

Allied Forces and the world during the post WWII times. He had also lost his position. By 1950, however, the world began to see that Furtwängler was neither a Nazi nor a politician, but an incredibly gifted musician who could not have rejected honors that were given to him by the Hitler regime. As a gesture of "forgiveness," Furtwängler was invited to conduct the New York Philharmonic Orchestra. However, when his boat reached New York, huge crowds of demonstrators objected to Furtwängler's arrival and threw tomatoes and eggs as he prepared to leave the ship. It was decided that he would

Stanley and Hedda in London

not risk further humiliation—or his life—and he stayed aboard the ship and returned to Germany.

The more forgiving Londoners decided to have the ship stop in England and invited Furtwängler to play. Long queues formed immediately. Hans and I stood in line to obtain standing-room tickets as all seats were sold out. I still weep when I remember that performance. Beethoven's music and Schiller's *An die Freude* (*Ode to Joy*) evoked such unbelievable emotions in the six-thousand listeners who all left with the sincere hope and wish for love and peace among men. The text is so idealistic and romantic. Schiller (1759-1805) was dreaming of peace and love for all mankind. Schiller's poem is always sung in German. It was wonderful to have shared this experience with Hans. Whatever it was that we shared together as friends now seemed stronger. (When Leonard Bernstein performed this symphony in Berlin when the wall between east and west had been removed, he replaced "Joy" [Freude] with "freedom" [Freiheit]. I saw this performance on television and was deeply touched.)

I wrote to my girlfriend Erika Hinrichsen at home and encouraged her to come to London. Since German girls could only enter Great Britain as mother's helpers or hospital employees, I asked the Joneses whether they knew of a family. They did recommend several, whom I visited. I liked one very much but feared that they might not be kind to a German girl since they were Jewish. I mentioned this to Erica and Alan. They burst out laughing and told me that they were Jewish and wasn't I happy with them? My friend,

Erika, arrived a few months later. Once she was settled in, we decided to meet so I could show her London. We would both take the tube and agreed to meet at Piccadilly Circus. Being very anxious to meet her, I arrived a good half hour early and decided to stand at the top of the entrance to the tube. It seemed like the best spot to see my friend. Suddenly, somebody gave me a shove and I heard her most unpleasant voice shouting, "This is my place, Ducky!" I was bewildered, to put it mildly. Here I was, clad in a simple trench coat, no makeup, plain shoes, and a shoulder bag, while she wore a mini skirt, high black boots, a very tight shirt, and plenty of make-up. How could she take me for one of her colleagues? I had twenty more minutes to wait and I could not leave "my" spot. So I

Erika and Hedda
in Trafalger Square, 1951

ran down and up the stairs in frustration until Erika came. My nemesis was gone by that time. A new "lady" had taken her place. My friend and I quickly exited, only to find similar "ladies" in Trafalgar Square. At least now I was not alone. My friend, Erika, was not happy as a mother's helper even though the family was very nice. Instead, she began working as an orderly in a hospital. As a hospital employee, she received room and board, fairly good pay, and more time off.

When Erica Jones informed me that she was pregnant again, she asked whether I would take care of the baby. I shared her happiness but said that I could not give up the freedom I had been enjoying. It was agreed that I would help to look for a new German girl and stay on for the first two weeks after the new baby arrived. That gave me about five months. I found a new nanny for Erica who gave birth to a healthy baby girl.

The two English literature courses I had initially signed up for at the university proved to be too ambitious. My knowledge of the English language had severe shortcomings. So I withdrew from "HOLM" (Hamlet, Othello, Lear, and Macbeth) and continued only with the Chaucer course which emphasized the wonderful *Canterbury Tales*. Reading the original texts from the fourteenth century was in many ways easier for me because the language was so much closer to German. I was fascinated by the professor's attempt to recreate the language of so long ago. It was at that time that I began to get interested in the study of linguistics.

Teaching a German course was a huge challenge. It was a non-credit course since I lacked all teaching credentials. The participants were officers who would be assigned to the occupation army in Germany and businessmen who were interested in rebuilding Germany. The class met once a week for two hours. I had eighteen students and, since I assigned a lot of homework, the class kept me rather busy. It was a most eager and hard-working group and they seemed to benefit from my teaching. I was proud. To manage my time better, I quit my job at the Inns of Court but kept on with my interesting involvement at the Student Movement House.

My friendship with Stanley had grown stronger and stronger. We explored London, visited Oxford and Cambridge, and "hopped over" to Paris for long weekends. I moved in with Stanley, although I told him that I would probably return home to Travemünde in the not-to-distant future. My friend Erika absolutely disapproved.

Several students and I again "hopped over to Paris" for an extended weekend in January 1950. Since the French despised all Germans, it was decided that I would go as an "Irish" girl. I did not see too much of Paris during that visit. Money was scarce and wine was considerably cheaper than coffee. With two glasses of wine for breakfast, the Eiffel tower appeared to be swaying, so Stanley took me back to the hotel. A bit wealthier than the rest of us, he had a single room which we didn't leave until it was time to return to London.

A letter from Hans was waiting for me, announcing his arrival. I was in a bind and totally confused. What was happening to me, in love with two so totally different men? Then there was Helmuth at home in Germany, the only one with whom I could possibly realize my dream of starting a "normal" life as a mother of many children. But, I did not love Helmuth. Yet, neither Stanley nor Hans were men I could or would marry. Hans was married (twice already with children my age) and Stanley was going back to Ceylon which was entirely too foreign for me. I don't remember how I managed Hans' visit, but I did somehow and, when he left, I was more confused than ever. I confided in Mrs. Littlejohn (Erica's mother) who determined that I should go home to Travemünde for a two-week visit. She paid for the trip. It was great to be home. Brigitte had passed the final examinations and was working as a pediatrician in a Hamburg hospital. Emmeli was working as a psychiatrist at a hospital in Kiel where I visited briefly during my trip home. Hinrich was still in school, excelling in math and science. I had a great time with Helmuth who was home during a semester break. We took long walks along the beach and parted the best of friends. I also saw Hans in Hamburg, of course.

In early 1951, my mother wrote that my sister Brigitte was again pregnant and had decided to return to her husband Ewald in Rostock, East Germany. Obviously her son Hans would go with her. My mother had been taking care of Hans while Brigitte was studying to be a pediatrician in Hamburg. It was hard for my mother to part from her three-year-old grandson, in addition to the fact that she did not think my sister would find happiness with her husband. Ewald had lost his left arm during the war. He had chosen psychiatry as his specialty. He was not an easy person to know. Matthias was born August 8, 1951, and a third son, Christian, was born May 25, 1953. It was a difficult time for all of us as East Germany was out of bounds for us to visit. We missed Brigitte.

After some more time in London, and in spite of Stanley's interesting company, I realized I needed a change. After confiding to Hans in a letter about my confusion, I decided to leave England and Stanley decided to accompany me on my trip home. We spent a week in Paris, mostly visiting the Louvre and other smaller art galleries, then went to München where we viewed the Bavarian Alps, and finally on to Travemünde. Mutter was shocked when she met Stanley, who certainly looked different. However, his charm endeared him to friends and family. Even my grandfather, Heinrich Martens, whom we visited several times in Lübeck, liked him very much and was not shocked to meet this dark-skinned friend of mine. Stanley stayed for almost a month, earning quite a bit of money by sketching family and friends in watercolors and oils. When it was time for him to leave, I looked once again at the universities and was admitted for the fall of 1952. I would never enroll as my path instead took me to the United States.

I kept in close touch with Erica and Alan and their sweet little girl. The new nanny worked out very well and yet another baby was on the way. The big news was that Erica's best friend, Anne, had given birth to a boy. The father of this boy was a physician but married. Anne, who also was a medical doctor, managed with the help of her mother. Soon after Erica's second daughter was born, I learned that Anne had a second son. The identity of the father remained a mystery. I was already in the United States when Erica wrote that she was getting a divorce. Anne had disclosed the mystery: the father of her children was Erica's husband, Alan. Not only did Erica lose her husband but also her very best friend. However, Erica recovered. A year after this catastrophe she married a surgeon who was kind and good to her and her children. She wrote me such a happy letter and was anxious to leave on their honeymoon to Africa. Two weeks later, I had a letter from Mrs. Littlejohn. Erica's new husband had been bitten by a snake and help had come too late. Erica was a grieving widow. That was devastating news.

Erica came for a week-long visit to Rochester in 1973. She had visited her younger daughter who was attending college in Amherst, MA. She was glad to meet my daughter Anna. She had met Anna's father in London. She visited my sister's pediatric office and, since she was most interested to learn more about the workings of the practice, we had Brigitte's partners over for dinner. Brigitte had just recently been invited to join Drs. Richard Meltzer and Kenneth Woodward in their office. The background of the patients was diverse. Dr. Meltzer's patients were primarily Jewish, Dr. Woodward's were black, and my sister had many families of German background since the mothers and grandmothers enjoyed speaking German to her. "Were there any racial problems?" Erica inquired, or "Did any of the Jewish patients hesitate to have a German physician?" It was an interesting discussion, to say the least. But all three physicians agreed that there were no serious problems. Kenneth revealed that he had encountered serious difficulties as an intern at the University of Rochester in the 1950s when he was told that he could not assist in the deliveries of white mothers because he was black.

Erica opened her solo practice as a sex therapist in London. However, she died two years later of cervical cancer which had also taken the life of her dear mother, Mrs. Littlejohn, a few years earlier. Erica and I had been very good friends.

In May 1951 I left England to return to Lübeck. It was sooner than anticipated, but my grandfather's serious illness had prompted my early departure. Stanley Abeyasinghe accompanied me on this trip. We also went together to the hospital. My grandfather was happy to see us again. He became quite animated and talked about his brother, Robert, who had lived many years in Colombo, Ceylon, as an import-export merchant. "Do not go so far away," my grandfather cautioned. I assured him that I would not.

Portraits

Two portraits are hanging on one wall in my room. I wonder what the respective artists would say if they found out that the two people they portrayed would actually get involved in a close relationship.

The two men who created these portraits were completely different yet shared two common traits. First, they were both in their thirties when they created their respective pieces. Second, they were both in Germany when they created the portraits. However, one artist worked on his drawing in Berlin during the turbulent times in 1932-1934, while the other painted the watercolor portrait in 1951 in Travemünde, a serene fishing town by the Baltic Sea.

The watercolor painting depicts a young girl who appears to view the world full of good expectations. The other, a strong charcoal drawing, shows a determined, resolute young man.

Hedda in Watercolor

Hans Harmsen in Charcoal

The latter is by the artist Maholy-Nagy (1895-1946), a Hungarian-born painter and sculptor described as an all-around modernizing visionary. Maholy-Nagy studied in Berlin but was forced to move to the Netherlands in 1934. He left for England and finally in 1937 immigrated to the United States. In 1937 he directed the New Bauhaus School in Chicago, and in 1939 he founded the School of Design which is still part of the Chicago Institute of Technology today.

I am not sure what prompted eager brown-shirted thugs to attack Maholy-Nagy in Berlin, leaving him badly beaten and almost unconscious in the gutter where a young medical student happened to find him and take him to his modest room. He nurtured him back to health and protected him from further attacks by the Nazis. The artist thanked the young man by drawing his portrait. The young man portrayed is Hans Harmsen, who would become my friend and ultimately Anna's father.

The watercolor of me was painted by Stanley Abeyesinghe (1914-1993) who was born and worked in Sri Lanka (formerly Ceylon). After a one-man exhibition in 1945 in Colombo, the capital of Sri Lanka, Stanley's talent was instantly recognized. He became a sought-after portraitist. Following the recommendations of a well-known sculptor and several writers, the government of Sri Lanka decided to sponsor him in many ways. Stanley received a substantial grant to study abroad and I met him in London in 1950. We became fast friends. Stanley worked at the British Museum for a year and we enjoyed many hours at the museum looking at and admiring the art.

Stanley and Hedda in Travemünde, 1952

Hinrich in Watercolor

Emmeli in Watercolor

When I left England in 1951 to make preparations for my immigration to America, Stanley came with me. We visited Paris once more, traveled to Munich, and from there to Lübeck and my home in Travemünde. There he painted my brother Hinrich, my sister Emmeli and me, a beautiful full-length oil painting of my mother, and another painting of me in oil. Unfortunately, Brigitte took the portrait of our mother to East Germany and she had to leave it behind when she left. It is fortunate that we have a photograph of the lovely portrait.

Lisa in Oil

Hedda in Oil

It was magical to watch Stanley work. Friends and neighbors lined up to have him paint them and he did please some. Stanley came once more to Travemünde in 1952 to bid me farewell. At that time he did an oil painting of my handsome brother Hinrich.

Hinrich in Oil

Hedda, Stanley, Emmeli, Hinrich in Travemünde

We met again in 1956 when he visited me in Rochester, NY. He brought me a beautiful porcelain dragon that he had found when he visited Kyoto, Japan. He also painted my three nephews, Hans, Matthias, and

Christian, as well as an oil painting of my sister, Brigitte. That painting still hangs in the Highland Avenue house in Rochester where our family shared our lives for fifty years. Today the house is owned by Christian. Unfortunately the portrait of Matthias was lost.

Hans in Oil

Christian in Oil

Porcelain Figurine

Brigitte in Oil

I have two other pieces that Stanley painted for me. I had asked him to paint something that reminded him of his home. One is an oil painting of elephants in the jungle. The other depicts a Perahera Festival, a Buddhist celebration in Sri Lanka featuring jugglers, dancers, musicians, and lavishly decorated elephants. The amazing thing about this painting is that Stanley painted it on a small piece of aluminum foil. The amount of detail he was able to create is incredible. I am grateful to have so many pieces of Stanley's art. He died in 1993 in Sri Lanka. I have many wonderful memories.

Elephants in Oil. Stanley added the baby elephant at my request.

Perahera Festival on Foil

Hans Bartelt, My Uncle, Makes His Way to America

Of her three siblings, my mother, Lisa, was always closest to her brother Hans, who was two years younger. Hans was an excellent student and chose to study medicine following high school in 1922. He went to medical school in both Heidelberg and Munich in southern Germany. While in medical school, inflation hit Germany.

This thousand-mark bank note indicates that it was valid from September 15, 1922, to January 5, 1923, and reminds us of the inflation that devastated Germany. Crippled by the Treaty of Versailles in 1918, this was the time in history that enabled Hitler to convince so many politicians to allow him to rise to power.

Hans Becomes a Physician in 1928   *Hans Marries Dori in 1933*

Hans Bartelt, My Uncle, Makes His Way to America

When my Onkel Hans was in medical school in Munich, his father sent him money to buy food. By the time the money arrived, my uncle told us he would need a laundry basket filled with the paper money to pay for a loaf of bread!

Hans finished medical school in 1928 and began to practice internal medicine in Hamburg. In 1933, Hans married a Dutch graphic artist, Johanna Theodora De Jong, whom we called Dori. Käthe, his eldest sister, and her six-year-old son, Rudolf, lived with them. Käthe helped him with some household chores and managed his practice.

Unfortunately, circumstances changed for Hans in the years leading up to WWII and he made his way to India where he could continue to work as a physician since his German medical license was accepted there. Dori followed Hans to India and later was able to immigrate to the United States as well.

Onkel Hans in India

Hans treated many army officials and diplomats. One of his patients, American consul Roy Bower was most grateful that Hans had diagnosed him correctly and consequently cured him. Roy offered to help Hans immigrate to the United States and take the necessary board examinations there to maintain his medial license.

Dr. Hans Bartelt arrived in New York City in the summer of 1948. Roy Bower's sister welcomed him to share her apartment on Riverside Drive. Roy got busy with all the necessary paperwork and together they learned that Hans would be admitted to the New York State Board examination without further schooling since he had received his medical degree in Germany before Hitler came to power in 1933. They secured text books from the medical school, and Hans began studying for the test, which he passed in December 1948.

Hans did not have the desire to start a private practice again and decided to take a job as a physician in the Tuberculosis Hospital in Mount Morris, NY. The hospital offered a pleasant apartment on the fifth floor of the main building plus a good, if modest, salary. Hans was welcomed by all the other physicians and nurses and became very good friends with the director,

Lynn Armstrong, as well as the pathologist, Dr. Matthias, who had fled Austria in 1938. Life was good. Lynn encouraged him to take up golf and the nurses pleaded with him to join their bowling league. Hans had never been a fan of athletic activities but most certainly was intrigued by golf.

Hans and his sister, Lisa, corresponded with a regular exchange of letters and began dreaming of a possible life together. My grandfather died in July 1951, just shy of his 82nd birthday. We inherited a little money and my mother made plans to visit her brother in the US later that year. I spent the summer studying for and passing the interpreter examination and preparing the documents necessary for my immigration. I also made several trips to Hamburg to meet secretly with Hans Harmsen.

On September 25, 1951, Hinrich and I took my mother to Travemünde where she made what turned out to be a very dangerous trip aboard the freighter *Lucy Esberger* to visit her brother. We were both shocked by how small the ship looked. We met the captain and the other passengers who assured us that everything would be fine. I left my mother, feeling a bit comforted that all would be well. The ship left on September 26 at 6:45 a.m. My mother kept a detailed diary of her harrowing trip. It was supposed to last fifteen days, but many days of very bad weather, including a hurricane that forced them to change course, made the journey last nineteen days.

Lucy Esberger

At long last, on October 14, 1951, the ship landed in Boston and Hans and Lisa were once again together. They toured Boston, New York City, Rochester, and Niagara Falls. Lisa loved Letchworth Park and Mt. Morris where Hans worked. She had been thoroughly enchanted by her visit. It was

Lisa and Hans

very difficult for her to leave and I believe that it was then that Hans and Lisa determined that she should immigrate with her children and live with Hans. My mother's return trip took twenty days and was not much better than the trip to America. The ship encountered fierce winds from another hurricane, as well as fire caused by lightning strikes. Hinrich and I picked our mother up on January 5, 1952, in Hamburg, Germany, and took the train back to Travemünde. On the train, the wheels were set in motion for my immigration to America. My mother and brother would soon decide to follow.

Lisa with Hans in Mt. Morris, 1951

A New Life in the United States of America

Hedda Departs for America on May 2, 1952

In November 1951, I finalized my plans to accept Onkel Hans' invitation to immigrate to the United States. After my two-and-a-half years in England, I felt like an outsider in Germany, where I did not see any future for myself. Mutter had visited her brother in America. Reassured that I would have a good life in the USA with Onkel Hans, Mutter supported my plans to leave Germany. Stanley came once more for a visit to Travemünde, but by then my mind was made up to leave Europe and start anew without all of these attachments.

I was twenty-four years old. My sisters were working as physicians. All I had were a few credits from the University of London and a paper proving I had passed an examination as an interpreter. It was high time to show some accomplishments and to leave behind unrealistic relationships. There was Stanley Abeyesinghe, the Ceylonese artist, and Hans Harmsen, a married professor at the University of Hamburg.

Hedda Says Goodbye to her Mother, Lisa

On May 2, 1952, my mother and my brother, Hinrich, accompanied me on the train to Blankensee, Hamburg's harbor. I had only one suitcase. After a tearful embrace, I boarded the *Italia*, a fairly big ship, filled with some 2,000 souls, also venturing out into the unknown, destined for either Canada or the United States, full of dreams and hope. I was shown my bed in a dormitory, left my suitcase, and hurried on deck to look for Mutter and Hinrich to wave a final goodbye. Next to me stood a man who asked if I could please tell him if I saw a tall man in the crowd wearing a short-sleeve shirt and no tie. I

Hedda Meets Hermann Dillenberg at the Ship Railing

informed him that I too was looking for a man with the same description (a secret which I had not shared with either Mutter or Hinrich). Hans stood out in the huge crowd gathered ashore. What a coincidence, the man next to me and I had both been looking for Hans Harmsen, who had promised both of us he would be at the pier. We spotted him in the crowd and began talking about him. I all but forgot about Mutter and Hinrich. I introduced Hans as my sister's professor, since I could not possibly admit otherwise; while my new acquaintance told me that he and Hans Harmsen had been together on the medical team with Rommel in Africa.

My new companion finally introduced himself. "I am Herman Dillenberg, a bacteriologist, serving here as the ship's physician." His name was familiar to me from stories that my Hans had told me about his time with Field Marshal Rommel in Africa. After the defeat in Africa (Tunisia), both he and Hans were sent to Greece, where German troops were suffering serious diseases while in retreat. They were separated in the spring of 1944 and did not meet again until 1946, when Hans founded the Hygienie Institut in Hamburg and had resumed work as professor of social medicine at the University of Hamburg. Hermann Dillenberg had not been as fortunate, since West Germany had no means to offer him a good position. He applied and was accepted as professor of bacteriology at the University of Regina in Saskachewan, Canada. The school provided for his trip and gave him the position as the ship's physician.

Herman and I became instant friends. Learning of my dormitory-style accommodations, he requested that my suitcase be brought up to his suite which consisted of a bedroom and a living room. In other words, I was now in "very proper" accommodations. It was definitely an enormous upgrade moving from fourth to first class. Herman and I talked and talked and enjoyed several of the ship's recreational offerings. Rather enjoyable was the fact that I now ate at the Captain's table as the friend of the ship's physician. Curious and jealous people asked, "How did you arrange this?"

Hedda and Hermann Enjoy a Sauna on Italia

A fast romance developed. In hindsight, I can probably describe us as two insecure individuals; I was twenty four and Hermann, thirty six, both looking at our futures in a new country with great anxiety. At least my English was good since I had spent over two years in England. Hermann's English was limited to what he had learned in secondary school many years earlier. On the third day of our trip, prior to reaching Calais, he proposed marriage to me. I accepted. He wrote a letter to my mother asking rather formally for my hand. He gave as a reference Professor Hans Harmsen. The boat trip was wonderful; we dined at the captain's table, enjoyed the pool and the sauna, and each other's company. The captain offered to marry us, but I felt I had better wait. Onkel Hans was waiting for me in New York and I thought it wise to discuss my new adventure with him. I also wanted to know what Hans Harmsen had to say. After ten days, we reached Halifax, said goodbye, and promised to meet as soon as possible in Niagara Falls. Our farewell was filled with promises of love and faithfulness forever. Meanwhile, my dear mother took the train to Hamburg to find out more about this Dr. Dillenberg. Hans Harmsen assured her that Herman was a good man and a good choice for her daughter.

Arriving in New York was very emotional, seeing the Statue of Liberty greeting the "huddled masses." I quickly found my uncle. I had not seen him since 1936, but I recognized him from photos. My uncle welcomed me with open arms. We spent two days in New York City and became acquainted and very fond of each other. He was delighted to have a family member with him. It all felt like a dream. We also stopped to visit Hedda Mohr and her husband Jackob who had a basement apartment on Riverside Drive which served also as Dr. Mohr's office. He was an internist. (More about them later.) We also visited the friend and benefactor of Onkel Hans, Roy Bower. Roy had served as US consul to India and had met Onkel Hans in Madras. It was the first time I had to speak English since my arrival in the US. We continued on our trip along the beautiful Hudson River to Mount Morris, a small town south of Rochester, NY. I think I waited until we reached Elmira before telling Onkel Hans about my engagement to Hermann Dillenberg and our plan to live in Winnipeg. I felt guilty and embarrassed telling my story since I really wanted to stay with Onkel Hans longer and get to know him.

He told me that four letters were waiting for me. My mother had written as well as Herman Dillenberg, Stanley Abeyesinghe, and Hans Harmsen. My mother sent her best wishes but asked me to talk to my uncle before making any drastic plans. To say I was confused was a huge understatement. I was very grateful to my uncle for sponsoring my new life in America and I was determined to make him proud. The nurses and my uncle's colleagues at the Mt. Morris hospital welcomed me with open arms. I spent most of the month of May in Mt. Morris where my uncle was a resident physician at the Tuberculosis Hospital on Murray Hill. We shared living quarters on the fifth floor of the hospital. My uncle was waiting to move into one of the doctors' houses in preparation for my mother and brother joining him in December of that year. Of course, there was the gnawing question regarding my future plans.

We changed the topic and Onkel Hans told me about his memories of my childhood in Lübeck. He had been a physician in Hamburg, had just opened his private practice, and made frequent visits on his motorcycle to Lübeck to visit his mother who resided in the same house as our family. I did not remember him but loved his stories from 1930 to 1936. I learned that I had been a flower girl at his wedding to Johanna Theodora DeJong (Dori) in 1934, and that my mother had not been able to attend the celebration because my brother Hinrich was about to be born. He told me about Hinrich's very serious illness as a newborn. He was an "RH" baby and was very yellow and sick. It was a miracle for him to survive. In 1934, the blood-type problem (Rhesus factor) had not been discovered, let alone solved. Onkel Hans continued to tell me how he and his friend, Walter Stratz, a Swiss dentist, enjoyed my singing of all the Christmas songs, totally off-key but with such fervor and enthusiasm. Most important to me, however, were his stories about my father, whom he described as a most wonderful, loving man. How puzzled he and all the physicians had been about my father's illness: MS symptoms, possible brain tumor, and scar tissue from measles. Even the autopsy (my father died September 16, 1936) did not result in a diagnosis. My father's death and funeral had been Onkel Hans' last participation in a family function. He left for India soon thereafter. I learned from him much later why he left.

My uncle and I arrived in Mount Morris, NY, at dinner time and my uncle's colleague, Lynn, and his wife, Lucy Armstrong, were waiting for us with an enormous dinner. Their two daughters, about two and three years old were eating with us, which I found rather odd. European children did not usually participate in dinner parties, thus avoiding the constant parental admonitions. As it was, the two children dominated the "conversation." After dinner, they were taken to bed by their father while the hostess attended to the dishes. I was surprised that Lynn, the director of the hospital, did not have a maid. I was anxious to read the letters and I was also tired. Onkel Hans and I left soon after dinner. The news from Germany (the letters had been sent via airmail instead of a slow ship like the *Italia*) was very strange. In his letter to Mutter, Hermann Dillenberg had given Hans Harmsen as a reference. Mutter, who knew nothing of my four-year friendship with Hans Harmsen, immediately took the train to Hamburg to see him. He read Hermann's letter and assured Mutter that Hermann was an excellent choice and that he would be good for me. He advised Mutter, however, to tell me to wait, which she did. She cautioned me to let at least six months go by before I left for Canada.

The letter from Hans Harmsen asked me to join him in New York City in two weeks where we would stay in his brother-in-law's, photographer Ted von Borsig's, apartment while he was on an assignment in Europe. Enclosed in the letter was a bank draft for $200 to cover my flight to NYC. The next day there was a phone call from Hermann arranging a meeting in Niagara Falls. He could not enter the USA and I could not enter Canada. Five days later,

A New Life in the United States of America

Onkel Hans drove me to the Rainbow Bridge between Canada and the US. I met Hermann at the customs house where Onkel Hans left us to talk for many hours. Hermann had also received a letter from Hans Harmsen and insisted that I not meet with him in NYC. Infatuated (in love?) I swore up and down that I would not go to NYC. Back in the car, Onkel Hans was not willing to advise me. "You have to decide for yourself."

I went to New York City. Hans and I stayed one week, explored the splendid city, and I decided to write a letter to Hermann, bringing my brief, oh-so-wonderful ship-board relationship/romance to an end. Back in Mount Morris, Onkel Hans was relieved that I would be staying in the US. I made plans to build a life.

My First Years in the United States

I ended up having a variety of jobs while I explored opportunities at the University of Rochester, hoping that I too would be a student someday.

A position offered by the Rochester Children's Center sounded attractive since it offered room and board. I became a housemother's aide at Hillside, located on Monroe and Highland Avenues in Rochester. My room was in between the two dormitories that held a total of sixteen boys ranging in age from seven to sixteen. They all came from very troubled backgrounds and appeared to be unwanted by their respective families. The housemother was a kindly elderly woman who did not stay overnight at the house. My job consisted of supervising the daily routine which began by making breakfast. The lunch "menu" was the same every day: slices of Wonder Bread with peanut butter and mint jelly. I can still smell this combination and have not touched peanut butter since.

While helping the boys collect their dirty laundry one day, I noticed a strong odor of urine. It turned out that several boys were bedwetters who, fearing either shame and/or punishment, simply covered their beds. One day when the weather was great, I decided to have the boys help me take the mattresses out and wash them and collect their sheets for the laundry. The director, Miss Adelaide Kaiser, came storming out. "What do you think you are doing!?" she screamed. "When the boys wet their beds, they have to suffer the consequences." Although I was not familiar with this particular problem afflicting some of the boys, I lost all respect for Miss Kaiser and wondered how she got the position as director (I later learned her father had been a well-known pediatrician in Rochester). I continued to take care of the wet beds and the boys were most grateful to me.

I was off two afternoons a week and every other weekend, when the housemother stayed overnight. I used the free time to look into furthering my education. The University of Rochester had two different campuses at that time: the River Campus for men and the Women's Campus. The latter was within walking distance from my residence. My first course at the university was a summer semester class on European history held on the women's campus on Prince and University Street. I was able to pay the tuition of $80 in installments. I purchased a used book for little money and felt very proud. I read the first chapters and did not anticipate any problems, but my first lecture was most difficult. Since all the Greek and mythological figures were pronounced in a most unfamiliar way; <u>Zeus</u> was [zooos] and not [tsois], <u>Socrates</u> was [sokratteez] not [zo:kra:tes] etc., etc. However, I managed and, eight weeks later, received my first American college credit.

My educational record was evaluated and I learned that I needed sixteen more credits to graduate with a bachelor of science degree. I was advised to take psychology 101 to start. I have to mention the first test. Having never taken a multiple-choice examination before, I requested extra paper. The instructor was puzzled but cautioned me to hand all my notes in at the end. There were one-hundred questions. I had answered twenty-six by the time the hour was up. When the papers were returned, the instructor was surprised to see (as she later told me) that I appeared totally normal. I had answered each question in detail: "a) is not feasible because…, b) this is an absurd statement…, c) could be possible if…, d) I opt for this as being the correct answer…" Since all answers that I had given were correct, she gave me a passing grade but told me to take a speed-reading course and learn how to take multiple-choice tests. I shall never forget my experience in psych 101.

In September I had a serious altercation with Miss Kaiser, the Director of Hillside. It was a Saturday afternoon and, as a special treat, I had made vanilla pudding for the boys. Since I had purchased the ingredients with my own money, I did not think that I was doing anything wrong. The boys and I were having a good time when Miss Kaiser stopped in. She told me in no uncertain terms that it was against the rules to give special treatment and "spoil" the children. I left the next day.

For a while, I lived at the YWCA and worked as "Miss Want Ad" at the *Democrat & Chronicle* newspaper. It proved to be most challenging and way over my head. Clients phoned in their requests and I typed them. My command of the English language was simply not good enough. The girl sitting next to me often came to my rescue. Her name was Josephine Lippa. She was the star Miss Want Ad and had been at this job for quite some time.

Josephine took me under her wing. I was invited to spaghetti dinners with her family when I saw for the first time how Italians eat this food without looking like slobs. (I have as yet to master the trick with the spoon.) Although I had only been in this country for less than a year and the prospect of owning my own car seemed out of reach, Josephine decided to teach me how to drive.

My lessons took place in the evenings, from 9:00 to about midnight. I do not recall getting a learner's permit. It's possible that way back then such a thing did not yet exist. Josephine picked me up, made me get into the driver's seat of her much loved "Bella," and start the engine. Her car had a stick shift so it took a while before I managed a relatively smooth departure. Once that hurdle was overcome, her commands began: "Turn left; stop next to the tree; drive next to the car there; park behind that car; do not, I mean DO NOT scrape the car; DO NOT hit the curb; slow down, don't forget to look; keep your hands on the wheel in the ten and two position…" She was a strict and demanding instructor. The only time we practiced in the daytime was when we went for my test which was successful. I still think I passed because the instructor was intrigued by my accent and could not stop talking about his experience as a soldier with the occupation army in Germany. Thanks to Josephine, I have driven all these years accident-free, except for one speeding ticket in East Aurora. The latter was changed to a lesser charge when I went to traffic court. It was called a "moving violation."

I employed Josephine's teaching techniques on several members of my family: my two sisters, my brother, my mother, my daughter, and three nephews. All did well, with the exception of my brother, who was too stubborn and thought it demeaning to follow my orders and, I have to admit, my daughter, Anna. In her case I probably was not abiding by Josephine's strict rules.

The YWCA did not approve of my late hours so I looked for an apartment near downtown and my job. I found one near the old RIT (Rochester Institute of Technology) campus. It was a first-floor apartment with a living room, kitchen, bath, and bedroom at $50 a month. It was an excellent arrangement, and far better than the Y, since I could now cook at home.

Even with Josephine's help in the ad department, my extraordinarily patient supervisor suggested that this might not be the right job for me after six weeks. I had just goofed by placing an ad for a car hop in a cafeteria instead of a gaseteria, causing a furious customer to complain about "the girl with the foreign accent." I had no idea that there was such a word as gaseteria.

I also had a second job. Three times a week I went downtown in the evening to write up the business proceedings of the day at the court house. This job was fairly well paid and, best of all, I met a lawyer whose clientele were German immigrants who needed help translating their birth, marriage-divorce, death, etc. certificates. This became a rather lucrative business for me. The pay was all under the table and I earned about $80 a week, clear profit after I paid for my typewriter.

Soon I looked around for another job and another apartment. I found a pleasant two-room apartment with kitchen and bath on Troup Street. It was located in the vicinity of the beginnings of the Rochester Institute of Technology. My landlord, Mr. Winters, rented to several students and I began to feel right at home in this new community. I went to work as a "foreign correspondent" (fancy title!) with Ritter Dental. There were four people in the office. One took care of the French correspondence; another handled Spanish and Portuguese; I translated incoming German correspondence into English and, after our director Mr. Yakoubian had dictated his replies, translated his responses into German. The fourth member of our group was the best typist ever, Irene. She knew only English but typed in all four languages with equal speed.

Emmeli, Lisa, Hinrich, December 1952
Emmeli says Goodbye

Lisa on Ship to America

In December of 1952, my mother and brother immigrated to America and joined my uncle in Mt. Morris. After all these years, my mother had a house again! And my brother was now a senior in the Mt. Morris Central

School. I bought a car, a new Chevrolet. I named her "Putzi." It made life considerably easier to get to work, to visit Mt. Morris, and to begin classes which were now at River Campus. The Women's Campus had closed and was now combined with the River Campus.

Mount Morris House: They Lived on the Left Side.

Hinrich on Ship to America   *Mount Morris High School*

In 1953, my sister Emmeli also immigrated to the US and came to Rochester. I had encouraged her to join me as the local hospitals greatly needed physicians. She moved in with me and began her four-year internship at Rochester General Hospital, conveniently located on Troup Street, within walking distance from our apartment. Emmeli spent the first two months in the Pathology Department with Dr. Abel. While she mostly spoke German with Dr. Abel, it gave her plenty of time to improve her English. After completing the required two years of residency in family practice at St. Mary's Hospital, she applied to take her State Boards. She was admitted to the State Boards in Illinois.

Emmeli Leaves Germany, July 1953

Hedda and Emmeli in NYC 1st day in USA, 1953

Emmeli begins Internship at Rochester General Hospital

Dr. Yakoubian was in the process of being transferred to Brazil and our nice little office of translators was closed. I looked for a job at the University of Rochester. Employees had the benefit of free tuition, a great deal. I first worked with Dr. Theodor Dunham in his microspectroscopic laboratory, where I did all sorts of things for him. I was his secretary, lab assistant, and supervisor of the many microscopes that he purchased with enormous funds from the Office of Naval Research and the USPHS (United State Public Health Services). Dr. Dunham held an MD as well as a PhD in astrophysics. He was a brilliant yet most peculiar man. He managed to write grant proposals based on "research" that had never taken place. Often, I was typing at his house until shortly before midnight, and then he would take the proposal to the post office so that he would meet the deadline. His wife would serve dinner and keep their two adopted children quiet. His graduate assistant, Douglas Scott, and I both questioned whether he was inventing his "research," but we were glad to have jobs and decided to keep quiet. In May of 1955 Dr. Dunham mysteriously disappeared, taking all of his lab contents with him. I will elaborate on this story later.

I was then asked to join Dr. Tom Keenan to start the university's Computer Lab. It was a noisy environment with the huge IBM 650 humming away, the Burroughs E 101 clicking, and the card-sorting machines rattling. Most uncomfortable was the fact that the large room had to be kept on the cool side. However, Tom and I had a very good working relationship serving the academic community. One day, Professor Lincoln Canfield, the Chair of the Language Department, came to the computing center and was shocked to see me working there. He said, "What on earth are you doing here? You ought

Dr Keenan and Hedda in the Computing Center

to be teaching in our high schools!" He advised me to begin taking the courses I needed to become certified to teach, beginning with methodology. I took a methodology class with him which was taught in Spanish (very challenging for me as I was the only non-native Spanish speaker in the class). Amazingly, I managed to pass the class.

Emmeli and Hedda visit Niagara Falls, 1955

Emmeli was in her last year of residency at St. Mary's Hospital and she and I shared an apartment on Troup Street. We had our car, Putzi, and life was good to both of us. I continued to take classes at the U of R. Emmeli and I spent many weekends in Mount Morris with Onkel Hans and Mutter. Emmeli and I also visited Niagara Falls.

My First Years in the United States

My friend Douglas Scott and his wife Margaret introduced me to another couple, Claire and Michael Watson. The Watson's lived in a huge mansion in Pittsford. Claire, an aspiring singer, took German lessons and diction from me which provided me with extra income, enabling me to send clothing to Brigitte and her sons Hans, Matthias, and Christian.

Brigitte was my only sibling left in Germany. She lived in the Russian Zone. She and her husband both worked as psychiatrists in a Rostock clinic. Her marital problems, her life with the three boys in the Russian Zone, and her longing for all of us were a constant concern to Mutter. Emmeli and I were determined to bring Brigitte and her boys to Rochester.

Brigitte and her Children Immigrate to America

On July 1, 1956, Emmeli began practicing medicine in Mount Morris. She was studying for the State Boards, earned an excellent salary, and lived in the nurses' home on Murray Hill on the beautiful hospital grounds.

Claire and Michael Watson owned a beautiful house (I should say mansion) in Rochester. Claire had been taking German lessons from me as well as singing lessons at the university. They decided that Dr. Michael Watson, a radiologist, would take a sabbatical from the University of Rochester to do research in Frankfurt and Claire would further her operatic career there. They were leaving in August 1956 and asked me and a couple, Douglas and Margaret Scott, also friends of mine from the university, to care for their house while they were gone. The Scotts, their little daughter Dulcey, and I moved in to this beautiful house while the Watson family moved to Germany with their four children for a year of study. I was more than happy to exchange my rather modest apartment for this considerably more luxurious living arrangement. Best of all, Margaret and I became fast and very good friends. Margaret was a war bride from Brighton, England. She was homesick and not happy to be a housewife. Her very sweet two-year-old daughter did her best to provide some happiness for her mother. It certainly helped that I had visited Brighton often while I lived in London and we could talk about familiar places such as the beach, the many booths on the pier, and the treacherous, rather cold water.

As mentioned before, I was working as an assistant at the computing center. I dealt with a variety of faculty members and befriended several. I was also able to register for courses. My tuition was free since I taught German in evening classes. Professor Lincoln Canfield, the Chairman of the Foreign Language Department, encouraged me to apply for a teaching position at the Pittsford High School. I was hired to teach German and French beginning in September 1956 with a starting salary of $4,500. Although I had met several very interesting and friendly people at the computing center, I did not like the work. The rooms had to be kept cool and the machines, the Burroughs E 101 and the IBM 650, were extremely noisy, as was the card-sorting machine. I was looking forward to teaching.

Then a letter came from Brigitte. Her marriage, which had been difficult from the very beginning, had now become too difficult for her to endure. Brigitte had three sons: Hans, whose birth I had witnessed and assisted with on February 8, 1948, in Travemünde; Matthias, born on August 9, 1951, in Rostock (located in the Russian Zone); and Christian, born on May 25, 1953, also in Rostock. Our sister asked for help. I remember that Emmeli and I met in a restaurant for lunch to think of a plan to help Brigitte. The Russian Zone was not yet totally blocked off from the west. It was still possible to obtain a visitor's pass to cross the border in either direction.

After much back and forth, we decided to inform our mother that we would send Brigitte the following telegram: "Mother seriously ill. You must visit in Lübeck." Our mother was living in Mt. Morris with her brother, Dr. Hans Bartelt (our Onkel Hans). My uncle, who now was the proud owner of an American passport, and mother agreed with our idea and the two made plans to fly to Germany. The telegram was sent. Brigitte and her sons received a forty-eight-hour pass to visit them. Her luggage was checked at the border to make sure that she had clothes only for the allotted time and her husband gave his permission. Brigitte was able to smuggle some money hidden in

Brigitte in Niendorf Deciding to Emmigrate to America. Left to Right: Hans, Christian Bartelt (cousin), Matthias, Brigitte, Christian, Lisa

her clothes seams. Ilse, her sister-in-law, came a few days later with more clothes, money, and other essentials. My mother and uncle rented a modest place in Niendorf, located on the Baltic Sea. My mother was happy to see her daughter again and hoped that Brigitte would not return to her husband, Ewald. Meanwhile, the three boys enjoyed the beach, oblivious to the strange happenings. Soon Brigitte decided not to return to her husband. Plans were made to have her join us in the United States.

Permission was quickly granted for eight-year-old Hans and he flew back with our uncle and mother in August of 1956. My mother had taken care of Hans for the first three years of his life and there was a special bond between the two. My sister had to stay behind. She needed to obtain a divorce and finish her doctoral thesis. Our former maid, Agathe Dirksen, had a little farmhouse and graciously offered to take care of the two little boys to enable Brigitte to prepare the necessary paperwork. I wrote to my dear friend, Hans Harmsen at the University of Hamburg, asking his advice regarding the thesis. He immediately agreed to help and his wife invited Brigitte to stay with their family (he had four children at home). It was a very, very lonely and difficult time for Brigitte, as she would tell me later. She was separated from her two little boys and her oldest son Hans had gone to live in America. As I am writing this, I literally feel her pain. Brigitte persevered. With the help of Hans Harmsen, she finished her thesis, the divorce was granted, and the necessary paperwork for the immigration was completed. I became an American citizen

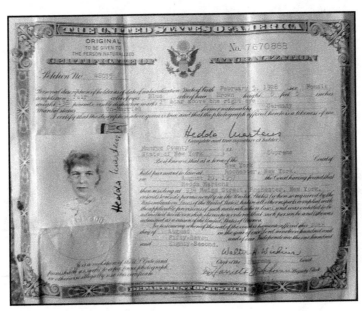

Hedda Naturalization Papers, 1957

in 1957 and was thus able to become the sponsor for Brigitte and her children. My mother received monthly payments from our grandfather's firm, Martens & Prahl, which enabled her to pay for Brigitte's passage on the freighter *Catharina Oldendorff* from Hamburg to Norfolk, VA. Brigitte left Germany with Matthias and Christian in early March 1957.

Catharina Oldendorff

Christian and Matthias on the Catharina Oldendorff

Plans had to be made for Brigitte and the three boys. It was determined that Hans would stay with my mother and uncle in Mt. Morris and Brigitte would reside with me in Rochester with the two little boys. I could receive them in style in the Watson mansion. While the Watsons were still in Rochester, I had met the Chairman of the Department of Internal Medicine at the Genesee Hospital. While Brigitte was crossing the Atlantic, I went to see him to inquire whether there was a possibility for Brigitte to begin her internship at the hospital. He seemed interested and told me to come with Brigitte as soon as she was settled.

When I made plans to go to Norfolk, Margaret wanted to join me. On March 20, 1957, we dropped her daughter, Dulcey, at my mother's in Mt. Morris. We then took off in the big Watson station wagon for Norfolk to meet Brigitte and the boys, scheduled to arrive within the next three days on the small freighter, *Catharina Oldendorff*. Margaret would be the driver. She was familiar with that car. Her husband, Douglas, checked the oil and the tires and filled the gas tank. I had a road map and $200. By today's standards, our preparation for the trip was comparable to the dark ages: NO seat belts, NO cell phone, NO hotel/motel reservations, NO credit cards, NO GPS, and, can you believe it, NO water bottles! We were wonderfully naïve and did not anticipate any trouble.

I remember enjoying the beautiful countryside that was beginning to show early signs of spring and, most of all, the fact that I could relax and did not have to drive. As we were passing through Painted Post, Margaret asked me to take the wheel. She complained of a stomach ache. We stopped at a restaurant in Corning and I told my friend that I needed to go on and suggested she call Douglas to pick her up. "No, I'll be allright. I want to go on!" A little while later, already in Pennsylvania, Margaret decided to rest lying down in the back of the car. I had brought pillows and blankets for the children.

As we were approaching Harrisburg, I heard her moaning. I stopped the car and asked for directions to the nearest hospital. Attendants in the emergency department helped Margaret who by that time could hardly stand. She had suffered a miscarriage. The nurses were less than sympathetic: "We know your kind. You do something in one city and then come to another state for help!" Margaret was not given a bed. She "rested" on a gurney. I was allowed to sit in a reasonably comfortable chair. This is how we spent the night. Again, Margaret did not want me to call her husband. She was allowed to leave early the next day and advised to take it easy. I needed to drive and go on. I was worried that we might not make the anticipated time of the freighter's arrival. I don't remember how, but we made it! We arrived shortly before midnight in Norfolk and found a cheap hotel for $15 a night. Margaret was feeling better. The pain was now "discomfort." We were very hungry and had a good breakfast before driving to the waterfront to make inquiries about *Catharina Oldendorff.*

"Can you see the ship out in the bay?" asked Margaret. Yes, I could, but the water was rough and the freighter could not come closer. Brigitte, Christian, Matthias, and their luggage were transported in a small motorboat. I was waiting anxiously since I hadn't seen my sister in a very long time. Several men were eager to help once the little boat arrived. Suddenly, I heard Matthias scream, "I don't want that black man to touch me!" He had never seen a black person before.

Matthias, Brigitte, Christian, 1958

I was glad to see my sister again. All their belongings fit into the station wagon. The children could stretch out in the back. It was before the "fasten your seat belt" time. We stopped for food (ice cream, of course) and found a lovely motel after some driving. My friend Margaret felt somewhat left out since we now talked in German all the time. I translated, of course, but that is not the same.

Our mother met us in Painted Post, right after the Pennsylvania border.

She brought Brigitte's son Hans who had not seen his mother for seven months! The three brothers were very happy to see each other again and my mother was glad to have Brigitte in the United States. We all rejoiced to have one another. Onkel Hans and Emmeli were waiting in Mount Morris; Margaret was glad to see her little daughter. Unfortunately, I had to drive back to Rochester. Margaret still did not feel well enough and I also needed to go to work. However, I felt pleased and satisfied.

Christian, Hans, Matthias Reunited in Mt. Morris, 1958

The next weekend, I went to get Brigitte and the two little boys to live with me in Rochester in the Watson mansion. Matthias and Christian enjoyed the big house and the garden while I began to teach English to Brigitte. Unlike Emmeli and me, Brigitte had not shown any interest in learning English, an obligatory subject in school. She knew the fundamentals, of course, and could read quite well. So we practiced and practiced for hours. Margaret and her husband, Douglas, pretended to be administrators of the hospital for mock interviews which was most helpful. After a week, we decided that Brigitte was ready to go for the interview. It worked out well. The interviewing physician practiced his German he had studied in college which made everybody comfortable and at ease. An agreement was reached and Brigitte would start her internship on July 1. The hospital would pay $50 per month, supply uniforms, and room and board (every other night), and once a week, the family would be able to get a free meal.

I was also very fortunate as the Pittsford School Board, the superintendent, the principal, and all my colleagues at Pittsford were most generous and helpful, especially when my sister Brigitte arrived in Rochester with her three boys. Brigitte entered her internship at Genesee Hospital. The Pittsford School graciously and immediately changed my "single" health insurance contract to "family" so that the boys were covered. Pittsford also paid for the courses I needed to become certified as a teacher.

Michael and Claire Watson planned to return to Rochester by August.

Brigitte and her Children Immigrate to America

It was time to find an apartment for Brigitte, the boys, and me. I looked at two possibilities. Our home had to be near the university and close to the hospital. However, I learned that children, especially boys, were not welcome at either place. I mentioned my problem to a man named Ralph (I never knew his last name). He was in charge of the copying center at the university and we talked while I was waiting for the copies that I needed. Ralph told me his landlady was selling her house on Meigs Street, a most desirable location for us. Mrs. Ward, the owner, was planning to move in with her children. We looked at the house and it was ideal for us. It had two apartments, a nice little backyard, and a garage. I would be able to have an income by renting the lower apartment.

I bought the house on 934 Meigs Street for $13,000. How did I manage to buy the house we so definitely needed? I had become good friends with Hewitt Kenyon, an Assistant Professor of mathematics who was most willing to lend me $5,000 which would constitute a second mortgage. I saw a lawyer to ask whether it was feasible to buy a house without any down payment. He went with me to the bank then called Lincoln Rochester. The bank officer agreed, provided my loan was cosigned by my brother, his wife, and Brigitte. At that time, only Nancy, Hinrich's wife, and I had an income. None of us had any collateral to offer, but the bank felt that our education and future earnings were more than enough. So we moved into 934 Meigs Street, where we were to reside for the next eight years.

934 Meigs Street

I rented the downstairs to my brother and his wife, a registered nurse. My brother had a scholarship for graduate work in mechanical engineering to obtain his master's degree, and my uncle and mother helped out by taking care of the children every weekend and during all school vacations. After a year, my brother went to Michigan to pursue his PhD and Tom Bannister and his wife, Mary, became my new tenants. Tom was a Professor of biology at the university. Mary gave piano lessons. My two younger nephews became her pupils. They had the advantage of being able to practice on Mary's piano since we did not own one.

Since Brigitte and I were both working full time, we needed to find daycare for the boys. Hans stayed in Mt. Morris with my mother and uncle. The Rochester Children's Nursery was just around the corner from us and they accepted the children. Christian was enrolled in kindergarten. Miss Gruber, a lovely teacher, welcomed him with open arms; however, Christian did not want to stay. Quite a bit of coaxing was necessary to convince him that he would have a good time. After having settled Christian, I went with Matthias to his first-grade class which was held in the same building. To my horror, a very black teacher greeted us with a big smile. Thinking of Matthias' reaction when a black man was trying to help him in Norfolk, I feared the worst, but all worked out very well. Matthias and his teacher, Harry, were best of friends from the start.

Since we did not have a lot of money, the nursery agreed to take care of the children for $25 per week which was doable. Once my teaching in Pittsford began, I dropped the children off every morning at 7:15 and picked them up at 4:00 p.m. Both children adjusted well to this routine. But we all looked forward to our weekends in Mt. Morris, when the three brothers would be together. They loved Mt. Morris and the beautiful surroundings of the hospital. There were other children from the resident physicians and the boys had to speak English which they learned quickly. Hans organized their adventures which were filled with excitement and fun. Brigitte joined us occasionally for a weekend when her very busy schedule allowed two days off. Her internship was very hard work and she was usually exhausted and in dire need of sleep when she was home.

****

One day, Brigitte was on evening duty in the emergency room during her rotating internship. A young nun from the home of the Sisters of Mercy was brought in by an ambulance. Two older sisters had heard cries and had found the patient lying in her bed bleeding profusely. The examination by the physicians established quickly that the nun had just given birth. The two nuns who had accompanied the patient were in total disbelief and denial. Nevertheless, the big question was, "Where is the baby?" Two police officers were dispatched to inspect the nun's room. It did not take them long to discover the body of a perfectly formed newborn hidden under towels in the waste-paper basket.

The nun admitted to having smothered the infant. All nuns in the home claimed that they had not been aware of the pregnancy. There were many ugly jokes making the rounds in the hospital with reference to a holy ghost, and yes, even the stork, as my sister told me. The nun was not imprisoned or sentenced by a court of law. She was whisked away to Elmira for meditation and atonement for her "sins." Sadly, the newspapers report fairly often about desperate young girls who committed the tragic act of killing their newborn babies because of fear from their parents' and society's wrath or other untold psychological problems. Having to serve time in prison is usually the punishment for their criminal act

This heartbreaking event reminded of a time back in Lübeck when I was about six. It was the custom that we would walk over to my grandfather's house for a family Sunday dinner. We were always dressed in our Sunday best. It took us about thirty minutes to reach our destination. I usually had my father all to myself, since my sisters chose to walk way ahead of us two. It was special and very wonderful.

We lived north of the original wall and grandfather's house was located in the south-western part, outside the wall. For a while, we walked on Wall Strasse, just inside the city wall and there was this mysterious, unassuming brick building bearing the strange inscription, "Ein Heim für Gefallene Mädchen" (a place for fallen women), in big letters. I had fallen off my bicycle numerous times. I was worried that I might have to live in that dreary home. He comforted me by saying, "No, these girls were probably bitten by a stork and needed help with taking care of their babies." I remembered seeing pictures in children's books depicting a stork carrying babies. My mother had just recently given birth to my brother and she was still recuperating and in need of help. So I was satisfied with the answer. My attention quickly turned to the "largest" waterfall (about two meters high) that was nearby. It carried the water from the Krähenteich into one of the arms of the river Trave. We always came with dried bread to feed the ducks and swans, swimming in the small pond. This wonderful stop made us late for dinner at times but my grandfather was quickly appeased by my father's several colorful excuses.

****

The first year of our lives together in Rochester went very well. Brigitte's charming personality had endeared her to her colleagues as well as the supporting staff at the hospital. Her English was up to par now and she began her residency in pediatrics which she loved. There was a little more money now and she could help with the finances of the household. Brigitte's workload, however, stayed much the same. She loved her work with the exception of night duties. She disliked being "on call" at the hospital which allowed for very little sleep.

Matthias, now a second grader, was transported daily to a different school where the atmosphere was not pleasant. The teachers treated the children from the nursery differently since they were from "broken homes." I visited his school and decided to make other arrangements. Right next to our house was School #24. We enrolled both boys there. One problem was the lunch. The school did not supply lunch. I cooked spaghetti and meatballs and put it into a thermos bottle so that nobody needed to use the stove. Dessert was ready in the refrigerator. The boys were able to walk home for lunch and our dear neighbor, Mrs. Crombach, was always home and kept an eye on them. She reported to me that Matthias was a bit domineering and ordered Christian about which caused unnecessary fights and tears. But on the whole, this setup worked and Matthias was responsible. I was usually able to be home when the boys came back from school.

While Christian no longer experienced any difficulties with English (I think the year in kindergarten had helped greatly), Matthias' teacher told me to keep on practicing English with him. One funny thing happened for Halloween. The children in Matthias' class were asked to bring some candy to the school for the Halloween party. He saw a bar of chocolate and asked whether he could break that into small pieces and take it to school. I told him he should only pick the candy that was already wrapped. He remembered seeing Ex-Lax in my bathroom, beautifully wrapped in silver paper. He took that. Fortunately, I found the empty cardboard container in the bathroom and ran to school. The teacher and I went through the collected candy and removed the Ex-Lax chocolate before any damage could be done.

Mt. Morris: Hans, Christian, Matthias, 1957

Weekends were regularly spent in Mt. Morris and, if the boys were sick, my mother would come to get them. My mother took the boys all summer long. She loved it, as did my uncle. The boys had the greatest time and for me it was an opportunity to continue my studies at the University of Rochester and take required education courses so that I could be certified as a teacher.

While we encountered many challenges in our new country, Emmeli and I were grateful that the plan we had hatched to bring Brigitte and her sons to America had been successful and that we were all together again.

Investigations

I have experienced two uncomfortable situations when I was asked to give information concerning other people. One occurred in 1957. I had just come home from Pittsford High School where I was teaching French and German. I was busy with my two nephews whom I had just picked up from the Rochester Children's Nursery when the doorbell rang. There were two men who identified themselves as representatives of the FBI. I was petrified and wondered what I could have done wrong.

There had been a bank robbery in Rochester and I was told that the alleged thief was also born in Lübeck in the year of 1928. We did not have a newspaper at that time and rarely listened to the news on the radio. As the prosecution and the defense were preparing for trial, the accused had claimed that he was still suffering from shock he experienced during the traumatic bombing of Lübeck in March 1942. Could I tell them something about that air raid? They came equipped with a map of my hometown and indicated where that unfortunate man had lived. They also knew my old address and that my home had been destroyed. An eerie feeling crept up my spine. Had I not grown up in a country where your very existence was an open book to investigators? Was it possible that the horrendous event some fifteen years ago could have affected that poor man in such a way that he would commit this crime? I learned that he had not lost his home that night. I told them that life for fourteen-year-old school children resumed in a relatively normal way soon thereafter since not a single school was bombed. I doubt that my testimony contributed to the guilty verdict. I hope that he is a free man now.

The other investigation was closer to home. It affected me deeply since the integrity of a brilliant man was in question. He had been my boss at the University of Rochester. I have to relate the whole story:

As I have said before, prior to meeting Dr. Theodore (Ted) Dunham in 1953, I was a foreign correspondent at the now defunct company of Ritter Dental where dental chairs and other equipment for dental offices were produced. However, when Dr. Yakoubian, the head of the company, accepted a transfer to Rio de Janeiro, I looked once again at the want ads.

"Secretary and Research Assistant needed for the Microspectroscopic Laboratory. Moderate compensation and free tuition for two courses per semester. Dr. T. Dunham." I called at once and was invited for an interview. The lab was located in Strong Memorial Hospital. The first person whom I asked for directions at the information desk had no idea what I was talking about. My difficulty pronouncing microspectroscopic no doubt contributed to the confusion; I also mispronounced Dr. Dunham's name by saying Dun-ham instead of Dunnam. The next person, however, directed me to the third floor of the R-Wing which was under construction. The entire five-story wing of the building was to be the Department of Psychiatry under the direction of Dr. Romano, hence R-Wing.

When I exited the elevator on the third floor, I was indeed standing in and on a construction site not remotely conducive to a sparkling research laboratory. A note attached to a steel post showed an arrow pointing to the lab. My beautifully polished shoes quickly became dusty from the debris and I was a bit worried about my dark-blue "interview suit." The left side of this huge place was totally open. The outdoor walls were up but the open spaces lacked window panes. On the right side was what seemed to be a makeshift wall that housed the laboratory.

In stark contrast to the always impeccably dressed Dr. Yakoubian, Dr. Dunham was in shirt sleeves with an ill-fitting tie. "You come highly recommended. Can we start right away?" That was the interview. It was October 1954. His office was cramped and his desk piled high with papers and books. My desk with a typewriter was right next to his. Not a believer in dictaphones, he thought it was best to dictate directly to me. When he was not in the office, it was my duty to check the temperature in the large lab, which was filled with many microscopes (almost like a museum). The BURCH reflecting microscope was Dr. Dunham's treasure. I was to dust around it but not disturb it in any way. There also was a small darkroom at the very end of the lab. I was introduced to Douglas Scott, Dr. Dunham's research assistant and a graduate student from the Department of Optics. Science had never sparked my interest and, as it turned out, my ignorance appeared to be the right attribute for this job. I understood next to nothing of the reports and letters that I typed. However, I enjoyed working there. Several months into my job, Dr. Dunham asked me to stay later and type at his house. Miriam, his wife, provided supper. I was delighted and felt very important. I also met their two children: Mary, called "Polly," a strikingly beautiful ten-year-old, and Ted who had just turned eight.

Immediately after supper, Mrs. Dunham and the children disappeared upstairs and work began. Dr. Dunham dictated a proposal for a grant to the Office of Naval Research (ONR). He described in detail the research that had taken place (including failures as well as successfully completed tests) and outlined plans for further research to attain the desired goal. By 11:00 p.m. and after some twenty pages of typing, he reread the proposal and said that we needed to go to the Main Post Office so that the proposal could be mailed before midnight, since it was due that very day. After that, he took me home and said that I should take the next day off. He thanked me profusely. When I was at home alone, I wondered about the "research" that was so eloquently described. I had not witnessed it. The preceding scene requesting grants from the Rockefeller Foundation and others took place several times. They were always at the last minute, involving a trip to the post office before midnight.

I wondered about this mysterious research and asked Douglas Scott. "It's in his head," was the answer. Dr. Dunham did not dictate from notes. His work was well funded. When officials from the ONR visited, they were always satisfied. Dr. Dunham was held in high regard. He deserved it. He once said of Cecil Burch, the British Physicist: "He thinks with his left hand and does it with the other in ten minutes. He is a real genius." Dr. Dunham was brilliant himself. He had graduated from Harvard, summa cum laude, with a degree in chemistry, received his MD degree from Cornell University, and then returned to his first love, astronomy, and obtained his PhD in physics in 1927 from Princeton University. He returned to Harvard as a Warren Fellow, applying physical methods to medical research. At the University of Rochester, in conjunction with the School of Medicine and the Institute of Optics, he developed instrumentation for spectrophotometric analysis of small regions of biological cells, never abandoning his love for lens designs for telescopes. He traveled to Iceland and brought back huge slabs of obsidian which filled the vacant construction site on the third floor next to the lab. Lens grinders at Bausch & Lomb were employed to follow his designs for telescopic lenses that he ordered for the Mt. Wilson Observatory in California where he also had an appointment.

I became acquainted with a number of workers at Bausch & Lomb. Most of them were German immigrants and German was the language at their place of work. (Much later, I would revisit them when I worked on my PhD in linguistics.)

My brother, Hinrich, was a sophomore in mechanical engineering at the University of Rochester at the time. I got him a part-time job at the lab. He was not involved in any research, but was asked to design more shelving units for additional microscopes that would be acquired with the help of the grants.

In March 1955, I was invited to join the Dunham family on a four-week trip to California. I took the train to Flagstaff, AZ, and awaited the family who had come by car all the way from Rochester. I was a research assistant but mostly served as storyteller and entertainer for the children. When Mrs. Dunham overheard my rendition of the Grimm Fairy Tales, she took me aside and asked me not to stress the evil stepmothers too much since both children were adopted. That was not an easy task. In the 19th century, many mothers died in childbirth and the widowers "in need of help" married again, thus providing the stepmothers. The Brothers Grimm related real life stories in all their tales. The good fathers were either absent or not involved in their children's upbringing (*Snow White*) or frequently away from home in search for work (*Hänsel and Gretel*). With permission from the parents, I invented numerous stories about little children who had found happiness and stability with new parents. Polly was delighted and shouted proudly, "I flew in from Paris." Polly had been adopted in France.

Leaving Flagstaff, we went south to marvel at Oak Creek Canyon, Sedona, and then a little east to view the Sunset Crater. From there, we explored a part of the Grand Canyon. When it suddenly became dark and cold, Dr. Dunham decided to seek shelter in a meeting house for the Navajo Indians which was packed full. Heading west, we visited the Hoover Dam, Lake Mead, and stopped in Las Vegas for a clean bed, shower, and some food. Las Vegas was small at that time, with primitive-looking gambling places and not many paved roads. Next we drove through the Mojave Desert which was fascinating and beautiful with blooming yellow cacti. Before reaching Dr. Dunham's destination, the Mt. Wilson Observatory, we crossed Death Valley. Mrs. Dunham, the children, and I relaxed for a couple of days in a nearby motel while Dr. Dunham was busy at the observatory. San Francisco was our final destination. They rented a room in a nice hotel near the Golden Gate Bridge for the children and me. I was given the name, address, and telephone number of Mrs. Dunham's mother whose residence was nearby. I was to call for an appointment to visit the lady. The parents left for Oregon. I was given enough money to entertain and feed the children. We explored the surroundings, went to the beach (by taxi), and visited Mrs. Dunham's mother in her most elegant house.

A maid, dressed in an outfit one sees on movie sets, ushered us into the dining room where a table had been set with delicious cakes. It was a strange reception. The children were polite but subdued and we were all relieved when the hour for the reception was up and we were asked to leave. We were not invited to return.

We returned to Rochester on April 1 and settled back to work. A graduate student asked me whether I was interested in investing one week's salary in a company called Haloid. To this day, I regret that I did not have the courage, since Haloid became Xerox!

One Monday in May 1955, I reported to work as usual. Upon leaving the elevator, I noticed that the large obsidians were gone and I did not need my keys to open the lab. Dr. Dunham's office was cleaned out except for the typewriter and the lab that had housed so many marvelous microscopes was almost empty. I called the Security Office and the room was quickly filled with officials from the university. Everybody seemed perplexed and puzzled. Dr. Dunham's home phone was disconnected and university investigators reported that his house was empty. It was an enormous embarrassment to the university and I was asked not to mention anything outside that room. Mr. LeRoy Thompson, in charge of all the grants obtained by the faculty, mentioned that the microscopes were the property of the university.

Over and over again, I was asked whether I knew anything about this abrupt departure. I was as puzzled as everyone else. It was a painful and difficult time for me. I felt cheated. It seemed inconceivable that this brilliant man could betray so many people.

Dr. Dunham had gone to Canberra, Australia. In 1957, he joined the faculty of the Australian National University and designed and installed a spectrograph in Mount Stromlo Observatory. I never heard from the Dunhams again. Neither did Dr. R. Hopkins, Director of the Optics Institute at the university, who had been good friends with Dr. Dunham.

Who had helped Dr. Dunham in the execution of this secret departure?

Investigations

While thorough investigations took place, I never found out the real story.

According to *The New York Times,* Theodore Dunham died on April 9, 1984, at his home in Chocorua, NH. He was eighty-six years old. The obituary mentions his tenure at the University of Rochester, but no details about his sudden departure and subsequent work at the Australian National University. That remains a mystery.

Searching for a Hobby

Rochester, NY, 1952. As I was completing my application for admission to the University of Rochester, I stumbled upon the question: "What are your hobbies?" I found myself unable to give an answer. My work as an assistant housemother at the Hillside Children's Center was so overwhelming that I would not have had the time for a hobby, even if I had one. Outside of taking a bath, I knew of no other source of relaxation. Since I could not really write that into my application, I conjured up the absurd hobby of stamp collecting. To sound a bit more sophisticated, I used the fancy name for it, philately. As far as I can remember, this was the only time I put a falsehood in writing. In spite of my fib, I was admitted as a part-time student to the University's Women's Campus.

The most frequently mentioned hobby is reading. Most of my reading had been required for school. The only novel that I had read entirely for pleasure was the German translation of *Gone with the Wind*. My classmate Hilke Juhl had lent me the book in 1941, and as predicted by Hilke, I was totally in love with Rhett Butler. I remember reading the book with a flashlight in my bed since my mother adhered strictly to the eight-hour sleep requirement for all school children.

During my time in England (1949-1951), my friend Erica Jones recommended Agatha Christie's thrilling murder mysteries. "It will enrich your vocabulary," she said. She was right, to be sure, although reading those novels was very hard work for me. I had to refer to the dictionary frequently. Other hobbies, such as singing, dancing, and painting, required talent that I did not have. Knitting, baking, cooking, and sewing needed material and/ or money. Thus, philately was a reasonable choice. All one needed to do was collect old stamped envelopes.

Sewing

I had learned sewing in school (mostly aprons) and at home. However, it was not until the summer of 1945 in Travemünde, that I started a "mass production" of blouses and nightgowns. Our neighbor, Käthe Wittekind, lent me her machine. It still had foot pedals but it worked. Frau Wittekind's husband managed the bank. His first name was really Adolf, but he changed it to B-dolf at the end of the war. My brother Hinrich and friends had "organized" (we refrained from using the ugly word "stolen") two parachutes from old German planes that were destined to be destroyed. Since we could not buy any clothing, the enormous quantity of sturdy fabric contained in a parachute was a dream come true. One chute had a camouflage pattern. I planned to make blouses out of that. The other was white, most suitable for nightgowns. I do not remember who gave me the patterns. At any rate, they were for "one size fits all." I did not lack eager customers who anxiously waited for their nightgowns. I envisioned great success. It would be a barter system, since money was not useful for anything.

It was a hot day in July of 1945 when my first long-sleeved gown was finished and my sister Emmeli was the first to try it. The next morning I overheard my mother and Emmeli whispering, "How will we tell Hedda?" The truth was that Emmeli had worn the gown less than twenty minutes. The "wonderful" material proved to be totally unsuitable for human attire. I was heartbroken. I did however manage to wear one of the blouses to Brigitte's wedding in 1947, although it was very uncomfortable. My mother found someone to remove the chutes from our apartment.

Twelve years passed before I once again tried my hand at sewing in 1957. I had bought a house on 934 Meigs Street in Rochester, NY, and since the houses were relatively close together, I needed to make curtains for the bedrooms. Sears had drapes and curtains in their store, but they were either much too expensive or downright ugly and cheap looking. I managed to acquire an electric sewing machine at a garage sale, measured the windows and bought the necessary rods and fabric. My finished curtains not only filled the purpose, they were actually rather attractive. Furthermore, the machine came in handy to lengthen or shorten the boys' jeans, and I learned to put patches on the pants' knees where the material had worn thin, made flannel shirts, and wrap-around skirts. When you have to count pennies, you become creative.

It was not until my grandson, Carl, was born in 1996, that I started to sew again. This came about when my son-in-law, Bruce, complained about the poor material and design of the onesies. He found it so difficult to change the baby during the night. "It's too hard and takes too long to get his feet into the outfit. Can you help?" So I designed "easy-to-put-on" outfits that would gradually evolve into most beloved pajamas for both Carl and Erika, made out of the best flannel material. Erika's had a little lace around the neckline, while I used plain binding for Carl's pajamas. I think Carl was ten years old when I stopped producing my "Mumu-wear."

Carl and Erika Wearing Mumu Pajamas

Painting

I had always admired the professional painters while growing up in Germany. However, I was never allowed to paint with one of their brushes. A three-year apprenticeship was required before you could call yourself a painter. The Meigs Street house was in dire need of paint inside and out. So I bought two brushes, one paint roller, and paint for the ceilings and walls and instantly beautified the rooms. Using oil-based paint for the woodwork was considerably more difficult. I needed different brushes and had to learn (the hard way) to avoid dripping and spilling. That's when turpentine came to the rescue. It was on the whole a most gratifying job. I have fond memories.

Eight years later, in 1965, we moved into a big house on Highland Ave in Rochester. Without any neighbors nearby, we did not need any curtains. However, we wanted brighter colors in most all of the rooms. Our improved finances allowed us to hire a painter. After the master's "apprentice" made a mess of things, we decided to paint ourselves. That meant, I would be the one to do it. After living for fifty years in the house, I can proudly say that there was not a wall, ceiling, or corner that I had not painted.

I need to mention that I also crocheted at least ten large afghans, as requested by many family members.

After all this, do I have a hobby? The dictionary defines a hobby as a pursuit outside one's regular occupation, especially for relaxation. I have come to the conclusion that my hobby is not outside my occupation. My hobby is my chosen profession: **Teaching**.

My Teaching Career

After the war, the outlook for a normal, productive life seemed remote. Unable to find a place at a university, I worked in a veterans' hospital. I began by reading to the blind men and feeding those who had lost their arms: holding cigarettes, writing letters, and taking care of bedpans. Since there was a serious shortage of doctors and nurses, I was soon required to perform nursing duties. We worked non-stop from 6:00 a.m. until 7:00 p.m. It was volunteer work; however, we received our uniforms and food. Unlike my sisters who both chose to study medicine, I was hoping to become a teacher of languages and literature.

In the fall of 1946, I was able to get a position as an assistant fifth-grade teacher at the elementary school in Travemünde, my first official teaching job. I enjoyed it very much indeed and had forty boys in my class. One day at the end of September, we went on a field trip that involved taking the ferry across the river Trave. The children were cautioned to stay in the middle of the deck since the ferry always shook and rattled when the engine started. Suddenly, there was a horrible scream. One little ten-year-old boy fell overboard and was swept under the ferry. He was killed instantly. I shall never forget my master teacher, Mr. Gröning's comment, "He was just a refugee." The screaming children were calmed down and the field trip went on as planned. There was no counseling and I did not get permission to find the grief-stricken mother. The death of this little boy was swept under the carpet. After all, he was "just a refugee" and did not really belong to the community.

Fast forward to 1957 and the beginning of my tenure teaching at Pittsford High School.

My interviews had been successful and I was looking forward to starting. My starting salary was $4,500 per year on the condition that I would continue studying for my degree and take the required courses necessary to obtain my license. I was also asked to pledge that I intended to become an American citizen. I finally finished all of the required classes by the end of my fourth year of teaching.

I remember wearing a light blue cotton dress to a reception for new teachers at the beginning of the school year. Despite the rather warm weather, I wore my white cardigan to hide the fact that I was sweating profusely. The Superintendent, Mr. Bettinger; the High School Principal, Mr. Carlson; the Middle School Principal, Mr. Kinsella; and Mrs. Brummit, the Chairman of the Board, welcomed the new teachers with heartfelt words and encouragement. A reception was to follow. As I got up from my seat in the auditorium, I noticed something sticky on the back of my dress. I had been sitting on chewing gum. A kindly soul sent me to the nurse who attacked the spot with alcohol. Now my skirt was wet as well. I missed the reception but was in time to receive my schedule for the coming month.

My day began with two French classes at Allens Creek Middle School, instructing seventh graders. Then I drove about three-quarters of a mile to the high school to teach beginning German to ninth graders and the so-called second year of German to tenth graders. Since the normal load for a teacher consisted of five classes, world history was added. For some reason, the appointment of a qualified history teacher had fallen through. I was stunned when I was handed a history book and told that I would begin with the unit about the power struggle of European kings. This included the Magna Carta, Joan of Arc, Ivan the Terrible, and the Holy Roman Empire, which was "neither holy, nor Roman, nor an empire," as the eighteenth-century French writer Voltaire described it. The final "class" of the day was study hall. "What is that?" I asked. "Just see to it that the kids are quiet and do their homework," was the response. It was new to me that one was given time in school to study. Finally, it was suggested that all teachers leave their lesson plans for the following day with the secretary so that a substitute would be able to give instructions. I was horrified by that idea and determined that I would never miss a day and thus could not be penalized for not handing in a plan. In my five years at Pittsford, I was never absent.

There were a few days before school actually began. I was sure about my plans for the language classes but very worried about how I would make my history class interesting. The material presented in the textbook seemed so dry and uninspiring. It would not be easy to tell tenth graders that Medieval Europe was an isolated world whose people had little knowledge of, or contacts with, other lands and peoples. I regretted that I had not paid better attention when Herr Dr. Bülow, my high school history teacher, told us about

216

the power struggles of the two Ivans, the good and evil czars, and other kings. As it was, I burned the midnight oil and was glad when a real history teacher arrived just before Thanksgiving. My "free" hour was filled with cafeteria duty. I disliked this assignment because I had great difficulty watching the children fill the garbage cans with perfectly good food when I was struggling to feed my own household of three nephews and my sister. What a waste.

I remember my first day as a teacher very well. My new shoes were painfully uncomfortable, my nylons too hot, and my hands left wet spots on the blackboard. But, all in all, I got the children interested and involved. We sang *Frère Jacques*, learned about places where French was spoken, and simply got acquainted. The second-year German students needed to review what they had learned; actually, we needed to start from the beginning. That group, as well as the true beginners, was a delight. I had been given a gift. Close to fifty bright children, all of whom wanted to learn. It was a teacher's dream come true. By the way, my nickname was "Miss Whom," since I constantly corrected my students' deteriorating grammar and reminded them of the rules of the direct object.

I taught French for only two years. I had been able to build the German program and there were enough classes to justify my position as the German teacher. I was even relieved of the unpleasant cafeteria duty. The school board paid for the required education classes that I attended on Saturday mornings. I do not remember a single class that taught me anything I did not already know. In short, my precious Saturday mornings were a complete waste of time. The following incident will prove my point. The instructor was giving the final test. Eager to go home, I answered the questions written on the blackboards. A little later, another student from the class asked me, "What did you write for question five?" I was panic stricken since I never noticed that there had been a fifth question. Instead of going home, I waited with wobbly knees to speak to the professor and hoped that he would give me a chance to answer that question. There was no need. Before I opened my mouth, he patted me on my shoulder saying, "Great job, Hedda!" It was obvious that he never read the entire exam at all.

The students' favorite "classes" were gym, music, or lunch. For me it was lunch with my colleagues. Several had become my very good friends. We discussed some students, the flaws of the administrators and, of course, the problems of the world. One day, the chemistry teacher, a very entertaining man, did not join our table. Instead, he sat by himself deeply engrossed in a book. We could not ascertain the title of the book, as it was carefully covered by a newspaper page, so we pestered him. Reluctantly, he admitted that he was reading strictly prohibited literature: *Lady Chatterly's Lover*, by D.H. Lawrence, a banned author. It turned out that several other teachers had already signed up to get the book. I put my name on the list. Readers were given no more than twenty-four hours. My turn came and I was prepared to read through the night. My nephews, Christian and Matthias, who were in first and second grade, needed help with their assignments. My sister, who was home for the night after a long shift as an intern at the hospital, wanted to go to bed. "Can I just look at the book?" she asked. Thinking she would be asleep within minutes, I agreed. However, when I was ready, my sister pleaded with me to let her go on reading. The next day, I signed my name again at the bottom of the waiting list. It was fun to partake in a forbidden fruit.

I was very grateful to Pittsford for five wonderful years. But it was time to go back to the university full time. I had the lofty ambition of becoming a college professor.

Hedda in the Pittsford Yearbook, 1961

The University of Rochester registrar allowed about eighty credits for previous studies, leaving fifty credits left to earn my bachelor's degree. I registered for two English courses given by Professor Hinman who obviously enjoyed teaching. In one class, we read Chaucer's wonderful poem, "The Canterbury Tales," in the original Middle English of the 14th century. My German background proved most helpful in this class and I managed to get a B+ in the course. I did not fare as well in the beginning composition class.

Every week, we had to write a paragraph on a given topic. He collected our papers on Tuesdays and discussed them on Thursday. His written comments (in red ink) were usually longer than my actual writing. However, I learned a lot and advanced from a D to a respectable C, good enough for an undergraduate. I selected German poetry for my third class, with Professor Wilhelm Braun as instructor. The students in that group were for the most part advanced in their German language studies. It was an exercise in translating from German to English. Although it meant an easy A for me, the class was sheer torture. Goethe, Heine, Rilke, and others must have turned over in their graves.

To pay for my tuition, I became a teaching assistant to Professor Arthur Hanhardt, Chairman of the German Department. This assignment was a rude awakening for me. The boring, uninspiring text was neatly divided into thirty lessons, fifteen per semester. I was handed a syllabus, as well as samples of the various tests that I was supposed to give. It was like wearing a straight jacket, to put it mildly. It was very hard for me to follow these rules after I had enjoyed five years of free reign. In addition, the majority of my students in German 101 were there to get the foreign language requirement out of the way. Just a handful truly enjoyed learning the language. At that time, German was a requirement for students majoring in the sciences and those who planned to go to medical school. To lighten the tedious grammatical drills, I taught them some poems, which they greatly appreciated. However, one student said, "Can you give me one good reason, why I, a future pediatrician, should learn Heinrich Heine's 'Lorelei'?" Years later, while I was riding in an elevator at Strong Memorial Hospital, a physician, still clad in operating room attire, tapped me on the shoulder and began to recite, with perfect pronunciation, "Ich weiss nicht, was soll es bedeuten, dass ich so traurig bin…" My former student had become a pediatric surgeon. I was very, very happy.

The German classes were scheduled every day from 8:00 to 10:00 a.m. I almost got into serious trouble. During the warm days in spring, I had the windows open and we could hear the members of the ROTC exercising. These war games were accompanied by dreadful shrieks and yelling. Still in uniform, one student came to my 9:00 session and I voiced my displeasure and disgust about these military drills. The next day I was called to the Dean's office where my student and a high-ranking officer were also present. I was told that "my anti-American comments" could cost me my recently acquired citizenship. Fortunately, they accepted my sincere apology.

I earned extra money by teaching German in the University Evening School. The students were totally different. They were in their forties and fifties and tired after a long day's work. Most of them were employed by either Bausch & Lomb or Eastman Kodak and had years of experience. However, they did not have college degrees and their managerial positions were on the line. Recent college graduates threatened to replace them. Many of these men were of German descent and some had a scant knowledge of the language. The founders of these companies, J.J. Bausch and Adolf Lomb, as well as George Eastman did not have the luxury of higher education. In fact, Bausch had been a poor immigrant from Germany. He was sixteen, with very little schooling, when he began his life as a turner (one who fashions or shapes objects on a lathe) in Rochester and Buffalo before becoming a pioneer in the American optical industry by using vulcanite rubber to make eyeglass frames more affordable. I enjoyed teaching these evening classes very much.

Of all the courses I took, I found world literature the most interesting. Among a variety of authors the professor had selected were Ibsen's *Hedda Gabler*, Flaubert's *Emma Bovary*, and Tolstoy's *Anna Karenina*. The heroines of these novels were all involved in unhappy marriages and committed adultery. This topic appeared to be most disconcerting to many of the freshmen who were my classmates. Some protested and did not want to read such "trash," stating that they would never ever do such a thing. However, the professor prevailed.

I completed the requirements for the bachelor's degree in 1964 and, after passing the GREs (graduate record exams), I began to study for an MA in linguistics. I retained my appointment at the evening school and Professor Hanhardt assigned me to teach two advanced German classes. I was allowed to select my own texts and given free reign. In addition to courses in linguistics, I was required to learn yet another language. I took Russian with Professor Antanas Klimas, a refugee from Lithuania. I took two courses in summer school and a third in the fall. After mastering the Cyrillic alphabet, I did not encounter any difficulties, and actually liked the class. My family called it my "Russian Summer."

We bought a new house in the spring of 1966 and I sold the house on Meigs Street. It had served us well for eight years. The move was scheduled during my master's degree examinations. I don't remember how I was able to manage it all, but I did get the MA in June 1966. Upon the recommendations of my professors, I was accepted into the PhD program.

During all this time, I never went to bed without writing to my friend, Hans Harmsen. We traveled together in Europe during August of 1966.

In December 1966, I passed my PhD examinations, but still had six credits left to take and five years to finish my dissertation.

The University of Rochester offered me a position as an instructor for $5,000, but I opted for the position of Assistant Professor for SUNY at Brockport for $7,000 in the fall of 1967. My reasons for choosing Brockport were twofold. The Foreign Language Department was a thriving and congenial group without any "I am better than thou" attitude. There were four German instructors, a large Spanish group that included three refugees from Cuba, four professors of French, and also instructors of Russian and Chinese. Regrettably, due to lack of student interest, the latter two languages did not survive. I loved teaching at Brockport and trained several good teachers. I taught beginning German, German literature, and a methodology class for aspiring French and Spanish teachers. To my dismay, I found that the majority of these students, especially those who were native Spanish speakers, lacked a solid background in English as well as a general education. I was advised, however, not to voice my concerns. After all, I was just beginning my own career. To this day, I regret not speaking up. I have come across many teachers who ought not to be guiding and instructing children. In addition, the college senate decided that a C average was good enough for future teachers. I did not agree.

Whenever I read or hear about possible cuts to the course offerings and staff in educational institutions, I am reminded of the terrible phone call I received in early August of 1982. I was requested to attend an important meeting with the President of Brockport College. Quite a large group of faculty members representing various departments were at the meeting. Among them were my German colleagues, Chris Kayser and Thomas Freeman. Also present were members of the Geography, History, English, Music, French, and Arts Departments. We were informed that then Governor Mario Cuomo had ordered that the curriculum at Brockport be reduced and various positions cut. The non-tenured instructors simply lost their jobs, while the tenured professors were given a salary for one full year and the option to retrain at the expense of New York State. I was a tenured Associate Professor. As a Band-Aid®, I was also given life-time medical insurance benefits and was the only dismissed instructor awarded the bittersweet emeritus honor (retired or honorably discharged from active professional duty, but retaining the title of one's office or position). The latter entitled me to take advantage of secretarial services as well as office space and free parking. Nevertheless, I was devastated. I never went back.

I returned to the University of Rochester in 1983 where I immediately became an adjunct professor at the Eastman School. One year later, I became a full-time professor there. My years at the music school were some of the best in my teaching career. My classes were filled with gifted, enthusiastic students. I taught German, required for students of music history, and German diction, required for singers who wanted to specialize in opera, especially Wagner, Mozart, Strauss, and Beethoven, and those students who endeavored to become Liedersänger, who primarily sing the works of Schubert, Schumann, Strauss, Beethoven, and other masters. My only training for teaching these classes took place in 1955 when Claire Watson, an aspiring soprano in Rochester, hired me to teach her German diction and be her German coach. She went on to become a highly celebrated opera singer in Germany. Even today, I am thrilled to see some of my former Eastman students performing on the Cable TV Arts Channel.

During this time, a friend at RIT (Rochester Institute of Technology) also offered me two German classes as an Adjunct Professor and MCC (Monroe Community College) offered me an adjunct position as well. I was busy teaching at both schools, earning good money and, best of all, knowing I was wanted.

Setting our Roots in Rochester

In the summer of 1958, Hinrich and Nancy moved to Lansing, MI, where he attended Michigan State University and in 1962 completed his PhD in Electrical and Mechanical Engineering. In 1962, Hinrich accepted a faculty position at the University of Buffalo. He remained at the University of Buffalo for his entire career. In 2000, he retired as a Professor Associate Vice President for Computing and Information Technology.

With the departure of Hinrich and Nancy, we needed new tenants for our house. My new tenants were the Bannisters. He was a Professor of Biology at the University of Rochester and Mary was a piano teacher. I charged a higher rent and managed to pay off one of the loans. Their newborn baby, Nathan, became Brigitte's first patient. Neither Brigitte nor I had ever met such impractical parents before. It was a great joy to help them out. The Bannisters stayed in our downstairs apartment for four years.

I was busy! Teaching, taking care of Matthias and Christian (Hans was living with Mutter and Onkel Hans), and taking classes. Matthias and Christian did well at their school. Matthias loved the social life and school while Christian always looked forward to the weekend or a day without school. He did not care for the daily routine at all, although he had no difficulties in any subject. Brigitte earned a little bit more money and we could afford a few more luxuries, a new dress or an extra pair of shoes. The growing boys were also in need of new clothes. I managed quite well with the mortgage payments and our dear sister Emmeli never failed to send her monthly support. I also worked as a translator for a lawyer who settled affairs for German immigrants and refugees. That was good money; he always paid cash.

In the summer of 1959, Brigitte began her second year as resident physician and her sons stayed in Mount Morris with our mother. This allowed me to take advantage of a special opportunity offered to me: six weeks at the Language Institute at Princeton University.

On October 4, 1957, the Russian Sputnik "World Wanderer" took off for space exploration. The US became aware of the fact that it was necessary to study foreign languages in order to keep up with the world. Russian was introduced in many universities and, in general, the foreign language teachers received a boost. I received a letter from Princeton inviting me to participate in a special language program. I had been recommended by my professor, Dr. Lincoln Canfield, who taught Methods to Teach a Foreign Language at the University of Rochester. The six weeks of study was free of charge, including room and board, for approximately one hundred selected participants. Half would be taking German and the other half French. The idea was to prepare us for a career as foreign language teachers. Many of the participants were refugees from Austria and Germany who were Jewish and hoped to make a new career in America as teachers. For the first time in my life, I was able to be a real college student with no outside responsibilities. By "real" I mean that I lived in a dormitory and shared a suite with two other students. We were advised of the location of the cafeteria, the hours for breakfast and dinner, laundry facilities and, of course, most importantly, our class schedule. On our first day, our professors were introduced to us at a special dinner. My six weeks at the Language Institute at Princeton University turned out to be a most wonderful experience. I had been planning to be a teacher anyway, but this experience allowed me to advance my career a bit faster.

Emmeli took the Illinois medical board exam in 1957 and passed. At that time, New York State only permitted a certain number of foreign students to take the medical board each year. They had filled their quota and Emmeli would have to wait at least another year before she could try again in New York. However, Illinois had openings for the exam and Emmeli decided not

Hans Visits Emmeli in Her New Office in Downs, IL, 1959

to wait any longer and took the Illinois board. She moved to Jacksonville, IL, where she worked as an associate for another physician. After one year, Emmeli opened her own practice in Downs, IL, where she worked as a general practitioner in that small town until cancer forced her to end her practice in 1998. She was a huge part of the community and the outpouring of support from everyone was amazing.

Hans Does a Flip in Mt .Morris

We still spent most weekends in Mount Morris. In 1958, my Onkel Rolf came from Germany with his wife, Annemarie, to visit his sister, Lisa, and his brother, Hans. My uncle's three-bedroom house was filled to capacity so we waited until Sunday morning to drive down and visit for breakfast. It was the happiest and longest breakfast in a long time. I recall operating the new toaster that could handle four slices at the time. We had an assortment of jams and marmalades and plenty of coffee. Most important of all, wonderful conversation was abundant.

The children asked to be excused. Hans, age thirteen, said they had to get ready for the upcoming funeral. "Who died? You didn't tell us. I didn't bring a black dress," my aunt blurted out. "You can watch from the window if you like; there is no need to change your clothing," Hans said. Looking out, we soon saw the children from the neighboring doctors' houses assemble in the backyard. I recognized Martha Armstrong, also thirteen, her sisters, Susan and Judith, the twins, Christopher and Jeffrey Judd, as well as six others whose names I have forgotten. Hans instructed the mourning group to form a line. They then proceeded to walk three times around my mother's garden table. What appeared to be a shoebox, decorated with some greenery, was sitting on top. When Hans picked up the shoebox that held a dead bird, the children, their heads bowed, followed him single file to the burial spot. My mother had already given permission to dig a hole between two hedges. Once the children reached the designated grave, and the box was in the hole, each mourner put a bit of dirt on a shovel and dropped it on the "coffin."

The most touching ceremony was completed and the very subdued children came to life. "So what do we do now?" they asked. Hans said, "Let's go swimming; I think my grandmother will watch us." Indeed, my mother was only too happy to go to the nearby pond with the children. She knew that a game of serious Bridge was planned. She was not fond of playing cards, although she was always available when a fourth was needed.

Brigitte completed her residency in the summer of 1960. Highly recommended by her superiors at the hospital, she was accepted by New York State to take the examination for the medical state board, provided she attend a special one-year course for foreign physicians at NYU. The problem was money. How could we afford room, food, and tuition in New York? Onkel Hans' estranged wife, Dori, had a friend named Camilla in NYC. Camilla graciously offered a room, free of charge, conveniently located near NYU, so that Brigitte could walk to classes. Emmeli contributed for Brigitte's food and I paid for her bus fare and school supplies.Thus began a most difficult year for Brigitte. She was lonely and had a demanding course load. (To give the reader an idea: seventy physicians started the course; only twenty-eight completed it.) One of her fellow students, a German Jew whose family had fled to Argentina during the Hitler regime, had a car and he drove Brigitte to Mt. Morris for Christmas for four wonderful days. In April 1960, the great German actor, Gustav Gründgens was performing Goethe's *Faust* in New York. I obtained permission from the Pittsford School to take twenty-five of my top German students to see the play. We went by bus and I took Hans along so that he could see his mother. That was wonderful for both mother and son.

Brigitte passed the final examinations at NYU and came back home to Rochester. The state board examination took place in May in the armory on Main Street in Rochester and lasted four days. I took Brigitte every morning before school so that she would be on time for the tests that began at 8:00 a.m. I remember being in awe of the cold atmosphere in the vast buildings. Many rows were set up, each with several proctors. There were only sixteen physicians among the huge group. There were architects, nurses, teachers, and others who took their assigned seats. I thought the whole scene was mind boggling. The results would not be made available until two months later. Meanwhile, Brigitte got a job as an Assistant Physician at the tuberculosis hospital in Rochester, located at the corner of South Avenue and Elmwood Street. I do not remember how much Brigitte earned but it was a fairly decent salary and we felt "rich." After waiting for seven weeks for news from Albany, Brigitte no longer wanted to look at our mailbox. When **the** letter did arrive, I called her from downstairs. I distinctly recall the scene. Brigitte sat down on the stairs and asked me to open the letter. "Don't tear it," she cautioned, because I was anxious to rip it open. I began reading, "We are pleased to…" Brigitte almost stumbled down the stairs. We were very happy and relieved.

Since she passed the state boards, Brigitte was now licensed to practice pediatrics. Another pediatrician, Dr. George Anderson, invited her to join his practice, located just across from the hospital on Alexander Street. Both physicians made house calls and Brigitte was more than busy. I acted as her answering service when she was out on calls. Brigitte left all of the children's school activities to me while she concentrated on her work. She earned extra money by working at clinics so we could afford a trip to Illinois. We drove non-stop for seventeen hours one way. It was fun to visit Emmeli. Brigitte had to learn how to drive quickly. She soon bought her first car, a VW Beetle, for $900. I still had "Putzi," a most reliable Chevrolet. After a year with Dr. Anderson, the two parted company. Their individual work ethics were too different and they had rather opposite ideas regarding treatment for their patients.

Brigitte rented office space in Strathallan Park. It was fun gathering and finding appropriate office furniture. We were ready for patients in August 1962. Hinrich and Nancy had just moved from Michigan to Buffalo, where Hinrich was appointed as Assistant Professor at the University of Buffalo. Nancy came with their young sons, David and Philip, the first patients to try out the new office. We decided that we needed more toys, but otherwise the trial run went smoothly. In no time, Brigitte's practice was very busy. Obstetricians recommended her, colleagues who wanted a little time off sent their patients to her, and she was frequently on call for other pediatricians. She often did not come home before 8:00 p.m. or even later. Brigitte also continued making endless house calls. I kept functioning as her answering service and kept her books. Our financial situation improved rapidly and Brigitte bought her first piece of furniture from Mangurians. Up to that point we had only bought necessities at garage or estate sales. We referred to this very attractive cabinet as our "Goldschrank," gold cabinet, which kept important papers through all of Brigitte's life.

In 1962 my tenants, the Bannisters, moved out and I moved into the lower apartment. Most important of all, Hans, now fourteen years old, moved to Meigs Street so that he could attend Monroe High School. We had finished a very nice room in the attic for Hans and we were all happy that the brothers were now always together. After painting the room, we put down linoleum tiles. We had put our radio at one end of the room and at 6:00 p.m., a Catholic service began. I could not walk on the freshly glued tiles so we had to listen to "Blessed art thou Mother of Jesus..." again and again. Neither one of us forgot that half hour.

I finished paying my second mortgage to Hewitt Kenyon and Brigitte began savings plans for her three sons. We even bought some flowers and installed flower beds in the front and back yards and painted the house, using a lot of paint on us, I am afraid. My friend Erika Hinrichsen, was working with a company in Hamilton, Canada, and came to visit and helped us paint the window frames. It was all a lot of fun. Most weekends and, of course, the summer vacations were still spent in Mt. Morris. Matthias and Christian did well in school, although Christian still preferred to play with Legos. We bought an electric train for them which

Matthias and Christian with their Train Set

we set up in the basement. The two boys often had a difficult time playing together. Matthias wanted to build the scenery (mountains, tunnels, trees, and houses) while Christian wanted to run the locomotive and organize the train routes. I frequently had to go down to the basement to bring some peace. Christian was content playing by himself. Matthias brought several friends home and enjoyed their company. One day, when I went to the basement to do laundry, I found a huge sign on the door, "Women Haters Club." However, it did not last long until girls were invited back to our house. Hans meanwhile enjoyed his life at the high school. Handsome and charming, he quickly endeared himself to all teachers.

Brigitte also started a job as a school physician. She worked in two schools on Thursdays when she was officially "off." After her retirement, we referred to her small pension of $56 a month as her "tulip money." It was the money she used to buy bulbs for her beloved garden; however, she was never able to stay within the allotted budget. In the summer of 1963, Brigitte took her first vacation with her boys. They went to Cape Cod for a week at the ocean. I stayed at home since I was taking summer school courses at the

Leaving for Cape Cod, 1963

Beach in Cape Cod

university. I took two Russian courses as well as an English poetry class and was very busy. After five years of teaching at the Pittsford High School, I got a scholarship from the University of Rochester and was hired as an instructor of German. Since I continued teaching German at the University's Evening School, I did not have to pay tuition.

On November 22, 1963, a horrible American tragedy occurred. President John F. Kennedy was assassinated. I remember that I was listening to the radio while correcting papers when I heard the dreadful news. I called Brigitte at her office. She was, however, too busy with her patients to talk. So I ran to our neighbors and we commiserated together. Brigitte and I talked for hours that evening and listened to the radio. Suddenly things had gone awry in our acquired country where we had sought a safe haven.

In the summer of 1964, Brigitte and her sons joined Hinrich and Nancy and their three sons (Clark was born on February 15, 1964) for a vacation at Kirk Cove in Ontario, Canada. I could not go since I was teaching summer school and also taking a Spanish class. But I did make the eight-hour round trip over the weekend and took Matthias home with me since he had injured his front tooth on a rock. He announced that he was "ruined for life." Fortunately, that was not the case. They had a great time, learning and mastering water skiing. Even our mother, who had gone along, gave the sport a valiant try.

Kirk Cove, 1964
From Left: Matthias, Lisa, Hinrich (Clark on shoulders),
Hans, Brigitte, Onkel Hans, Nancy
In Front: Christian, Philip, David

After a year of running her own practice without any time off, Brigitte joined the pediatric practice of Dr. Kenneth Woodward and Dr. Richard Meltzer. Their office was located on East Avenue in somewhat cramped quarters. Brigitte was now off every third night and more weekends. The group discontinued making house calls; however, they would see patients at the office after hours and on weekends. Two years later, they moved their office to the Doctors' Building adjacent to the Genesee Hospital. This location proved most convenient for all concerned. Brigitte became very involved with the nursery and also neo-natal care.

In the spring of 1965, Brigitte bought 1320 Highland Avenue. I sold the Meigs Street house for $28,000 and was able to add $5,000 to the down payment of the new house. Hans' friends helped us move. The former owner, Mrs. Squire, was mortified when she saw the boys with dirty shoes stomping on her very expensive white carpets. I do not remember the reason for her presence. She wanted to sell us her huge round table. My sister and I always regretted that we did not buy the beautiful piece of furniture at the time. I had my final examinations for my master's degree during our moving week. It was quite hectic. Nobody had time to actually celebrate my accomplishment.

1320 Highland Avenue

Our new home was great. There was lots of room, a very big front yard, and a terraced garden in the back that led up the hill bordering the Hillside Children's Center property, my first employer. Brigitte and I always referred to our new neighbors as "Adelaide." This unpleasant lady had retired, which was fortunate for the children. Brigitte loved planning her flowerbeds and it was delightful to decorate our house. For our first Christmas, Brigitte and her boys overestimated the size of our living room and came home with a giant tree that needed a serious trimming job. Christian completed his last year at school #24 and had to be transported daily. He had lunch every day with our old neighbor, Mrs. Crombach. Matthias had already transferred to the Monroe Middle School. Hans graduated in 1966 from Monroe High School. We put on a big garden party for him.

Hans's Senior Prom, 1966

Meanwhile, Matthias had also become a student at Monroe High School. Unlike his brother Hans, Matthias had frequent disagreements with some of his teachers and I had to go to school to straighten things out. He continued to like school, however, and had many friends. He began his studies at SUNY Brockport but left before graduating to pursue his love for photography. Matthias did well as a photographer in Europe and returned to graduate with a degree in Economics from Brockport. He later had success as a photographer in New York City.

Christian did not like Monroe High School. The students had changed in the past year and many rowdy and unpleasant boys had joined the group. When other boys took his milk money, we decided that it was time to find another school. Brigitte and I enrolled him in McQuaid High School, a private school, where he would not be bullied by anyone. Christian enjoyed

57 Eastland Ave: Home of Lisa and Onkel Hans

this school and did well. Later, he would graduate with a master's degree in computing and education from the University of Rochester.

In 1968 Brigitte bought another house on Eastland Avenue in Brighton in a section called Home Acres. This house became home for my mother and uncle who had retired from the hospital in Mt. Morris. Located just ten minutes by foot from the Highland Avenue house, it became a wonderful home for my mother and uncle. They visited daily and particularly enjoyed swimming in our pool and admiring Brigitte's beautiful garden.

Home Acres was an appropriate name. We all had settled in Rochester and were happy and grateful to be together.

My Daughter Anna is Born

Brigitte was very busy building her practice in 1966 and now was financially able to support the household. Since I had supported her family for many years, she decided that it was now time for her to help and support me. I had a teaching assistantship at the University of Rochester which paid for my tuition plus a little allowance (which at the time was tax-free). Brigitte's sons were all in high school. Hans and Matthias were a senior and a sophomore respectively at Monroe High School. The youngest, Christian, was now attending McQuaid High School. After the Principal, Dr. Ira Berman, retired from Monroe High School, the population changed (not for the better) and Christian was just not able to cope with the rather rude crowd.

My friend Hans Harmsen had visited me at least twice a year for the past several years. He met my whole family and was well liked. So it was decided that I deserved a trip to Europe. It so happened that the University of Rochester and Syracuse University had organized a charter flight from Syracuse to Zürich, Switzerland. Participants would be on their own for six weeks in Europe. It was ideal for me. I remember being appalled because the drinks were free and flowing during the flight and, by the time we arrived in Zürich, the majority of the passengers were stone drunk.

Hans met me in Zürich. We went to Strasbourg, in Alsace Lorraine, where he gave several lectures as president of the European version of Planned Parenthood. The week in Strasbourg was wonderful! I had been there before with Emmeli when she was a student in Freiburg in the summer of 1943. During the middle of WWII, Strasbourg was German and the beautiful windows of the cathedral had been taken out to protect them from the bombs. Fortunately, Strasbourg was never bombed and managed to escape most of the horrors of war. Located directly on the Rhein, which serves as a border between France and Germany, one can cross the bridge to Kehl on the German side.

From Strasbourg we travelled by train to Geneva, Switzerland, where

Hans was busy for a few days at the World Health Organization (WHO). He had served on a number of advisory committees regarding the dissolution of the labor camps, organizing the repatriation of the former inmates and/or finding appropriate living quarters for those who wished to stay in Germany. As Director of the Institute for Mental Health and Social Hygiene, he represented Germany. I was permitted to accompany Hans to the conference. I was fascinated by the enormous building and, in particular, the many cubicles reserved for interpreters. I think that some twelve languages were represented. I had just recently passed an interpreters' examination at the University of Kiel, but I realized that it would take much more training before I would ever be able to work in a place like that. Hans Harmsen, an MD, PhD, spoke briefly about his work with Planned Parenthood. He was promoting the "pill" in an effort to avoid the conception of unwanted children. He was strongly against abortion, not necessarily for religious reasons, but because of the emotional turmoil, as well as physical hardship, such an invasive event caused the mother. But, most of all, Hans felt that one should not plant a seed only to trample on it as soon as it showed signs of life.

From Geneva, we flew to Belgrade, then the capital of Yugoslavia, to attend yet another conference organized by WHO. Hans was the keynote speaker at the International Conference for Social Hygiene. All participants were residing at the Hotel Moskau, with the exception of the Russian contingent who had to stay aboard their ship. The accommodations were modest; six rooms shared one bathroom and towels were a prized commodity.

Marshal Josip Broz Tito was the President (dictator) of Yugoslavia. After WWII, Poland and Yugoslavia were in peril. The Russians had not provided any assistance when the Poles rose against the Nazis in Warsaw in 1944. Instead, the Russians advanced through Poland in 1945 and the prospect of an independent Polish regime became very dim. Yugoslavia was another case in point. The Communist Party, led by Tito, gained control over rival ethnic groups, especially the Serbs and Croats, and he was elected Premier in 1948. Tito was able to unite the provinces of Kossovo, Volvodina, Croatia, Bosnia and Hercegovina, Macedonia, Slovenia, and Montenegro. "Unified" Yugoslovia was ruled under his tight dictatorship. He nationalized all industry and suppressed, imprisoned, or executed all dissidents, yet he defied the USSR in many ways. Yugoslavia had become the most liberal of communist states. Tito ruled until his death in 1980.

I did not attend the meetings. Instead I explored Belgrade with its many drab-looking apartment buildings, each window displaying identical curtains and lamps. But the people whom I watched while sitting along the beautiful Danube seemed happy and well-dressed.

On the second day, Hans informed me that I was invited to attend the reception at the palace. We rushed to buy a simple black dress and black heels so that I was appropriately dressed. The reception was a gala affair. The palace was beautifully decorated and furnished in the most exclusive style. Many elegantly clad waiters offered delicious bites to eat as well as champagne, a stark difference from what I had observed on the outside. Tito welcomed the participants and then the music started. I watched Tito taking some of the ladies for a quick spin and suddenly he stood before me and asked me to dance. Yes, I danced with Marshall Tito! I kept my "Tito-dress" for many years.

The day following the reception, the Russians invited the group to go for a ride on their jet-powered boat along the Danube to a tiny village in Rumania, offering some spectacular scenery. The Danube rises in the Black Forest in Germany, passes through Vienna (Austria), Budapest (Hungary), Belgrade (Yugoslavia), and empties into the Black Sea. The 130 km section of the Danube is known as the Iron Gates. The narrow gorges were breathtaking. The trip along the Danube was one of my most memorable sightseeing trips. With three semesters of Russian behind me, it was nice to be able to engage in some conversations with our hosts. However, the language used by most was English and I was able to serve as an interpreter for the German contingent. That was a lot of fun.

The participants, consisting of mostly physicians and some sociologists, appeared pleased with the outcome of the conference they had just attended. They were going to advocate hand washing, especially in hospitals, and they seemed particularly pleased with the invention of the dishwasher. They had no doubt that households would become more germ-free. I wondered how many households in the country would be able to enjoy this new luxury item. However, I concentrated on the very beautiful and exciting trip.

After about two hours on the boat, we went ashore to visit a primitive Rumanian village. Two large tables were set outside and we were invited to sit down for lunch. There were three large bowls filled with a hearty soup on each table and the "place settings" consisted of a spoon for each person. Two women, whose hands had not seen any water for some time, went around with large loaves of delicious bread from which they carved thick slices for each one of us. There were no plates. We would simply use our spoons to take soup from the bowl nearest to us. The soup was delicious and the bread was the best ever. I could not help but be amused to watch the other participants. Some declined to eat—they missed out on a marvelous meal! Hygiene and cleanliness went out the window.

With an hour to look at the village (no photographs were allowed) we just saw the inside of a small, very primitive house and the dismantled, deserted church which had its doors torn off. It was obvious that no religious services had occurred there in many years. All items within the church had been removed and it was desolate and felt violated. As the country was communist, all reminders of Christianity had been destroyed. Our family would experience this lack of Christianity in the communist countries first hand when, in 2001, my nephew hosted an exchange student from Slovenia. Urška was twenty-one at the time. She spent her first Christmas with us and we learned that the whole celebration had no meaning to her whatsoever. My nephew's son, Stefan, fell in love with her, and they were married in 2007.

Hans and I flew to Dubrovnik after this memorable trip on the Danube. Dubrovnik dates back to the eleventh century. A walled city, it is located directly on the Adriatic Sea in the south of Croatia. As a most desirable seaport and fortress, Dubrovnik had changed "ownership" many times over the centuries. The Austro-Hungarian rule under the Hapsburgs lasted for more than a century. The population was diverse: Catholic Croats, Serbian Orthodox, and Muslim Serbo-Croats. During WWII, Dubrovnik had become a Nazi puppet state until the partisans, led by Tito, were victorious. Tito sentenced some eighty citizens, including a Catholic priest, to death and Dubrovnik became part of Yugoslavia in 1944. While listening to some of these gruesome stories, I marveled at the beauty of the city and enjoyed the happy people selling their goods to tourists. At one time, we stopped and looked toward the sea and Hans said, "I think we should have a baby together." Well, we did just that, as evidenced by my beautiful daughter born nine months later in April of 1967.

We flew back to Hamburg. Hans returned to work and I had a few days to visit with friends and family. I took two days to visit my friend Inge. She lived in West Berlin at the time which was supported by West Germany and mostly the United States. For DM 20.00 (deutsche mark), one could book a round-trip flight from Hamburg to West Berlin. Since I had never been to Berlin, I decided to go.

Inge met me at the airport, looking lovely. She was the fourth daughter of our neighbors in Lübeck and then Travemünde and my dear friend, Erika's, sister. We had grown up together during the Hitler times. Erika was my age and Inge two years younger. Inge had just recently married Edmund Dunlop who had actually been Erika's friend, which made the situation somewhat awkward. Erika had been working as a foreign correspondent for a large firm in Köln when Inge joined her sister to get a job there as well. Inge worked for two months when she decided to get married to Edmund.

"We only have a small guest room, Hedda," she said almost apologetically. I suppose she assumed that I was used to grand rooms and surely a stately guest room, coming from the land where money grows on trees. I explained to her that we did not have a spare room and that the children had to vacate their beds if guests were coming. The truth was that I had known only one person in all my life who had a guest room—my grandfather. It was specifically made for his grandchildren. Emmeli, Brigitte, and I alternated sleeping over from Saturday to Sunday. My sisters disliked the visit which took time away from their friends. I, however, found it quite interesting. On Sunday mornings, I must have been ten or eleven, I went with my grandfather to his "Stammtisch" in a bar. He met up with four other men to talk over a glass of beer while I was treated to a wonderful glass of lemonade. After WWII, I learned that these kindly men were Freemasons, an organization which was strictly prohibited by the Nazi regime. In any event, I am glad that I was young and innocent enough to be taken along to those meetings.

The Dunlop family was "old money and prestige" and Inge's wedding had taken place at a small castle near the Rhein. After the wedding, the couple moved to Berlin, where Inge's husband held a job as CPA for a very big firm. Their apartment was small but pleasant. The guest room appeared quite cozy. Spread out on the dining room were architectural drawings and I learned that they had bought land and were building a house, expected to be finished within a few months. Inge told me that she had just purchased a beautiful entrance door from an antique dealer. We had a good time together but at about 4:00 p.m., when Inge was fixing a cup of coffee, she became apprehensive and ill at ease. "Can you do me a big favor?" she asked. Inge wanted me to confirm that we had spent a week together in Travemünde in case her husband asked about it. There was no time for any further explanation since her husband arrived earlier than expected.

I was stunned when I met him. Beautiful, charming Inge had married an unattractive dud. The dinner conversation consisted of small talk and politics. I felt a relief when it was time to do the dishes. I never did have to lie, which was good. The guest room was located directly next to their bedroom and the wall was not very sturdy. I heard them talking and could make out that Inge was asking her husband for another week away from Berlin and she would fly with me to Hamburg. Breakfast was uncomfortable. Inge, dressed in an elegant robe, served rolls and coffee, while Edmund greeted me politely and then became engrossed in the newspaper. Soon after, Inge and I were off to explore West Berlin. New buildings had gone up; very few ruins served as a reminder of the war. There was of course the gruesome Wall, which divided Berlin. It made me feel most uncomfortable. At noon, we stopped in a fashionable restaurant. "I have to tell you something, Hedda," she said. "I spent one glorious week in Rome with Eberhard." It turned out that Eberhard was the owner of the factory where Edmund was employed. Inge had been swept off her feet by him. I was not surprised. I told her about my adulterous affair, about which she had heard rumors. Eberhard was also married with three children. I advised Inge to leave Edmund in any case and tell him the truth. She called her husband to say we would not be home for dinner and then called Eberhard and asked if he could meet us. I liked him immediatley. He was a charming man who made Inge come alive.

Inge's divorce was quick. She left everything she ever got from the Dunlop family and went to live with her parents for a while. Eberhard's divorce was contentious and expensive. Fortunately, money was really no object. Inge and Eberhard were happily married and had one daughter, Christine, in 1970.

After a brief visit to Lübeck to see some more relatives and friends, I returned to Hamburg where Hans and

Inge and Eberhard, 1982

I parted company. I flew to Zürich to catch the university-sponsored flight back home. While I am sure that the drinking occurred on the return flight as well, my mind was filled with so many memories and experiences that I don't remember anything about the actual flight.

Immediately after returning from my wonderful trip to Europe, I dropped in at the Language Department to get my teaching schedule from the secretary. It was just before Labor Day 1966. I had looked forward to seeing her again and telling her all about my great adventures. However, she did not seem to be in the mood to chat. I was told that there would be a department meeting on Friday at 4:00 p.m. in Dr. Canfield's office. Throughout the year, this special time had always been a happy hour, but the secretary's demeanor seemed to indicate that this might not be a happy meeting. Indeed, it was not.

Following many arguments and harsh disputes, the various professors had decided to split the Department of Foreign Languages into the (a) the Department of Languages and Linguistics and (b) the Department of Foreign Languages and Literature. This division came to be known as the "Painful Divorce." The graduate students, as well as some instructors who had not participated in these discussions, were upset. I learned that students could obtain a master's degree in French, German, Spanish, and Russian literature. A PhD would be attainable only through the Department of Linguistics. What was truly sad, in fact downright ridiculous, was that some of the members of the departments were no longer on speaking terms with one another! The literature team looked with disdain on the linguists and vice versa. Dr. Canfield stayed on as Chairman of the Linguistics Department. I never found out why a new departmental secretary had been hired. No wonder she had not been in a chatty mood when I visited her office.

I had already registered for several classes concentrating on the study of languages that would cover grammar, phonetics, and morphology (the study and description of word formation in language), as well as the history of the relations of languages to each other and the cultural place of languages in human behavior. In 1786, Sir William Jones had suggested a possible affinity of Sanskrit and Persian with Greek and Latin, wondering whether there was a genetic relationship between languages. His theories marked the beginning of the study of comparative historical linguistics. Jakob Grimm established the existence of the Indo-European family of languages which is a fascinating field. Professor Klimas stressed the study of Lithuanian, one of the oldest languages in that group. Professor Obrecht lectured on spectrography, and

My Daughter Anna is Born

Dr. Sapon did his best to make us understand the transformational generative grammar and the subconscious control of the speaker's actual use of the language as discussed by the American linguist, Noam Chomsky.

Professor Hanhardt had suffered a heart attack and I was asked to teach one of his classes: the History of the German Language. I received a most welcome stipend of $2,300. It was an extremely busy semester. I studied and studied. When at home, I remember going into our basement where nobody could hear me reciting the many things I had to memorize. Studying for my doctoral prelims, scheduled for December, was very hard indeed. I passed the PhD preliminary examinations in December 1966 and was now an ABD (all but dissertation). Best of all, I could enjoy Christmas with the whole family. My brother and his wife also came with their three little boys. Suddenly, Hinrich took me aside and said sternly, "You are pregnant, aren't you!?" So, the secret was out. Several people said, "How could you?" and I even heard an "Ach du lieber," but everybody was happy for me. My mother had known for some time and, two months earlier, I had confided in Brigitte. She sent me to an obstetrician, a partner of our neighbor Dr. Jack Hamilton, for pre-natal examinations. I had gained too much weight and was put on a super-strict diet. At that time, small babies were "in." When my condition became more obvious, my mother sewed two not very attractive dresses that helped hide my pregnancy, and I began to wear a large raincoat to classes. I was classified as an old mother, but I never had any doubts about my baby's health.

During the winter, I took to wearing oversized woolen sweaters and large coats when attending or teaching classes. I have to confess, I was worried about the reaction of my colleagues, advisors, and students. I think it was in late March when our department secretary put an end to my secret. My favorite professor, Lincoln Canfield, commented, "I was wondering why Hedda suddenly preferred water or juice over our customary wine during the department's happy hour on Fridays." Although that group was utterly surprised, they wished the best for me and my baby. Their curiosity about the baby's father was laid to rest when Hans, accompanied by Brigitte, came to pick me up from the university and meet several members of the department.

The so-called due date was May 5, 1967, her father's birthday. This date had not been difficult to calculate, since we knew exactly when we had decided to have a child together. Hans arrived by mid-April and I told my students that there was the possibility that I might not be there for classes soon. At the end of April, finals were coming soon and reviewing was essential. It was a good thing that Hans arrived earlier than expected, since Anna was born on April 24.

We had hosted a small dinner party on April 23. I felt the contractions begin while I was doing the dishes. Both Brigitte and Hans told me it wasn't the real thing. Of course, being doctors, they thought they knew best. Shortly after midnight, the pain was very intense and I phoned my OBGYN who, after listening to me, told me to put Brigitte on the phone. They worked together at the hospital. Reluctantly, Brigitte drove me to the hospital shortly after midnight. She parked as far away as possible and made me walk to the hospital entrance. Anna was born a mere three hours later. My sister, who was to be Anna's private pediatrician until she finished college, was with me. Hans came to take us home in the early afternoon the next day. He had a huge bunch of daffodils in his arms that Brigitte had reluctantly picked from her garden. She hated to pick her daffodils and brought that particular bouquet up year after year.

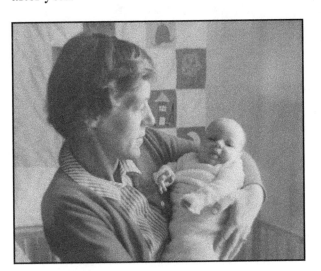

Hedda with her Daughter, Anna

My Mother, Lisa, Proudly Holds her First Granddaughter, Anna Lisa

Anna was healthy and, of course, the most beautiful baby ever. My mother had come from Mount Morris and was thrilled that she finally had a granddaughter after six grandsons. Everybody was very happy. Brigitte drove me to the university to teach my two classes two days later. The students would not believe my story, so they came to visit to see for themselves. It was very touching. Life was wonderful—until Hans left on May 6. His departure was most difficult, but there was one consolation; he would return in July. My classes were soon over and I thoroughly enjoyed my time with Anna.

Hedda Holding Anna

Anna's Father

Hans Harmsen and I met in 1948 when I was twenty years old. At that time, he had fathered seven children and taken in his brother's two daughters who had been orphaned two days before the war ended. Their parents had been killed in Berlin by the advancing Russian troops. Hans devoted all of his time to his work and used every opportunity to attend conferences around the world, which made his absences from Hamburg legitimate.

When my Anna was three, her father didn't like being so far away. He started suggesting that I move to Hamburg. Upon his request, we saw a lawyer in Rochester, NY, because Hans wanted Anna to have his last name. Brigitte advised against this because it would be too confusing for Anna to have a mother with a different name. The lawyer advised that Anna would have the option to change her name when she was sixteen. Anna decided not to change her name.

Anna and her Father, 1970

Anna and I were visiting relatives in Lübeck in 1972, when her father came to pick us up for a visit with his family. His wife had prepared a special lunch and Ernst-Friedrich and Arnold, their two sons, were also present. Ernst-Friedrich was blond and blue-eyed like his mother and Arnold bore a strong resemblance to Anna, both having large dark-brown eyes and heavy eyebrows. The sons were in their early twenties and viewed us with some suspicion, which was more than understandable. Hans' wife acted as if we were the best of friends. Anna was the only one who enjoyed the food and talking to the "boys." His wife had bought Anna two dresses (she thought they were "itchy") as well as a toy (which we still have) commenting that she thought it strange that Hans had not bought dresses for Anna before.

In total disbelief, I then heard his wife say that she knew Hans loved

Anna so very much and, since I was a working mother and she had a big home and could give "the child" security and a better upbringing, she suggested that I leave "the child" with them in Hamburg. The very idea that Anna was referred to as "the child" prompted me to put her on my lap. I took one look at Hans, got up, and said that I really did have to leave for Lübeck at once. Hans was also taken by surprise and totally stunned. Back in Rochester, I received a letter from his wife. She was sincerely and genuinely sorry for having suggested this plan and said that she would give Hans a divorce if I would marry him and move back to Germany, which was out of the question for me. Strange as it may seem, his wife and I continued to correspond until her death. Hans visited us soon thereafter in Rochester and realized that Anna was happiest there.

I also kept in touch with Ernst-Friedrich, who lamented the fact he never had a close relationship with his father and was happy to hear my stories about him. Hans was born on May 5, 1899, in Charlottenburg, a suburb of Berlin, Germany. His father, Friedrich (Fritz), a patent lawyer, stern and distant, was never able to have a close relationship with his music- and art-loving son. Hans' younger brother, Walter, was planning to follow in his father's footsteps and become a lawyer, but he was killed in the final week of WWII. A third boy, Fritz, died in infancy. Hans' mother, Therese, took care of the family.

Hans was always close to his mother, Therese, who lived to be 101 years old. When she celebrated her ninetieth birthday, Hans fulfilled her wish: a boat ride on the Wannsee in Berlin. She had been living as a widow in a home for seniors in Berlin for the past fourteen years. Hans supplied her with lots of yarn so she could knit hats and socks for needy people, plus many books to read when her fingers required a rest. When Hans told her about Anna and me, she said, "Ach, mein Hans, sei gut zu den beiden!" (Be good to both of them.) She lived another eight years in reasonably good health. She was ninety-seven when she gave me her wedding ring as a gesture of good will.

Hans' father, not a family man, was known to be obsessed with his work. Instead of spending time with his family, he used his free time to translate technical books from English into German. While he enjoyed walks with his sons, he never included his wife in these outings. Therese did her own cooking (an unusual thing for well-to-do families at that time) but, although she had a maid, she felt that she could not leave her household. Fritz was

Therese (Mother), Frida (Grandmother),
Hans, Anna (Aunt), Fritz (Father), 1916

respectful to others but did not allow anyone to get too close. He was a very strict disciplinarian and, unfortunately, he beat Hans if he failed to live up to his father's expectations. Hans was handsome and gifted and had a special fondness for music and the arts.

Hans told me that he had been very fond of his aunt, Anna. She had been an aspiring pianist but, unfortunately, her life was cut short when she succumbed to tuberculosis. One day in 1971, a huge parcel arrived from Ted von Borsig, Hans' brother-in-law, in New York City. He was a freelance photographer with residences in NYC as well as Berlin. I had never met him, but Hans and I had stayed in his apartment whenever we met in NYC. The carefully wrapped parcel contained a beautiful portrait of Anna Harmsen at age 26. Hans had given it to Ted with the request to forward it to me. It now hangs in my daughter Anna's home.

Anna's Great Aunt Anna

Hans was just fifteen in 1914 when WWI began. He could hardly wait to join the army and get away from home. His father did not approve of his free-spirited son who had no desire to become a lawyer or an engineer, the two professions his father had in mind for him. Glad to be allowed to take his final examinations at school early, he became a soldier in 1916 and fought on the Western Front.

Hans Harmsen, 1916

In early 1917, he was severely wounded. It took seventeen operations to reconstruct his jaw, chin, and nose. He suffered serious depression but determined to study medicine, which he began at the University of Marburg. It was customary to attend several universities for the first five semesters and he studied at Heidelberg, Munich, and Berlin. Thanks to the benefits he received from his war-time service, he was financially independent from his domineering father. Thus, he could also pursue his interest in fine arts and music. It was at this time that he began to collect woodcuts by Albrecht Dürer (1471-1529) as well as art from Ernst Barlach (1870-1938). He also joined a chorus and learned to play the mandolin.

While Hans was a student in Berlin in 1920, he helped the artist, Lészló Maholy-Nagy (pronounced naadge), who was born in Hungary but had come to study and work in Berlin. Hans found the artist badly beaten and lying in a pool of blood in the street. Maholy-Nagy had been involved in the attempted overthrow of the German government and was persecuted by the German Workers Party that would later become the Nazis. Hans took Maholy-Nagy to his apartment and nursed him back to health. Out of gratitude, Maholy-Nagy drew a charcoal sketch of Hans which was slashed by the Nazis when they searched for the artist in Hans' apartment. Hans protected Maholy-Nagy and saved his life by helping him get to Chicago, where he became a prominent teacher at the Bauhaus school. Maholy-Nagy's charcoal sketch now hangs in my daughter's home in East Aurora.

An unconventional student, Hans skipped many lectures at University Medical School, joining hiking clubs and music groups instead. However, his father's death, followed by financial difficulties, forced him to complete his medical studies by 1927. At that time, he fell in love with the daughter of a wealthy aristocrat who did not permit his daughter and Hans to marry, despite the fact that she was pregnant. He referred to Hans as a "poor nobody" and prohibited him from having any contact with his daughter. Hans was able to find the mother of his not-yet-born child in a home for "fallen women" in Magdeburg, where their daughter, Elizabeth, was born in 1928. Elizabeth was brought up by an aunt and uncle. Her mother married someone "in her class." Elizabeth remained a great worry throughout Hans' life. As an adult, she moved to Hamburg, a frail and emotionally unstable woman, totally dependent on her father's financial support. The difficulties he experienced with the birth of Elizabeth prompted him to study sociology and specialize in social medicine. Gifted and hardworking, he earned his doctorate in both fields.

With the beginning of the Hitler regime in 1933, Hans was not allowed to pursue his work with Planned Parenthood at the university. His many publications were prohibited by Joseph Goebbels, the Reich's Minister of Propaganda. With Hans' work curtailed, he began to support the painters Emil Nolde and Ernst Barlach, both persecuted by the Nazis. These artists both rewarded Hans with sculptures, paintings, and lithographs. Barlach's works were prohibited and many destroyed. Barlach's lithographs depicted poor people or cripples which, of course, were not to be seen during the Nazi regime; they were undesirable.

Hans married a social worker in 1936 with whom he had three sons in rapid succession: Dirk, Hans, and Hinrich. Their father was drafted into the Medical Corps in 1939. His marriage was not happy and he almost welcomed the opportunity to leave his home. As a high-ranking officer, he was in charge of the health and welfare, diet and hygienic conditions of the troops in France. Before joining Field Marshal Rommel in the Africa Corps, he had a four-week leave at home. During this time, he began a relationship with Anneliese von Borsig, the wealthy daughter of an airplane manufacturer, and also his wife's best friend. He had created a terrible muddle and managed to spread much unhappiness. Again, he welcomed his "escape" to Africa and, as he told me, he thought it would be best to die there when news reached him that Anneliese had given birth to a daughter, Ruth.

While in Africa, Hans met and befriended Hermann Dillenberg, a young bacteriologist in his command. Dr. Dillenberg was the doctor on the ship I took to immigrate to the United States.

As part of his love of art, Hans was instrumental in creating an Exhibition of Ernst Barlach artwork following WWII with most of the pieces coming from his own private collection. He had arranged that this exhibition would travel to several notable museums in America as well as Toronto. While visiting me in Rochester, Hans met with the Memorial Art Gallery located in Rochester, and arranged that the Barlach exhibit would have a special showing there. The museum curators were instructed that I was to select four Barlach lithographs as a gift. It was extraordinary to receive this valuable art. I remember being very nervous when I went to the museum to make the selections. In addition, Hans also brought me a porcelain Barlach sculpture in his luggage, wrapped in sweaters.

Barlach Lithograph: Sternreigen, 1918   *Barlach: Blind Beggar, 1913*

Barlach died in East Germany. Credit must be given to the Communist regime since they preserved whatever works, as well as many model forms used to pour ceramic sculptures, by Barlach that weren't destroyed by the Nazis.

When Anna was seven, a friend of Onkel Hans, a Hamburg lawyer, learned of her interesting background. He convinced me that Hans should pay child support since I most definitely had no intention of marrying him. Hans and I had never discussed money at all until then, but he started putting money into an account in Hamburg from which Anna benefitted when we visited there after her graduation from Columbia in 1989.

In 1975 Hans received Germany's highest honor, the German Cross for outstanding humanitarian services. The ceremony took place in Bonn, which served as the capitol of West Germany. I regret that I was unable to be present at that time. Retirement was obligatory for him and extremely difficult.

Hans continued to publish numerous articles, but his many travels around the world were severely curtailed. This meant that we had to make do with daily correspondence and few visits. Hans' last visit to Rochester was in 1972.

Hans Harmsen Receiving German Cross in 1976

Anna and I visited the Harmsen house in Hamburg for the last time in 1980 when Anna was thirteen. Hans' son Arnold lived there with his wife and two children. The house was in total disarray and disrepair. The garden was overgrown and sad looking. Hans was gone with his new wife, Frau von Aschenrade, and Frau Harmsen had died. She had moved to Hannover years before to live with her daughter. Hans's son Ernst, divorced with two children who lived in Freiburg, had come to Hamburg to pick us up from the airport and spend the night at his brother's house. Ernst, Arnold, Anna, and I had a long conversation. They couldn't hear enough about their father who was a stranger to them, having been so involved with his work and charitable pursuits. Anna, suffering from jet lag, retired after some hours, but the three of us continued talking until the wee hours of the morning. Neither man seemed truly able to cope with his life. I kept in touch with Ernst for several years.

Hans' third wife, Frau von Aschenrade, promised to take care of him. His health was failing and she literally kept him as a prisoner, not allowed to communicate with any of his children and definitely not with me. A year before his death, she gave me "permission" for Anna to see him, which I did not want. I did, however, travel to Germany and met him in a restaurant near his house from which he had managed to walk. I met a distraught, broken man. It was heartbreaking to see this once strong man without any energy or sparkle. Shortly after our meeting, Hans became bedridden and his wife would not allow his children into the house. His sons, Ernst and Arnold, told us later that they needed the help of the police to enter the house and see their father.

When Anna turned sixteen in 1983, a package arrived from her father. In it were several prints of Albrech Dürer woodcuts. Included was a nice letter of how proud he was of Anna.

Anna and I traveled to Germany in 1989, but did not see Hans or know of his death. I learned he had died when we returned home and I received a copy of his death notice. I am very grateful that Hans identified most of the many photos he gave me with little notes on the backs.

Hans Harmson died in Germany of natural causes in the summer of 1989 at the age of ninety. He was buried in Ratzeburg without anyone in attendance except his wife. She had the tombstone engraved with Prof. Dr. Dr. H.H., which was against his wishes. He was modest about his considerable accomplishments.

I loved Hans very much and he loved Anna and me. Every time I look at Anna, I see his wonderful eyes. Goethe wrote this little poem, which is so fitting:

Vom Vater hab' ich die Statur,
Des Lebens ernstes Führen.
Vom Mütterchen die Frohnatur,
Die Lust zu fabulieren.

From my father I have the stature,
To look at life critically.
From my dear mother, the good nature,
And desire to tell stories.

My Daughter, Anna

I was so happy to finally have time to spend with Anna when my semester of teaching was over. My hours with her were precious. Even before she could talk, we had long, wonderful "conversations." Her beautiful eyes expressed delight as well as sorrow and I was so glad to be there to comfort my sweet little daughter when she needed comforting. I could hardly wait until her father Hans would see her again in July.

In spring we began construction of an in-ground pool. Hans, Brigitte's oldest son, had built many panels for an attractive redwood four-foot-high picket fence and I helped by screwing the pickets to the six-foot panels. The pool was 20 x 40 feet, a good size for real swimming and diving. Anna acted as the "supervisor" of the workers from her carriage. One day, three-week-old Anna was outside in her carriage crying. One of the workers said, "I have six kids. She is hungry." Guilt stricken, I went into the kitchen, warmed up some milk, and filled a bottle. She gulped it down, burped, and fell asleep. Then I phoned Brigitte at her office. "I hope you mixed the milk with water. I'll bring home some formula," she reproached me. I remember being terribly worried that I had done something very wrong. Fortunately, Anna took it in stride and showed no ill effects. Unfortunately, my attempts to breastfeed had not been very successful, despite the support of my sister and Anna's father Hans who had even bought a special chair for me to use while breastfeeding. Now, some two months later, I would have to tell him that Anna was bottle-fed. He attributed my inability to nursing to the fact that I had been very busy at the university administering final exams to my students and we said no more about it.

Anna's eyes had become very dark brown, resembling her father's. I was so happy to show him our most beautiful baby. I had taken Anna to the airport with me. I really did not want to share Hans with anyone, but Brigitte had prepared a festive dinner and my mother and uncle arrived for a wonderful reception. I was rather disappointed when Hans stayed with the family in the dining room while I fed, bathed, and changed Anna to get her ready for bed. However, he did come to the bedroom and quietly attached a very pretty music box in the shape of a bell that played Brahms' *Lullaby*. Anna later used this little bell with her children, Carl and Erika.

The household was busy. My nephews, Matthias and Christian, were still in high school, while my nephew Hans had come home from college. Friends and neighbors were curious to meet "Hedda's friend." They had heard stories that Hans had been Brigitte's professor at the medical school in Hamburg, Germany; that he was the president of the European Organization of Planned Parenthood; instrumental in helping displaced persons in refugee camps; and helped starving artists whose work had been condemned, confiscated, and largely destroyed by the Nazi regime. I think that, most of all, they wanted to know this man with whom Hedda had fallen in love some twenty years ago and who was twenty-nine years her senior!

The week at home was hectic. Neighbors gave a lovely dinner party and my brother invited us to his home in Clarence. I longed to be alone with Hans and Anna. When Hans mentioned that he would like to visit an art historian in Ottawa and suggested that we visit the EXPO in Montreal, I was thrilled. It would be just like the summer before, when we traveled through Europe together! My heart sank when Hans told me that he had spoken with my mother and sister about taking care of Anna during my absence, adding that it was good that the baby liked the bottle and was not dependent on me.

To be sure, Anna would be left in the best of care: my mother and my pediatrician sister. But this would be hard on me. Everyone wished us a wonderful trip; however, as the car rolled down that fairly steep incline to Highland Avenue, I needed a tissue. "You will be fine," Hans consoled me, while putting his hand on my shoulder.

We did have a wonderful and interesting trip together. However, whenever I saw something particularly beautiful, I wanted to share that experience with my Anna. Montreal was fascinating, but I really felt the need to go home. Instead, we headed to Ottawa to visit with Naomi Jackson-Groves. While she and Hans discussed her work and talked about Barlach's novels, sculptures, woodcuts, and his life, I felt left out and soon was overcome with an incredible homesickness and longing to be with Anna. Mrs. Jackson-Groves was eager to continue the conversation and asked us to spend the night. Fortunately, Hans declined the kind invitation. I think he knew how anxious I was to get home. We had been gone for six days. At home, everything was fine, of course. Brigitte had changed to disposable diapers and, when we returned, I felt that my Anna said, "It's about time."

It was then that I realized that Anna would always be the most important human being in my life.

Anna was thriving. The in-ground pool was finished and Brigitte went for a swim with Anna in August. The pool became the main attraction for many family festivities and parties with friends, including competitive games and races. Thus began a life-long love affair for Anna and her swimming.

Brigitte Takes Anna for a Swim, 1967

I went for an interview with the Foreign Language Department at SUNY College at Brockport. I would start as Assistant Professor in September 1967. I found a good babysitter in Asha Prasad, the wife of an Indian graduate student. A number of Indians resided in the student graduate housing near the University of Rochester. Anna was well taken care of by several women who were all dressed in beautiful saris. None had ever done a bit of housework and taking care of a baby was totally new to them. Anna's clothes began to take on the odor of strong Indian spices and one day when I picked her up, I thought that the diaper bag (I had purchased a very expensive one) smelled rather badly. Asha had put a dirty diaper in the bag. I had to show her what to do with the contents. Anna was with Asha for a little over a year.

Asha and Anna

I was busy running the household. My sister was very involved with her medical practice and I continued to help out with her sons. Hans was already a student at the University of Rochester but he frequently came home. Matthias was seventeen. We had just transferred Christian (fifteen) to a private school since he had difficulties coping with the negative attitudes and belligerent behavior of his fellow students at the inner-city school. I prepared dinner, helped out with homework, and listened to what they wanted me to know about their days, causing me to either praise or admonish.

Anna loved to be at home and thoroughly enjoyed her big cousins. The evening routine was the same for her. Play, dinner, bath, cuddling, a story, and good night. That was always a wonderfully happy time for both of us.

The Tuberculosis Hospital in Mt. Morris closed in 1968 and my uncle retired. My mother and uncle moved to Rochester and lived at 57 Eastland Avenue, about five minutes from our house. It was an ideal situation for all of us. Our former neighbor on Meigs Street became Anna's new babysitter. Peggy Staudenmaier had six children ranging in age from thirteen to six. It was a wonderful place. Anna continued to learn English. However, she disliked Mr. S. and I was glad when my mother offered to take over for two days a week.

Since Anna heard German all day when she was with Mutter and Onkel Hans, she quickly picked up the language. Once I picked her up to take her home to our house, she met up with Matthias and Christian. Their favorite language had become English, so Anna picked up English as well. Our night-time stories consisted of one in German and one in English and Anna was happy with that. I referred to her as my "knutschpaket," a huggable package. I loved to hug her each night after we exchanged the stories of our day. Those were very happy times.

Anna with her Oma
(My Mother)

Anna and her Pappa Swimming, 1970

Anna's father visited at least twice a year between 1967 and 1970. He had become very fond of his little daughter. Anna was and is bilingual and communication presented no problem. Anna had inherited her father's facial features and especially his very prominent dark brown eyes which did not exist in my predominantly blue-eyed family. I continued to be busy teaching German, comparative literature, French, and methodology (training future language teachers, which also involved Spanish), and working on my dissertation. The latter was often most frustrating since much of my writing did not find the approval of the committee. (I regret now that I threw out all my own far more interesting notes.) Finally, the paper was done and I went before the committee to defend. I remember arriving in a new white blouse which Brigitte had carefully ironed for the occasion. I had come ten minutes too early and the secretary made small talk, trying to calm my nerves. Then she offered me a cup of coffee. I took the mug into my trembling hands and promptly spilled the coffee all over my blouse. To this day, I do not know whether the four-member committee took pity on me or whether they truly felt that my dissertation was good. In any event, I passed. We celebrated with a festive dinner that night.

*Anna and Hedda
After a Swim*

In 1971, I enrolled Anna in the Adelante program in Rochester. I had become acquainted with the director who had obtained a government grant for this bilingual program. For the pre-kindergarten class, she needed fifteen Spanish-speaking children and ten who spoke English only. The Spanish contingent consisted of mostly Puerto Ricans. A bus picked the children up at 7:30 a.m. and delivered them home at 12:30 p.m. This arrangement was great for my schedule. My mother was always there to welcome Anna home. She loved the school, sang Spanish songs and began to speak and understand Spanish. By the end of the year, in June 1973, a reporter from the newspaper came to write about the wonderful results of the program. The article in the newspaper featured Anna, who was asked whether she could count in Spanish. She said: "Do you want 'eins, zwei, drei,' or 'one, two, three,' or 'uno, dos, tres, quatro?" She really did not know which language was which. The Spanish-speaking children had not really learned English. It was decided to extend the program. However, I decided Anna needed more competition and I enrolled her in a regular kindergarten class in the Brighton School District.

*Anna on her First
Day of Kindergarten*

Immediately after the little graduation party from the Adelante program, Anna and I flew to Mallorca for a vacation with her father. Anna felt right at home speaking Spanish. She did all the ordering for us in fluent Spanish with a Puerto Rican dialect, while I tried my German-accented, carefully constructed Spanish. We toured the beautiful island and visited the house where the pianist and composer Frederic Chopin (1810-1849) had lived with Madame Dupin, better known as the novelist George Sand. The house is a museum now and truly a must-see, where Chopin composed his nocturnes, scherzos, polonaises, mazurkas, and many other beautiful, romantic pieces. After Hans left, we were joined by my uncle, mother, nephew Matthias, and friends from Lübeck. Inge came with her husband Eberhard and daughter Christine, who was just three years old and somewhat of a playmate for Anna. My friends had to depart after three days since Eberhard had some business in Sicily. After they left, the maid came to me with a hand full of gold (a bracelet and a large necklace). Christine had been playing with it and the maid had found it on the bed. This was during Generalissimo Franco's rule as a military dictator (1936-1975). If the maid had kept the jewelry, she could have been severely punished under Franco's iron-fisted rule. I returned the gold to Inge when Anna and I visited Lübeck and Hamburg two weeks later.

Anna entered kindergarten in 1972 at Brighton Twelve Corners Elementary School. She thrived in elementary school, making lots of friends and enjoying all school had to offer. The best part was that she now spent every afternoon after school at my mother and uncle's house where the bus dropped her off. My mother and uncle cherished this time with Anna and were most annoyed when, on rare occasions when my classes finished early, I would come to meet Anna at the bus. "This is our time!" they would say to me.

One day, when I picked her up from my mother and uncle, we drove to Twelve Corners shopping area to do errands. One of our stops included going to CVS Pharmacy for toothpaste and soap. When we returned to our car, a small Carmen Ghia, where Anna sat without seatbelts in the front seat, my little girl requested to return to the pharmacy. "I need to go alone and I want to buy something special," Anna said. It was getting dark and the thought of allowing my precious Anna to go alone into the drug store frightened me, but I could not deny her request. So I parked the car as close to the drug store's entrance as possible, put $1.00 into her coat pocket, and let her go. For the next few minutes, my eyes were glued to the big door. It was a huge relief when I finally saw Anna emerge from the store. She was holding a little paper bag and came running towards the car. "I've found something so beautiful and precious for you, Mom!" she blurted out. She even had some change left from the $1.00 that she gave back to me. "It's real silver, Mom!" My "silver" comb has been with me ever since. It is however, too precious to be used.

In first grade, Anna was riding the school bus and was disturbed by the bus driver's bad language. Here, you have to keep in mind that she was growing up in a house with three teenage boys (Brigitte's sons). In our house we spoke a mixture of English and German, often switching mid-sentence making it difficult to understand the conversation unless you knew both languages. One rule that Brigitte and I established with the boys was that the words, "shut up," were never permitted. We had grown very tired of the boys getting angry with each other or us and yelling those words. One day, Anna approached the school Principal, Miss Meyers, who greeted the children each day at the entrance of the school. She explained that she was very upset by the bad words that the bus driver was saying. Miss Meyers asked her to come to her office to explain. When asked what the driver was saying, Anna said it was "so bad" that she couldn't say it out loud, but that she could spell it. So she wrote, "SHUT UP." The principal agreed that that was indeed a bad word and asked if the bus driver said anything else bad. Anna said she didn't know but that he did say, "Shit, fuck, and sit on your ass." Miss Meyers did her best to not looked shocked. Anna had never heard those words before (swearing by the boys took place in German in our house) and didn't know they were bad to say. I believe the bus driver was fired.

Another wonderful story occurred when Anna was in second grade. The teacher and children planned a Thanksgiving feast and prepared a lot of food with the help of some volunteer parents. One of the other volunteer parents became my lifelong friend and we would get together often. We both remember well what happened after that feast with great amusement. Following the meal, the parents were asked to clean all the pots and utensils that had been used. One of the mothers turned to me and said, "Will you please do the dishes? My clothes are dry clean only." I was dumbfounded. My friend ran into that mother occasionally and, when we spoke of her, we always called her "dry clean only!"

Anna always loved swimming. One day, when she was about six, we were swimming at a public pool nearby. A man approached me and asked if Anna was on a swim team. I said no and he said she should be. I made some inquiries and in the fall I signed her up for the Town of Brighton Swim Club. Little did I know how invested she would become in the sport and how much we would both enjoy the many people we met and places we went for swim meets all over the country. Practices for her age group were three times a week from 5:00 to 6:00 p.m., which did not interfere with our dinner. We went to swim meets on many a weekend. I remember "ironing" her first heat ribbon (it was blue with gold lettering). It was the beginning of a quickly filled bulletin board in her room. Ribbons changed to first place trophies and, when she was eleven years old, she elected to join a nearby big club, "The MCC Marauders." This club was directed by Steve Lochte, (the proud father of the Olympic gold medal swimmer, Ryan Lochte) who was the swim coach at Monroe Community College. It was fun for her, since there were now enough girls in her age group to form relays. They had a formidable medley team: backstroke, Anna; breast, Maureen Cleary; butterfly, Chris Choromanskis; and freestyle,

Anna on Brighton Club Team, 1976

Lynn Hertwick. However, practice was now two hours every night from 6:00 to 8:00 in the evenings, which interfered severely with our family dinners.

Being a swim parent means countless hours sitting on the most uncomfortable bleachers, driving to and from the various pools at sometimes ungodly hours, and of course, comforting the swimmer when the race did not turn out in her favor.

By far my favorite races were those in the eight and under group. Many of those children could not really dive or were afraid to do so and during their "race" they looked at the swimmers in the other lanes, a serious "no no," and frequently rested a bit when they turned around to complete the required fifty yards. At the end, I loved to hug my wet and ever-so-proud little daughter when she came running to sit on my lap.

It must have been around 1980 when I was asked the following, "Mrs. Martens, can you please wake me just about ten minutes before you wake up so that I can use the bathroom and do my hair?" I shall never forget thirteen-year-old Maureen's touching request when we shared a hotel room in Syracuse to attend a swim meet. I had offered to take two of Anna's friends along since their parents were working. Maureen was first in the bathroom. She washed and dried her hair and looked positively lovely. I am afraid that Anna and Christine did not notice the gorgeous hairdo. Their time in the bathroom was short. They had simply changed into their bathing suits and put some sweatshirts and pants over. I don't believe they combed their hair. There was little time for me as well, since we had to be down for breakfast at 7:00. We were scheduled to leave for the nearby pool at 7:30 a.m. By 8:00 everyone was in the pool warming up. All swimmers wore their caps. I am still smiling when I think about Maureen's short-lived coiffure.

There were many, many races: dual meets (mercifully short); high

Jr. National Relay (from left): Anna, Maureen, Christine, Lynn

school competitions; city, county, and state championships; Junior and Senior Nationals; the Empire State Games; and the National Olympic Festival held in Houston, TX. I went along to competitions in Indianapolis, Princeton, San Francisco, and West Point, not to mention the numerous meets that were held in Syracuse, Buffalo, and Rochester. Anna's swimming career also took her to St. Croix, Puerto Rico, Trinidad, and Hawaii for training trips.

Anna received many letters from college coaches asking her to swim for their schools. She considered

Anna and Hedda, Columbia Dorm, 1986

several, but eventually chose to swim at Columbia University in New York City. A very exciting place to go to school and a wonderful place for me to visit. She swam all four years and was elected captain her junior and senior years.

She studied math and pre-med and eventually chose to go to the University of Michigan School of Public Health where she earned her master's degree in public health in epidemiology.

Columbia Swim Team Captains 88-89
Lorelei Koss, Laura Callif, Anna

Anna Columbia Records

Weddings at Highland Avenue and Elsewhere

Brigitte loved to garden in her time away from work. She found it very therapeutic. My primary role was admiring her handy-work and occasionally I was permitted (requested) to pull weeds. I also allowed myself to purchase a few raspberry plants. At first, Brigitte was reluctant to set aside a portion of her garden, but as the years went by, she gradually took credit for *her* wonderful raspberries. Some years the harvest was so bountiful that we could freeze many quarts to enjoy all through the winter (even after her grandchildren would eat their fill each day). My other major job was to inspect Brigitte's hands to see if they were clean enough to return to work. On days that she was on call, Brigitte would wear gloves to protect her hands, but on her days off, she would work without gloves, digging her hands into the dirt with joy. As a result of Brigitte's diligent gardening, our backyard was transformed into a paradise worthy of weddings and many garden and pool parties.

Brigitte's eldest son Hans married Ellen (Herling) in August 1974. Brigitte and I arranged a most wonderful garden wedding in our backyard. Ellen's parents, her four brothers, some cousins, several of their friends, and of course, our family came to the wedding. Some of my students helped and some members of the Rochester Philharmonic Orchestra played the music. (They were living in our neighbor's house for the summer, while the Music Director, David Zinman, and his wife were in Europe.) Another neighbor, New York State Supreme Court Justice Elizabeth Pine, officiated. We had a huge tent filled with beautifully decorated tables for all the guests. A friend of mine, Lusha Wieber,

Hans and Ellen Wedding

was our chef and also supplied many beautiful candleholders with beeswax candles which he made himself. A ten-minute rainstorm just before the ceremony did not disrupt the festivities. It was a most wonderful and happy occasion. Ellen's parents commented often that it was the best wedding they had ever attended.

Hinni and Maria Wedding

In September 1975, Hinrich and Maria (Bell) also got married in our backyard. It was the second marriage for them both. Hinrich had four children: David, Philip, Clark, and Polly; Maria had two children: Adam and Susan. All looked beautiful for the wedding. Maria's two sisters, Catherine and Ruth, came with their families and one of my former students who had acted as a nanny for Hinrich's children. This also was a very lovely occasion and our wish that the marriage would be good has become true. They celebrated their 40th wedding anniversary in 2015. Once again, New York State Supreme Court Justice, Elizabeth Pine, also officiated at this wedding. Following the wedding, everyone enjoyed the nice weather and our pool.

In June 1979, Christian and Katherine (Monroe) got married in Canton at the Monroe family residence. It was a very nice garden wedding followed by a big dinner at a pleasant restaurant. Kathy was the second oldest of seven children. She was working as a nurse in a Rochester Hospital, where Christian met her. The couple went on a wedding trip to Europe while our family spent a week at Cranberry Lake. It was the beginning of July, but regrettably very cold. We spent one day visiting Lake Placid which was preparing to host the winter Olympics in 1980. We looked longingly at all the winter hats, gloves, and scarves which adorned the storefront windows, but all stores were closed for the July 4th holiday. Back at Cranberry

Christian and Kathie Wedding

Lake, we went boating instead of swimming. It was an unforgettable scene when my sister, Emmeli, attempted to get into the boat as it was already drifting from the dock. In slow motion, we watched as her legs spread into a split and the inevitable happened when she ended up in the water! It was so comical. We could not stop laughing. Unfortunately, she had been wearing just about all the warm clothing we had. Warm, especially dry, clothing was not easily available. But dear Hans helped out with his warm socks!

In Back: Carol and Philip
From Left: Stefan, Teresa, Onkel Hans, Lisa, Lisa

David and Kathy
Wedding

Hinrich's eldest sons, Philip and David, each got married in 1984 Philip and Carol (O'Brien) in Toledo, OH, and David and Kathy (Gabel) in La Habra, CA. His other children all married in the nineties. Susan married Don

Polly and Tom's Wedding in Holiday Valley
From Left: Philip, Carol, Kathy, David, Maria, Hinrich, Polly, Tom, Adam, Annette,
Clark, Theresa, Don, Susan

(MacDougall) at Hinrich's beautiful house and garden in Clarence, NY. Adam married Annette (Vertino) at her family home in Amherst, NY. Clark married Theresa (Kantowski) in 1993, and Polly married Tom (Culver) in 1995 at the skiing resort of Holiday Valley, south of Buffalo, NY.

My daughter, Anna, married Bruce (Davidson) in 1994 in their backyard in East Aurora, NY. I will write more about this important event later.

Anna and Bruce Wedding

Matthias and Sara (Worl) got married in June 1999. The wedding also took place in the beautiful garden at Highland Avenue. Anna and I made the wedding cake which tasted fantastic and looked quite professional, considering it was our first attempt to use fondant to cover each layer. As it was hot outside, we had to store the cake in the laundry room which was in the basement and thus cool enough.

Brigitte and I were very proud to host three lovely weddings as well as numerous family gatherings. Our home at 1320 Highland Avenue remained a central family meeting place for over fifty years!

Matthias and Sara Cut Cake

Meeting Friends and Relatives from Lübeck in New Places

Hedda and Maria Corin, 2007

Maria Corin, My Second Cousin

Maria Corin and I led separate lives as children. Maria's father, Karl Blunck, and my father, Carl Martens, were cousins who married best friends, Annemarie Tegtmeyer (Maria's mother) and Lisa Bartelt (my mother). Both families lived in Lübeck. We saw one another occasionally but not very often. Our mothers remained close friends so we heard from and about each other occasionally. Maria and I both immigrated to the US in the early 1950s.

Maria met Claes Corin with whom she enjoyed a happy marriage. When Claes retired, they moved to St. James Plantation in Southport, NC, and built a beautiful, most comfortable house. Our mothers kept corresponding. Maria's mother stayed in Lübeck while my mother had moved to the US. When our mothers died, Maria and I kept in touch with letters, but it was not until 2007 when my sister Brigitte died and I moved to East Aurora that I began fostering our friendship. We both enjoyed speaking with one another on the phone in German sharing stories of our childhood in Lübeck in the same dialect.

Meeting Friends and Relatives from Lübeck in New Places

In 2007, I accompanied my family to visit Bruce's father for Thanksgiving on Fripp Island, SC. Since we went by car, Maria and I made plans to meet on our return trip. She traveled for a good two hours to meet us. I was concerned that this meeting might not turn out well because we didn't really know each other very well. I had a feeling that Maria had similar thoughts, but they proved to be wrong. I knew at once that all would be good between us as soon as I met her. We had a wonderful three days together. Maria showed me around the beautiful plantation, we went to the beach, and explored the lovely town of Southport.

Maria was busy preparing for her big eightieth birthday party in May 2008. With cousins coming from Germany and friends and relatives from far away, it was not too soon for planning. We visited the golf club where the party was to take place and I noticed that Maria was greatly respected and well-liked by the employees there. I was happy when Maria asked me to attend her party.

In January 2008, Maria suffered a most unfortunate accident. She was hospitalized with a severely broken kneecap which had to be surgically repaired. Weeks of rehab followed the painful hospital stay. I was amazed at her determination to continue with the plans for her birthday party. Oodles of little things had to be dealt with as I learned during our daily telephone conversations. There were days when her knee was swollen and painful and Maria seemed worried and apprehensive, but I admired her positive, calm, steadfast attitude.

During the week of the celebration, I was introduced to cousins from my home town that I had heard about but never met. Jochen Sostmann was of particular interest to me since we both were acquainted with two special people in the world of music. Knowing that Jochen had worked as secretary to the internationally known Austrian conductor, Karl Böhm (1894-1982), I asked whether he had heard of David Zinman, an American who was at the time the conductor of the Zürich Radio Orchestra in Switzerland. David Zinman was the conductor of the Rochester Philharmonic Orchestra for ten years before moving on to the Baltimore Orchestra in the 1970s. The Zinmans were our neighbors in Rochester and have remained my good friends. My cousin knew of his work and had nothing but praise for him.

We talked about the opera singer, Claire Watson, who also came from

Rochester, NY. I met Claire in 1955. She was eager to improve her German, especially her diction, hoping to join a German opera company while her husband, a radiologist, was planning to work in Germany for a year. I was glad to have the opportunity to teach a promising musician. Claire flew to New York City once each week for lessons and I saw her twice a week in Rochester. The Watsons traveled to Germany in 1956 and Claire was an immediate success in Munich, Frankfurt, Salzburg, and Vienna where she sang to great acclaim in many operas. After a year, the family returned to Rochester; however, Claire divorced her husband and returned to Europe. It was good to hear from Jochen that Claire had become a star in Europe. She regrettably died at age sixty-two after enjoying a triumphant, if brief, career as a soprano.

I was grateful to meet Maria's three children, get to know her grandchildren (all in their late teens and early twenties then), and her many most pleasant friends. Best of all, it was wonderful to see Maria so happy during the week I spent with her at her beloved Southport.

Annemarie Rieckenbach, a Chance Meeting

One lovely summer day in 1966, Hans Harmsen (Anna's father) and I were having lunch in an outdoor café in Zürich, Switzerland. We noticed that a woman at a neighboring table was looking closely at us. She suddenly came over, saying, "Excuse me, but I think I met you when you were a little girl in Lübeck." She joined us and told the following story: "I became intrigued when I heard you using the vernacular peculiar only to Lübeck but was reasonably sure, when your friend addressed you by your name, Hedda. I am Annemarie Rieckenbach."

She was also from Lübeck and was a good friend of my uncle, Rolf Bartelt. Annemarie had met me and my family when I was about seven years old. She had become a fairly successful reporter and, in 1938, was working on several assignments in Berlin. One report about Goebbels and Hitler got her into serious trouble and, thanks to Uncle Rolf and his connections to Switzerland from his work there in the early thirties, she was whisked out of the country. She "married" a Swiss carpenter, Johannes Rieckenbach, and found a safe haven with Walter Garrett, a well-to-do business man, who hired her as his secretary and Girl Friday.

Frau Rieckenbach took us to meet Mr. Garrett in his beautiful house which he shared with his third wife. Annemarie had her own spacious apartment on the premises. We became good friends. They visited us for Thanksgiving in Rochester, NY, in 1968. My niece, Polly, was born that very day in Buffalo, NY. Mr. Garrett expressed his wish to see the newborn because he had never seen one. We all took off for a surprise visit to the Buffalo maternity ward. Mr. Garrett had divorced his third wife and Annemarie hoped to marry him. This, however, was not to be, since Walter Garrett died soon after their trip to the US.

(The dialect Annemarie recognized is peculiar to Lübeck and just has few speakers, including me, left. We say "stop, spot, and Stefan," instead of High German, "shtop, shpot and Shtefan.")

Hedda Mohr, my Dear Friend

My Onkel Hans' former professor at the University of Munich was Jakob Mohr, a Jew. Both men were imprisoned during the war and both were released since they could prove they were leaving Germany. Extraordinary circumstances would bring these two men together again in New York City when my uncle spotted Jakob Mohr's wife, Hedda Neumann-Mohr, a very tall woman, on Riverside Drive. Hedda had been a childhood friend of both my uncle and my mother. I was named after her.

Her story follows.

Hedda Mohr, 1982

My Friend, Hedda Mohr

I heard about Hedda Neumann as a child. Her niece, Sigrid, was my classmate and friend. Hedda's cousin, Erna Heddinga-Bihler, was my godmother and my mother's classmate and friend. Hedda was five years younger than my mother. She was the daughter of Lübeck's illustrious mayor before WWI and the granddaughter of a wealthy chocolate manufacturer. She had five sisters and one brother, who was Sigrid's father. I did not meet Hedda until 1952 when I arrived in New York City and my uncle introduced me to her and her husband, Dr. Jakob Mohr. She came to visit in Mt. Morris frequently and, after my uncle's retirement, she often visited us in Rochester. In turn, we accepted her many invitations to come to New York City. When my daughter, Anna, became a student at Columbia University, I began to see Hedda often and found in her a most generous friend and benefactor.

The only one of her siblings not to attend the university, Hedda studied physical therapy at a well-known school in Sweden and then joined one of her sisters who was a student in Munich, as was my uncle at the time. Soon Hedda was hired as a physical therapist at the University Hospital, where she eventually met her future husband. He was, however, married and had a son, two-year-old, Hermann. After some time, he got a divorce and his wife left for the US. Against the wishes of her family, Hedda got married in 1935. At that time, it was already "undesirable" to marry a Jew. (Since 1933, Jews had been encouraged to leave Germany and many professors, lawyers, and journalists had lost their positions.) No member of her family attended her wedding. Hedda's husband lost his position at the hospital and was sent to the concentration camp in Dachau. Hedda was given the option to divorce him so that she would be "free of shame." She declined. Ostracized by her family, she stayed on in Munich, fighting for her husband's release. This was finally granted in 1938, provided they leave Germany immediately. Only one of her sisters came from Hamburg to say goodbye. They met in a park in Munich where they sat like strangers on a park bench.

Friends drove them to Bremerhaven, where the couple boarded a boat that would take them and many other "undesirables" to America. The ship stopped in Liverpool to leave some passengers and take on some others before heading out to the Atlantic Ocean. However, to the horror of the passengers, the ship headed back to Germany. The captain did not heed their pleas but followed orders. Upon arrival in Hamburg, SS men came on board and began hauling off many men, including Hedda's husband. Fortunately, Hedda had silver and money to bribe some corrupt SS men and her husband was allowed to stay aboard. Many others were less fortunate and the ship left the harbor with tearful, desperate people.

Arriving in New York, the passengers were denied permission to disembark and the ship sailed south. Hedda told me, "We could see the people on the beaches in Florida, but we were not permitted entry." Cuba was now the destination, where primitive accommodations awaited them in a camp. Hedda and her husband stayed there for almost a year, until Jakob's brother, who had been in New York since 1929, succeeded in obtaining visas for them. Once in New York, Dr. Mohr set up his medical practice on Riverside Drive and Hedda worked as a masseuse for well-to-do Jewish clients. (Among them the German actress, Grete Mosheim, who had been prominent in the Berlin theater until she was forced to leave because she was "half-Jew.")

The six years of war were most difficult for Hedda. She heard about the bombing of Lübeck but had no news from any member of her family. Her husband did not permit her to contact any of them after the war. He was unforgiving. Hedda secretly spent some of her own money to send care packages to some of her sisters, despite the fact that they had abandoned her during her time of need. She also began to correspond with her family. She learned that her mother had died, leaving all her personal belongings to her, but not a kind word. She also learned that her brother, Hans-Martin, a judge in Lübeck, had committed suicide in his chambers in order to avoid the imminent arrest by the De-Nazification committee. He had been suspected of cruel treatment of Norwegians while serving as an officer with the occupation army.

After some years, her husband relented and Hedda was allowed to visit her family in Germany. She rented a room in a villa in Sierksdorf, a seaside resort near Travemünde, located on the Baltic Sea. Her sisters visited with their families, including her sister, Gudrun, who was married to a former Nazi who had been sentenced to six years in prison by the Allies.

After her husband died, Hedda learned that he had been a very wealthy man and she inherited a considerable amount of money. She moved from her rather modest apartment on Riverside Drive to a beautiful apartment near Lincoln Center where I was her frequent guest. I got to know her friends and her stepson, Hermann, who was not very nice to her. I began to help her with her mail as her eyesight began to fade. Letters from her nieces in Germany asked for monetary help; they all knew that she had money. One letter came from Sigrid, my former friend and classmate. "I have lost my ring in a restroom. I know that you have the same one, since it is a family heirloom. Could I have yours?" Hedda asked me whether I was interested in having the ring. Since I was not, she got it from her jewelry box and flushed it down the toilet. Another asked for an advance on her certain inheritance, and one told her that she needed to recover from cancer treatment in the South of France and needed money for that as well as for a new vacuum cleaner. Hedda instructed me to write, "Do you feel the need to vacuum Heaven before you get there?" She did have a great sense of humor. I need to mention that Hedda always bought me the best tickets for the Metropolitan Opera. She herself was not musically inclined.

Hedda Mohr visited us often in Rochester. She spent many holidays with us and also travelled with us on a wonderful trip to Haiti in 1976. Each summer, she would come and enjoy our company and pool and get away from NYC. I loved these visits. We would spend hours and hours talking and playing Scrabble. These games would become incredibly competitive when my sister Emmeli was also visiting. To distinguish between the two Heddas, I was called Hedda Ma and she was called Hedda Mo. We shared many great times, especially when my daughter began college at Columbia University in NYC.

Anna would visit Hedda maybe once or twice a month in her wonderful apartment. One day, Anna called me afterwards to say she had just been taught how to tie her shoes by an eighty-year-old woman. Amazingly, Hedda Mohr's way of tying shoes prevented the shoelaces from coming undone without tying a knot. Anna would later pass this secret on to her husband and her children and particularly her children's preschool teachers, who were extremely appreciative and still remember her for the shoelace trick over fifteen years later.

My dear friend died just before Anna graduated from Columbia in 1989. She loved my daughter like her own. I am happy to say that I have some of her furniture and beloved trinkets in my home.

An Unforgettable Visit to New York

On May 27, 1975, I flew to New York to celebrate Hedda Mohr's sixty-sixth birthday with her. I brought a large bouquet of freshly picked white and purple lilacs from our garden and a cheesecake I had baked the day before. In those days, one could arrive at the airport just in time for boarding and have flowers on your arm as well as a cake still safely in its baking form. I splurged and took a taxi from LaGuardia to Manhattan for the sake of the flowers that were beginning to look a little sad. They recovered quickly, however, once they were in water, and Hedda's apartment was soon filled with their wonderful scent. I was in time to set the table for three and wondered who the other guest might be. I decorated the cake with fresh strawberries and was happy to have brought a most delicious-looking masterpiece.

She arrived at 3:30 sharp, a petite lady, no more than five-feet tall. Carefully applied makeup accented her large blue eyes, a prominent feature on her small face. Plastic surgery had removed all wrinkles; however, her neck and hands told the truth. I figured that she was about seventy years old. She was introduced to me as Grete Mosheim from Berlin. A champagne toast in honor of the birthday girl helped to get our conversation animated and enjoyable. Frau Mosheim was familiar with my background, family, and relationship with Hedda. She seemed genuinely interested in my daughter, wanting to see photographs of my special eight-year old, which endeared me to her at once. I was immediately angry with myself when I asked Frau Mosheim the rather dumb-sounding question, "And what brings you to America?" Too many people had posed that very question to me and never cared to listen to my answer. (I experience the same feeling when someone greets me with, "Hi, how are you?" and when I respond, the person is no longer within earshot.)

Grete put her fork down and began to talk. She forgave me for not knowing who she was. I learned that she and the famous German actress and singer, Marlene Dietrich, had become lifelong friends after they met as students of the Max Reinhardt School of Drama in 1922, especially after they discovered that both of them had had affairs with the director. Grete had become an instant superstar when she replaced the leading actress in the American play, *The Speaking Ape*. After that, she was pre-eminent in the Berlin theater scene. Tragically, her acting career came to an abrupt end in 1933. As a "half Jew" (I cringe using that ghastly terminology), she was no longer allowed to perform. Another actor, Oscar Homolka, who had left

Germany a little earlier, "married" her so that she could leave Germany for England. They divorced soon after.

Hedda, Hedda Mohr, Grete Mosheim

It was difficult for Grete to get acting roles, due to her language difficulties. In 1935, she met the American millionaire Howard Gould, also referred to as the "railroad king." They got married in 1936 but she had to promise to give up her acting ambitions. Instead, she lived a life of unbelievable wealth and luxury. Her intense desire to act again brought about the divorce in 1947. The settlement left her a very well-to-do lady. She co-founded the German-speaking ensemble, "The Players from Abroad," and began to appear again on the German stage, playing leading roles in plays by American dramatists.

My cheesecake remained uneaten on our plates. It was such a joy to listen to Grete's wonderful voice and impeccable diction. However, Hedda Mohr, familiar with the story, enjoyed the cake and commented that it was "wunderbar."

I was curious how these two women had met. Hedda was determined to use her skills as a masseuse and her husband, a physician in Manhattan, recommended her to his patients. One of them was Grete Mosheim and a strong friendship developed. After Jakob's death, Hedda found out that she too was a woman of means and was able to keep up with her friend's lifestyle. Both of them frequented the theaters and Hedda began to know a world she had not known before. She also began to make yearly trips to visit her sisters in Germany, getting to know her nieces and nephews.

Hours later, we were still sipping coffee (and champagne!). Grete

Mosheim asked me if I would be interested in helping her prepare for a role she would be performing in Germany. It was *The Gin Game* by Coburn, a play that made Hume Cronyn and Jessica Tandy famous. I was to read the male part (Weller Martin) while she memorized the role of his partner (Fonzia Dorsey). I was free for the summer and agreed to come for a few days. Needless to say, all my expenses were paid. I, the teacher, had become a prompter. Grete Mosheim was amazing! She enjoyed great success in Hamburg, Berlin, Düsseldorf, and Köln. Several years later, she performed in *On Golden Pond* in Germany. However, the play was not successful. Germans could not relate to a well-to-do academic wanting to spend his summer in a broken-down cottage in the middle of nowhere.

When Grete Mosheim left the birthday party many hours later, my cheesecake remained half eaten on her plate. I did not mind, since I felt privileged to listen to her fascinating stories. What an amazing woman.

An Unexpected Phone Call

I received a strange phone call in February 2012 regarding my dear friend Hedda Neumann-Mohr and her husband, Dr. Jakob Mohr. It was an unlisted number and I hesitated to answer. I am glad I did.

"Hi, this is Linda Mohr. Are you Hedda's niece?" It took me a while to understand that the caller was referring to Hedda Neumann-Mohr, my very good friend. "So, if you are not 'Little Hedda,' the niece from Hamburg, you must be the Hedda from Lübeck."

Linda explained that she was Hermann's daughter and Dr. Mohr's granddaughter. I remembered meeting her in Hedda's apartment when she was in her early twenties and about to get married. Linda had come with her mother. It was obvious that there was no love lost between them and my friend Hedda. Knowing that Hedda had become an extremely well-to-do widow, they came to discuss the wedding gift and suggested that $100,000 would be appropriate. Hedda did not agree; she was positively insulted.

Linda continued, "I have a second cousin in Israel. I didn't even know he existed. His name is Daniel Selig and he is anxious to hear about your stories about Nazi Germany. His mother is writing her memoirs and he wonders whether you might be able to tell them some of your stories. Could I give them your phone number?"

Linda had found my name among old papers that indicated that I had inherited some of Hedda Mohr's furniture. She located me with the help of Google. My head was spinning, to say the least. I thought of my friend and the difficult life she had led. I remembered her telling me that her husband had not been a practicing Jew; however, his son and daughter-in-law overruled Hedda's wishes and Jakob was buried in the Jewish cemetery in New York. At that time, Hermann's wife, Linda's mother, informed Hedda that she could not be buried there since she was not a Jew.

The next morning Daniel Selig called from Jerusalem. During our two-hour conversation, we switched back and forth between English and German. I learned that Dr. Jakob Mohr also had a sister, Liesel, who had left Munich and gone to Switzerland, where their mother lived. Liesel Selig was Daniel Selig's grandmother. I had met Jakob's brother, Max, who had left Germany in 1926 and now lived in NYC.

I told Daniel all I knew and remembered about Jakob and Hedda's heartbreaking travel to America, including their nearly one-year detention in Cuba, before Max was able to bring them to NYC.

Daniel promised me a copy of his mother's memoir. He told me that the story about Jakob and Hedda's departure from Germany had been the only missing link in the memoir and had been referred to as a "mysterious miracle."

The book, *Zarte Seele in Harten Zeiten, (Delicate Souls in Hard Times)*, written in German by Ella Selig, was published in 2013 and I am referenced as providing information. We live in a very small world.

The Fur Coat, 1986

During one of my frequent visits to Hedda Mohr's New York apartment, she announced that a furrier was coming soon and I must help her select a coat. The salesman came with a selection of three fur coats, all in the price range of $10,000 to $15,000. My friend opted for a beautiful coat, paid $13,000, and requested that Hedda M. be stitched into the lining. The transaction took no longer than one hour. What had prompted this strange purchase?

Grete Mosheim had called and reported that her two nieces would be visiting from southern California and, since they needed warm coats, she had ordered furs for them to wear to the theater. Not to be outdone, Hedda did the same for herself. On my next visit I learned that the nieces were rather unpleasant, the play was excellent, but Hedda's coat was too heavy and bothersome and she had put it in storage. "It has your initials stitched inside. You will inherit it," she said.

Hedda Mohr died in the winter of 1989. Her wish to see Anna graduate from Columbia did not come true. She was eighty years old. I took the coat with me to Rochester. It was a bit too long—almost floor length—but my mirror told me that I looked rich and stunning. I wore it on my next trip to Germany. It was a burden on the plane, definitely not made for tourist class. My friends, sisters Erika Hinrichsen and Inge Scholvien, came to the airport to greet me.

"Are you crazy?!" they blurted out as I walked millionairess-style toward them. "You have to take that coat off at once or it might be painted green!" They turned the coat inside out and we went as fast as we could to Inge's car. Erika lent me one of her cloth coats that would not incite the Green Party that was against cruelty to animals. Party members vented their anger by throwing paint on people who dared to wear fur coats. The French actress and animal activist, Brigitte Bardot, was behind this craze.

My flight home was uneventful. There were no green-paint-crazy people on the plane. But, once again, I found the coat too heavy and too big for tourist class. We had a fancy cedar closet in the basement at home and I thought that would be the best storage place. Furs were also shunned here at home.

When I went to the closet in the fall to put my summer things there, I noticed bare spots on the fur. "Oh, my!" Frantic, I grabbed the coat and hoped to enlist the aid of Rochester's most prominent furrier. The shop owner took one look at my sad-looking coat and shouted, "You must get out of our store at once!" while the saleslady opened the door. Once outside, I told them that I had stored the coat in our cedar closet. I learned that furs should never be stored in cedar chests as the cedar oil can greatly damage them.

Once home, I put the coat into a huge black plastic bag and threw it into our garbage can outside. Now I ask: Did you ever do something like that? I doubt it!

Rochester: My Second Hometown

Rochester, NY, was my home from 1953 to 2008. During that time, my sister and I managed to launch our careers in teaching and medicine and raise her three sons and my daughter, Anna. While teaching, I would often use the old legend about Till Eulenspiegel, known as the Pied Piper of Hamelin in English-speaking countries. Eule means "owl" and Spiegel means "mirror." His name could be interpreted as "seeing a wise guy when looking into the mirror." He is said to have lived in the fifteenth century and his grave is in a small town in North Germany. He was a prankster and amused people with his stunts. Once, Eulenspiegel promised the people in the town of Hamelin to help them get rid of all rats. However, when the townspeople refused to give him his rightful pay or reward, he punished them severely. The legend goes that he played on his pipe, lured all the children from the little town, and vanished with them.

I remember how excited we were when it was announced that Midtown Plaza, an indoor shopping mall, was set to open in April 1962. While we didn't have much if any disposable income at the time, it was fun to visit once in a while to see the grandeur. One of the highlights for children and adults was the "Clock of Nations," depicting twelve different countries. Much to our amazement, Japan and Germany were among them. It had not been that long ago that those two countries were despised enemies. The artist who designed the clock selected Till Eulenspiegel to represent Germany.

Clock of Nations

In the early sixties, Rochester enjoyed great fame and wealth thanks to thriving companies such as Eastman Kodak, Bausch & Lomb, Xerox, Sibley's, Forman's, and others. The city was healthy and wealthy. There were excellent high schools within the city, beautifully adorned movie theaters and, of course, the Eastman School of Music, and the Eastman Theater, home of the Rochester Philharmonic. The city was a safe place in which to live and the citizens were proud. According to Greek mythology, one of the evil qualities that escaped from Pandora's Box was pride, which is often defined as conceit or having excessive admiration for oneself. However, I have never understood why it is supposedly not a good thing to take pride in something. We should take pride in our country, the city or village where we reside, our homes, and our generation. When relatives and friends came to visit from Germany, I took great pride in showing visitors around my new home in America.

We enjoyed the city center in Rochester for many years. Midtown Plaza remained a destination for clothing, furniture, groceries, and many other needs and desires. Anna even had a school field trip to the plaza to see a special display of Washington, D.C. in miniature buildings. The plaza was host to many interesting displays. Unfortunately, in the early eighties, the excitement of the mall and the city center waned as bigger shopping malls opened outside of the city. However, the lilac festival continued to delight us every year. The park, open to the public, was just a mile down the street from our house. We learned when we bought our house that all the land on our side of the street had been owned by one family who planted lilacs everywhere. We certainly benefitted as we had many beautiful lilacs on our property giving off a wonderful fragrance each May.

Erika and Carl Enjoy the Lilacs of Rochester

In German, the word for "city/citadel" is burg, meaning a fortress.

Fortunate residents are called Burger (the Bourgeoisie or the middle class), who are protected by the Burgermeister. The word burg came to mean town in English (we have the boroughs and the syllable "bury" attached to many cities). As the middle class became more prosperous, their members wanted larger homes and gardens and they moved to the outskirts of the city that we now know as suburbs. Their once-great houses in the city were neglected and city officials allowed slumlords to reign. The better stores moved to sprawling plazas in the suburbs; a hideous jail was built, dwarfing the beautiful Rochester City Hall; and cheap housing was erected along the lovely Genesee River. Eventually, for a variety of reasons, everyone lost interest in downtown except as a place to work. After 5:00 p.m., the streets became deserted. Movie theaters and stores moved to the suburbs and Midtown Plaza became a deserted place. Sibley's and all the other stores closed. Other than an occasional concert or hockey game, no one went into the city after the workday. Even the Genesee Hospital, which had recently been refurbished by adding an ultra-modern birthing unit, was razed. I wonder what the mayors and councilmen were thinking when they permitted such waste.

The term inner city no longer meant "you are protected." It denoted poverty and safety was no longer guaranteed.

Where is the Clock of the Nations now? The clock has a permanent home at the airport where it continues to greet passengers arriving in Rochester and bring smiles to all who remember it from the thirty years it spent in downtown Rochester.

View of Downtown Rochester from Cobb's Hill

In recent years there has been renewed interest in downtown Rochester. A new baseball stadium was built, many old office buildings have been converted to luxury apartments, and a campus of Monroe Community College recently opened in a building purchased from Kodak. Eastman Theater has been renovated, a new convention center was built, and Midtown Plaza was torn down to make way for a Hilton hotel. The Strong Museum of Play, located downtown, is a great attraction for families. The eastern part of the Inner Loop, a seldom used expressway, has been filled in, reconnecting the neighborhood to downtown. The High Falls Historic district, buildings of original Rochester, has become a hub of offices. I am happy that my second hometown is once again becoming a place to be proud of.

A great view that always symbolized our house is one from Cobb's Hill looking towards the radio and television towers on Pinnacle Hill. As our house on Highland Avenue was essentially at the base of Pinnacle Hill, the towers served as a wonderful landmark pointing to the direction of our house. When Brigitte's eldest grandchild Stefan began to talk, he named the towers Begga's Towers. We have used the name in our family ever since.

Pinnacle Hill from Cobb's Hill
"Begga's Towers"

Rochester Neighbors

How fortunate we are that we can remember. Certain olfactory sensations, melodies, voices, events take us back to times gone by. Who would we be without the people we have met, the relationships we have enjoyed, the places we have lived and visited, the troubles we have overcome, the activities and joys we have experienced? The list, it seems, is never ending. Let me introduce you to some of my Rochester neighbors.

At my first home, 934 Meig Street, we met a few neighbors. On one side were Mr. and Mrs. Crombach, an elderly couple who occupied the house on the corner of Crawford Street. Mr. and Mrs. Schenk's backyard bordered ours and they were pleasant, kind, helpful people. But, after eight wonderful years at 934, Harry Staudemayer became the reason for our intense desire to move. Harry never did or said anything nasty to us. It was his loud and brutal behavior toward his family that became unbearable. He ruled his wife and six children (all under the age of ten) like the former Marine he was. On Sunday mornings we heard him shouting, "Get in the car, hurry up, or I'll wring your blasted necks!" He was not planning a family outing. As a devout Catholic, he was herding the family to church. Equally revolting was the "evening report." The four oldest children had to line up outside (rain or shine) and Peggy, their mother, had to report any misdeeds. Verbal and physical punishment was doled out right away. There was only peace when Harry, an engineer, was sent to Kuwait for several weeks. I met Harry's father during one of those absences and couldn't believe that such a pleasant man could have such a miserable son.

The bank determined that my sister and I were a good risk, so they lent us the money we needed to purchase 1320 Highland Avenue in 1965. We lived there together for over fifty years raising our children. My sister, Brigitte, in particular, was happy that we had an empty lot owned by Hillside Children's Center on one side of our property and we chose to build our pool next to that empty lot for maximum privacy. We were not thrilled with the tall metal fence that separated the properties, but were told it was necessary to keep the children safe. Much to my surprise, the center was still under the direction of Miss Adelaide Kayser. She was a most uncaring and, in my opinion, least suitable director when I worked there as an assistant housemother in 1952, shortly after my arrival in the US.

The large, empty lot was covered with lawn and many rather pretty wildflowers. (We gave the empty field the nickname Adelaide.) One day, Adelaide, the person, informed us that the children would be preparing a vegetable garden at the bottom of the hill. Indeed, a group of children got busy with shovels, manure, topsoil, and seeds, under the supervision of a non-participating adult. Unfortunately, they neglected to water the garden and the plants all died. Their next project was to bring in swings, rings, tires, and other equipment to build an obstacle course. The children came down once or twice, again under the "guidance" of a non-participating "teacher." It was Miss Kayser's last failed attempt to do "something wonderful for the dear children," as she told us.

Once Adelaide retired, politicians got involved and proposed a plan to build a school on the property. Congresswoman Louise Slaughter came several times to stress the need for the special school. We finally agreed to the project, provided the school be 180 yards from our house, halfway up the hill. A parking lot would be constructed for emergency vehicles and three cars with access to Highland Avenue. The unsightly metal fence, reminiscent of a prison, was replaced by an attractive, eight-foot-tall wooden fence. All projects turned out well and we were on very good terms with the "new" neighbors.

On the other side of our house was 1340 Highland Avenue. Our large picture window in the kitchen faced the driveway and back entrance to our neighbor's house and provided us with a good view of the happenings occurring there. Three wonderful, interesting, and somewhat eclectic families lived in that house during those fifty years.

Dr. John (Jack) Hamilton, a busy obstetrician, and his wife, Harriet, were our first neighbors at 1340. Their children, Kitty, Jane, and Andy, were about the same age as my sister's three boys and they befriended each other quickly.

Whether working in her garden, cleaning their swimming pool, or carting in groceries, Harriet was constantly on the go and never had much time for a neighborly chat. One day however, she told me that she had just bought a lot of live rats to store in the basement. I thought she was joking, but she wasn't. The rats were fresh meals for the huge Boa constrictor that lived in their upstairs guest room. "Boa" loved to eat live rats and we were welcome to come watch the feeding. None of us ever did.

Jack's partner, Dr. Webster, had delivered Anna in 1967. However, it was Jack Hamilton who visited me in the hospital and then at home. It was good to get to know him. Harriet, on the other hand, informed me (speaking from the other side of the hedge) that her daughters would not be babysitters. It was strange that little Anna befriended "Harry." She baked cookies for Anna and my little girl loved their visits. One day, when Anna was angry with me about something, she tied a little sack holding one pair of underwear, a toothbrush, and a shirt to the end of a pole and proudly declared she was running away. She marched over to the Hamilton's house, baked cookies with Harriet, and returned home happy.

Jack Hamilton and Anna's father, Hans Harmsen, enjoyed each other's company and got deeply involved in discussing various ways of preventing unwanted pregnancies. They agreed that promoting the pill and other prophylactic methods could help women from seeking unsafe and unlawful abortions.

In 1974, Harriet inherited a lot of land in the southern tier and the Hamiltons moved and became tree farmers, selling many for telephone poles and expanding to be a showcase for other tree farmers in the state. We kept in touch until Harriet's death in 1997.

Hedda with Harriet Hamilton

In 1974, 1340 Highland Avenue was sold to the University of Rochester and soon new owners appeared. We were curious and watched from our kitchen window which offered a direct view of the neighbor's driveway and house entrance. The realtor decided that his clients should meet their neighbors so we went out to greet Mary and David Zinman as we saw them approaching. Maestro David Zinman had just been appointed the new conductor of the Rochester Philharmonic Orchestra. The meeting was brief since David was headed out to LA to conduct the Los Angeles Philharmonic and Mary was flying back to Amsterdam in the Netherlands to finish her engagement as a violist with the Netherlands Chamber Orchestra. We thought the whole situation was most peculiar. Little did we know how wonderful it would be to live next to professional musicians.

The first two years were fairly uneventful. David and Mary were often gone for periods of time when he was a guest conductor and Mary played viola in Amsterdam. In July 1976, they had a son, Raphael, who was born in Amsterdam. We were excited to meet the new baby when they returned in August. Around this time we received a desperate call for help from David. His two children, Paul (age thirteen) and Rachel (age ten), had been living with their mother in New Jersey since their parents' divorce. Their mother had suffered a severe stroke and the children would be moving in with him. David was still in Los Angeles and couldn't return right away and Mary was still in Amsterdam. "Could you please take them for a day or two?" The distraught children stayed with us until Mary and David could return to Rochester. The children were devastated, but it was much more difficult for Paul. He kept to himself during the three days they were with us. Rachel warmed up to Anna and the girls played together. I was glad that Rachel let me hold and hug her since, outside of food, there was not much else I could give. Rachel and Paul's mother died following complications arising from surgery to remove a brain tumor in April 1977.

Mary, Rachel, Paul, David Zinman, 1977

Once David and Mary arrived, their house came alive. We were often called upon to babysit Raphael which we happily did. Anna and Rachel often took turns doting on Raphael. Years later, David's father, Sam, needed care following a stroke and an addition was built so that he could move into the house. David's sister, Judy, an aspiring artist, also moved in for a period of time.

When David was not conducting in Rochester, baby Raphael toured the world with them wherever he was guest conducting. My sister, Brigitte, joined them when they went to Hong Kong and Sydney, Australia. Rachel was at our house often. She had blossomed into a very beautiful girl and became an accomplished dancer. Anna and Rachel had totally different interests but they loved spending time together. One summer Rachel choreographed a dance and we all gathered in our backyard for the show. Anna played the athletic prince who did all the lifting, while Rachel played the charming princess. Mary still played viola with the Rochester Philharmonic and there were Thursday and Saturday concerts. We watched Raphael on Thursdays. Brigitte often preferred to stay home with Raphael so Anna and I could enjoy the Saturday concerts. Of course, we had the best seats in the house.

Anna and Rachel Perform a Dance

Actually though, the best seats in the house were right next door at 1340 when Mary called me and my Onkel Hans over to listen to their music-making. Sometimes as many as ten musicians, visiting friends, the week's soloist, or members of the orchestra were there. We were also the beneficiaries of wonderful rehearsals with soloists including Itzak Perlman, Yo-yo Ma, Jesse Norman, and others who often stayed at the Zinman house. I truly enjoyed being a spectator for these impromptu music concerts. It was wonderful.

One funny episode occurred in late fall sometime in the late 1970s. There was a tall hedge that separated our two driveways. My oldest nephew, Hans, was working for a tree and landscaping company and told his mother, that the hedge needed to be pruned to keep it healthy. The Zinmans were away, Brigitte was at work, and Hans started pruning. When my sister returned home, she was beside herself! The bushy green hedges that had been over ten feet tall when she left, were now two to three feet tall bare sticks. We were horrified that the Zinmans would be upset with us since, technically, the hedges were on their property. I remember how nervous we were when they returned home. We immediately went over to apologize about the hedges being trimmed so short. They laughed and said, "What hedges?" Landscaping was clearly not their forté and they were happy to enlist Hans as their private landscaper for many years. They gave him free reign to do whatever he thought best.

The Hedge Cut by Hans

The Zinmans stayed in Rochester until 1985 when David became the Music Director for the Baltimore Symphony. One wonderful tradition that David, Mary, and their children started back in 1976 was to come over to our house every Christmas Eve and play and sing Christmas carols for us and our whole family. Even after they moved away, the Zinmans always called and played and sang for us over the phone, no matter where in the world they were. While we no longer get the Christmas Eve phone call, I have kept in contact with Mary and David over the years and we still enjoy talking about some of the fun times we had on Highland Avenue. We are lifelong friends.

Mary, David, Raphael Zinman Return for a Visit, 1990

The Pine family lived next to the Zinmans. They had three daughters about the same age as Anna. It was nice that she was able to walk over to visit and play fairly often. Part of their backyard was level, not hilly like the rest of the neighborhood. So the Pine's yard was often the place for games of kickball, softball, and soccer for the neighborhood children. Their mother,

Elizabeth Pine, became a New York State Supreme Court Judge. She presided over the second marriage of my brother and also that of my nephew Hans.

Terry Platt and Dianne Edgar moved into 1340 Highland in 1985. Terry was a professor of Biochemistry at the University of Rochester, and Dianne had recently graduated from medical school and was applying for residency programs. Dianne started in the Surgery residency program but soon switched to Obstetrics and Gynecology. As we all know, babies rarely arrive between 8:00 a.m. and 5:00 p.m., so her schedule was quite unpredictable. Their son, Dana, was born in November 1986 as Dianne was beginning her grueling four years of training, and their daughter, Tammela, was born in June 1988. Various babysitter arrangements, on occasion including us, and the fact that Terry did have regular hours, helped them manage these often trying years.

Dana, Tammela, Dianne, and Terry Platt, 2006

We became and still are good friends. Dianne started her private practice and took her specialty boards. We enjoyed having children next door again and watching them grow. Both children were athletic and musical; Dana played the trumpet (his trumpet eventually became my grandson Carl's) and Tammela took up the clarinet. We liked listening to her practice through the open window in the summertime. Both children are grown and happy and

Dianne and Terry are now my nephew, Christian's, neighbor since he now lives at 1320.

Brigitte and I were very lucky to have had such wonderful neighbors over the years.

Platt Family Visits Hedda in East Aurora Home, 2007
Dianne, Tammela, Erika, Hedda, Dana, Terry

Stolen Jewelry

We were planning a festive dinner on Mother's Day in 1982. I had baked my mother's favorite—an apple cake that would be served with lots of whipped cream. Anna, my then fifteen-year-old daughter, was interested in gourmet cooking and had prepared delicious salads and appetizers. My sister Brigitte was setting the dining room table with candles, our best china, and little bouquets. The main meal, artichoke chicken, just needed heating since it had been prepared the day before. The kitchen was cleaned up and we were ready to receive the family by noon. We were also going to celebrate the birth of Teresa, my sister's third grandchild. Then came the phone call.

No, there had not been an accident. Nobody was hospitalized. The caller was my mother and she was distressed and very upset. It had been her custom to dress up for special occasions and put on her precious jewelry, consisting of a brooch (an heirloom from her mother), a golden bracelet her father had given to her on her wedding day in 1922, and my father's wedding ring which had the diamond from my father's tie clip attached to it. These three items were my mother's most beloved possessions. As she opened her jewelry box on the top of her dresser, her prized possessions were gone. We rushed over to her house and turned the jewelry box inside out, to no avail.

Who had been in her bedroom? Two days earlier, a window cleaner had been at the house. The owner had washed the outside on a ladder, while a teenager polished the windows from the inside. My mother had taken a liking to the young man and fixed him chocolate milk and a sandwich. We called the window cleaner. He got hold of his helper and both came to the house. We also called the police. The officer put the boy into his police car and informed us that he was a suspect in several thefts from stores and homes. He was sixteen and no longer in school. The officer listened to our stories, checked the box, and then went out to speak with the suspect. Upon his return, the officer told us that the boy had confessed after he had been told that his fingerprints were on the box. Unfortunately, he had taken the three pieces of jewelry to a place downtown and sold them. The officer explained that stolen property usually goes in the front door of such a store and soon disappears out the back to be resold by a fence, a person who knowingly buys stolen goods and later resells them for profit

Our party did take place. We were, however, not successful in calming our grief-stricken mother. Sweet little baby Teresa helped a bit. My mother had cherished those pieces of jewelry. She had rescued them from our burning house during the bombing in 1942 and then taken them to her new home in the United States. They were irreplaceable gifts from her mother, father, and husband. We tried hard to find replacements. My sister Emmeli searched in many antique stores. All our efforts were to no avail. I did find a goldsmith who managed to duplicate the bracelet with the help of several photographs. My mother was glad when she found it in her jewelry box.

The young culprit was sentenced to make weekly payments of $40, as well as twelve months of probation. Since his surname began with the last letter of the alphabet, I had to sit through a variety of defendants in Brighton Town Court: petty thieves, speeders, DWIs, and prostitutes (always with their respective attorneys). I had no idea that so many offenders resided in our neighborhood.

The payments to my mother stopped after just three weeks. The total restitution was to have been $5,000, which represented the value of the jewelry, plus a sum for causing extreme emotional distress to my eighty-year-old mother. The court could not help me any further since the boy had nothing and was allegedly unemployed. I decided to put the matter behind me.

Three months later, I was notified by the court that my mother's case would be settled. The boy was on crutches and had his right arm in a cast. He was sideswiped while riding on a stolen motorcycle, causing him rather severe injuries. His lawyer stressed the fact that his right arm had required many surgical procedures and that he would likely have permanent disabilities. The boy appeared thin and pale and was obviously in pain. I was admonished when I blurted out, "There goes your window-washing career." Should I have felt sorry for him? I did and, then again, I didn't.

The accident awarded the boy quite a bit of money. The result was that I was given $4,880 for my mother. Lawyers had done their job. I had a bad taste in my mouth.

Anna Meets Bruce Davidson

Anna attended Columbia University in New York City. I was thrilled with her decision as I had a built-in place to stay when I visited, namely with my friend Hedda Mohr. As is the case for most if not all parents, dropping Anna off at the start of the first semester was extremely difficult for me. Shortly after she began her college career, my uncle suffered a stroke and we had to move him to our house. Unfortunately, visiting Anna became more difficult as I had become the primary caregiver for my uncle and my mother. Anna was part of the swim team at Columbia and I did manage to attend a few meets each year. A special memory was spending each of the four Thanksgivings with her in NYC. We watched the Macy's Thanksgiving Parade and then found a restaurant to have a special dinner. Anna had to stay in NYC for Thanksgiving since her team had practice on Thursday, Friday, and then on Saturday they always had a conference swim meet. It was a nice time for us. We often visited Rockefeller Center to see the beautiful enormous Christmas tree.

Anna's cousin Hans and his wife Ellen drove Anna to Ann Arbor, MI, in the fall of 1989, where she planned on pursuing a master's degree in Public Health at the University of Michigan. She found a room in a nice house that she shared with three bachelors who were all older than she was. I was somewhat relieved to know that my nephews, David and Philip, were both living in Ann Arbor, and within walking distance of Anna's new accommodations. Philip had met the owners, Stuart Isaac and Bruce Davidson, and had given his approval. Little did I suspect then that Bruce would eventually become my son-in-law.

I think it was sometime in October 1989 that Anna had an accident with her bicycle. She called Bruce for help. He comforted her. When she called me that evening, her voice seemed an octave higher when she spoke about Bruce.

Since Hans and Ellen had met Bruce and Stuart when they took Anna to Ann Arbor, I pumped Ellen for information. Her immediate response was, "I hope it's the 'cute' one." A few weeks later, I asked my nephews David and Philip. "He's okay, a good guy, and I think they are an item." That was the first time I heard that phrase. Anna had told me that he was working in some kind of research, loved to ski (which he did in Utah), was an avid rock climber, and had scaled the Half Dome. I had no idea what

Bruce and Anna: Half Dome in the Background

that meant and where that rock was, but Anna assured me it was an enormous accomplishment. Bruce also enjoyed kayaking. All these sports meant danger and daring to me and I worried that my daughter would join him in these activities (which of course she did!).

Anna secured a research job in Ann Arbor for the summer of 1990. She had one week off and I made plans to visit so we could sightsee around the state. Of course, I was particularly interested in meeting her friend, Bruce. Before I could book a flight to Detroit, I had to make sure that my mother would be taken care of. Her health had declined dramatically due to Alzheimer's disease. We had a lovely home-healthcare aide who tended to my mother five days a week from 7:00 a.m. to 3:00 p.m. which left the weekends, evenings, and nights. The latter shift had been my obligation for some time. My sister Emmeli took leave from her family practice in Downs, IL, to take over for me. My sister Brigitte continued her office hours and took care of the household.

Anna picked me up at the airport with her first new car, a Toyota Tercel. When we arrived at Huron Street, I met Stuart and his lovely girlfriend, MoJo, who welcomed me. Where was Bruce, I wondered? Then he came, trying to rush by us. I heard him mutter, "I did not intend for you to see me like this." I think he was returning from rock climbing. But he soon joined us, freshly showered and very handsome, with an endearing smile. After some small talk with their friends, Bruce announced that it was time to go out for dinner. He was wearing a T-shirt and shorts, which surprised me somewhat. We got into his car and he started the engine and began backing out of the driveway when Anna shouted, "Bruce, my mom's leg is still hanging outside!" He is nervous, I thought to myself, and decided not to hold it against him. I do not remember whether the first restaurant that Bruce had selected for us was closed or too full; anyway, we drove to another location. I recall that Bruce went in ahead but failed to hold the door for Anna and me. We talked about life in Ann Arbor; Anna's cousins, David and Philip; and carefully avoided any topic that was actually dear to my heart. I did learn a little about his work as a research assistant in a lab at the university. I think they were studying the possible harmful effect that anesthesia might have on a patient's lungs. He was working with mice and rats. It sounded very interesting and definitely important. Bruce became very animated while talking about his work. It was obvious that Anna was fond of him. But I wondered whether he might want to stay a bachelor, devoted to his work and very definitely to his many sports.

Back home, it was time to go to bed. "You can sleep in my room, Mom," Anna said. I stayed awake for quite some time. How could I know that night that Bruce, a long-time bachelor, would morph into a most wonderful family man and become my very dear son-in-law?

One year later my sister, Brigitte; my future son-in law, Bruce; and I were listening to the endless graduation ceremonies as Anna received her master's degree in Epidemiology. We were carefully "checking each other out," you might say, while engaging in rather trivial conversation whenever there was a pause before yet another speaker took over. All of a sudden, Bruce said, "I hope Anna will get swimming out of her system. I find swim meets so very, very boring!" Anna had worked as an assistant coach to the Michigan swim team that had taken her to Hawaii. I wondered whether she would ever be able to part from the sport she loved. Swimming had occupied so much of her life. She had achieved outstanding results as the team's most valuable swimmer in each of her four years of swimming for Columbia University. His sports were skiing, rock climbing, golfing, playing soccer, kayaking, and even diving for his high school swim team. Anna had not been involved in any of those sports. She had traveled to Europe, Kenya, Egypt, and the Caribbean Islands. Bruce had never left the USA. I wondered whether Anna and Bruce would be the right match. I knew that Anna loved him.

Fast forward to 2013: Anna learned to ski, golf, and climb. She never gave up her love for swimming, however, and has been coaching the East Aurora Swim Team for over twenty years. Bruce actively and enthusiastically participated in Carl's swim meets, supports Anna's coaching, and tries not to miss any of Erika's lacrosse and soccer games since she opted out of swim meets. One never knows what the future has in store. The man who did not ever "in a million years" want to sit through another "boring" swim event was totally hooked.

The very exciting news that Bruce and Anna would be moving to Buffalo came in 1992. Bruce's boss, Dr. Paul Knight, had received an invitation to become chairman of the Anesthesiology Department and continue his research at the University of Buffalo. He asked Bruce to join him to set up and run the research office. This was too good to be true. Bruce and Anna lined up a real estate agent and came for a weekend to look for a house. They looked at a number of houses, at first those near the university, and finally found one on Geneva Road in East Aurora. The location was lovely.

In the spring of 1993, neighbors gave a welcoming party for Bruce and Anna. Bruce's parents happened to be visiting from Fripp Island, SC. I came from Rochester to meet them for the first time. We sat together at the neighborhood party and enjoyed getting to know one another. I asked Bruce's mother, Marilyn, to please tell her son to marry my daughter. "The last time Bruce did what I told him to do was when he was seventeen," was her response. However, Bruce and Anna did get engaged in August of 1993 while taking a trip to Lion's Head, located on the Georgian Bay on the appropriately named Bruce Peninsula, Canada. Immediately after their return, Bruce and Anna began to plan their wedding. They set the date for June 25th, 1994, and decided to hold the party in their large backyard. I was very busy at the time with my mother, who truly needed constant care. It was good that Bruce and Anna organized everything from caterers, bakers, and music to invitations and everything else. Brigitte even took care of the flowerbeds on the terraces.

My mother died in early spring 1994, and Bruce's parents invited Brigitte and me to visit Fripp Island, a lovely paradise, for a much needed time to get away from it all. Marilyn and Bob welcomed us with open arms and gave us a great time. We were all very happy that Bruce and Anna would be getting married. Marilyn was worried that there might be too many bugs spoiling the festivities for the planned outdoor wedding, but nobody could possibly imagine the torrential rain storm that would threaten to ruin the garden wedding.

Anna and Bruce Get Married

The elegant tents that would accommodate 118 guests, as well as a kitchen, were set up in the backyard of 140 Geneva Road. The flowerbeds on the terraced garden looked lovely, as did the many colorful plants that decorated the stairs leading from the house to the garden. My sister, an avid gardener, was rightfully pleased with the splendid results from her labor of love. Bruce and Anna had tasted and selected the cake and made all the necessary arrangements with the caterer, Tiddledybinks, from Tonawanda. A variety of beverages was in the house; the musicians, appropriately called the Creek Bend Band, had confirmed this important gig; and the florist promised that the bouquets for the bride and her entourage would arrive on time for the ceremony on the following day. I was glad that everything was so superbly organized. Out-of-town guests had arrived and found welcoming shelter with relatives and friends, while the Rochester contingent had rented rooms at the conveniently located Byrncliff in nearby Varysburg. Regrettably, the Roycroft Hotel located in East Aurora was still undergoing remodeling and would not open until August.

Then on June 24th, it rained a 123-year, record-breaking 2.57 inches in Buffalo (definitely more in East Aurora) and the rehearsal, directed by the groom, had to take place indoors. Soon thereafter we went to the Old Orchard Inn to enjoy a happy time and wonderful food at the rehearsal dinner, hosted by Bruce's parents, Bob and Marilyn.

Umbrellas were needed when we left the rehearsal dinner and drove in pouring rain to Byrncliff. I did not sleep that night at all. On June 25, the wedding day, the sky over East Aurora looked foreboding, dark clouds hovered over the town, but the rain had

Brigitte Shows how Deep the Water is in the Caterer's Tent Area

295

stopped. My sisters Emmeli and Brigitte and I were dressed for the festivities. However, as soon as we arrived, Brigitte changed into shorts and a T-shirt

Everybody Working to Get the Last of the Water

from Anna and she and the bridesmaids got busy pushing the ankle-deep water from the flooded backyard. The tents were standing in water. Casenovia Creek was raging and unforgiving. Anna left to rent three more pumps and buy squeegees from the hardware store. Instead of playing golf with friends, Bruce directed the clean-up. The tent company suggested we get wood pallets from the lumber yard and special flooring so that the guests' shoes, as well as their chairs, would not sink into the muddy ground. The many helping hands were successful and, by the time the guests came at 4:30 p.m., they had no idea that the backyard had been completely underwater in the morning. The

Chris and Dianne help Anna

Hedda and Anna Before Wedding

bride, her bridesmaids, and Brigitte got cleaned up and had a mere forty-five minutes to dress and hover over Anna. Bruce and his groom's men got changed in a neighbor's house. The chairs for the audience were set up, the arbor was put in place, and my brother, Hinrich, tested the loudspeaker equipment.

Hinrich in Charge of the Sound

The guests had no idea that a near catastrophe had taken place just hours before. In fact, there are no words to describe the scene. Only photographs can truly relate story.

Judge David Floyd arrived, ready to perform the ceremony. Lo and behold, the sun came out! Bruce's friend, Chris, played the guitar and sang while a canoe slowly made its way down Cazenovia Creek carrying Mark, the brother of the groom and best man, and Bruce. It was a touching scene. Those two took their places with Bruce's friends, Chris, Stuart, and John, to wait for the bridesmaids, Christine, Dianne, Mojo, and Kathy, the maid of honor. They

Bruce and Mark Arrive by Canoe

were followed by the radiant bride, Anna, and the pretty flowergirls, Lisa and Teresa, who held the train of Anna's gown. It was beautiful to see those three descending slowly down the steps to the garden. Brigitte and I awaited them at the bottom and took Anna to Bruce. I went against protocol and was totally out of order when I gave Bruce a hug. The ceremony was memorable and lovely. The nervous Bruce married "Lisa Anna" instead of Anna Lisa.

Manpower had overcome the deluge. All guests had a great time singing, square dancing, and enjoying each other's company. Bruce and his friend Chris entertained by singing duets. It was a wonderful wedding. Several friends and family members met again the following day to help unwrap the wedding presents.

Cazenovia Creek, no longer a raging river, was calm, quiet, and harmless.

On June 26th, *The Buffalo News* reported that East Aurora was hardest hit by the torrential rainstorm.

Bob, Marilyn, Anna, Bruce, Hedda, Brigitte

My Grandchildren, Carl Robert and Erika Rose

Carl, Mumu, Erika, 2008

Carl Robert

It was the middle of September 1995 when Bruce and Anna came to visit Brigitte and me in Rochester. After dinner Brigitte and I were getting ready to watch *Jeopardy!* when Bruce appeared and said in a moderately serious voice, "Can I talk to you?"

We were immediately concerned that something was wrong, but then Bruce shifted gears and, with a smile on his face, and his amusing way with words, he announced that Anna was pregnant and, if all went well, I would become a grandmother by the beginning of April. The official due date was April 1, 1996. What delightful news! I was touched that Bruce wanted to be the one to make the announcement; he was obviously very happy and I knew he would make a great father.

My Grandchildren, Carl Robert and Erika Rose

Anna's pregnancy went well. She continued to work and coach. Brigitte and I got busy knitting blankets, booties, and sweaters as well as purchasing many wonderful baby items. It was fun to finally be preparing for a new baby. Bruce called March 29th to say they were heading to the hospital. The call came shortly before 4:00 a.m. on March 30th that a beautiful, healthy boy named Carl Robert had arrived. He was named for my dear father and Bruce's father. A perfect name in my opinion.

Brigitte and I were too excited to drive, so her oldest son Hans drove us to Mercy Hospital, south of Buffalo, to see the new baby. We both thoroughly enjoyed taking turns holding Carl. Anna and Bruce were so very happy. I returned home for the night but drove back the next day to help Anna and Bruce with Carl. What a wonderful time. Carl was of course the most handsome and, above all, the smartest of all babies.

After two months, Anna returned to work part-time Tuesday, Wednesday, and Thursday. I was delighted to be the babysitter. I arrived Tuesday mornings at 7:15 a.m. so that Bruce and Anna could get to work by 8:00. They were able to commute together most days as they worked in adjacent buildings at the University of Buffalo south campus. I returned home to Rochester on Thursday evenings.

Carl was good with me, although he was apprehensive in the morning when he anticipated his mother leaving. I put him in the stroller and walked down the street and around the circle until they were gone. I loved every minute with him. I recited all the poems and songs that I knew. I also played the German version of "peek-a-boo" with him in which you say in German, "Mu-mu-mu-keek!" From this my most favorite name of "Mumu" was born. For the past twenty years many people use Mumu for my name instead of Hedda.

Mumu Walking Carl

Several months later Bruce said to me, "I don't even remember what my life was like before Carl." He was overwhelmed with happiness at being a father.

Carl loved gardening with "Begga," Anna's nickname for my sister, Brigitte, eating strawberries, and swimming in the pool. He also loved *Arthur, Winnie-the-Pooh, Pokémon,* and *Harry Potter* growing up. I was happy that I could visit often and was always present for important dates in school and holidays. While growing up, Carl tried skiing, snowboarding, soccer, swimming, and golf. He

Begga and Carl in the Garden

excelled in both swimming and golf in high school.

I knew Carl was musical right from the start. In preschool, he delighted me by singing *Leaving on a Jet Plane*. In fourth grade, he began playing trumpet and was always the happiest one in the band. Carl was part of a trio of trumpeters in high school who were so good that the teacher selected very challenging music for them. As part of the band, he went to Disney World to march in a parade. Now he plays ukulele and guitar and I look forward to his singing and playing for me whenever he comes home from college. I can never get enough of it. With the help of FaceTime, he plays a few songs for me every Sunday during our weekly call.

When Carl turned sixteen and received his driver's license, I was happy to stop driving and have him as my chauffeur. He was glad to oblige his "ancient" grandmother in exchange for the use of my car.

I am especially thrilled that he loves languages. He studied Latin and German in high school and Arabic, Spanish, and German in college. I am proud that he has

Mumu and Carl, 2013

301

chosen to major in German.

The summer between his sophomore and junior years in college, I helped arrange for him to spend six weeks in Egypt with his second cousins who have built a sustainable farm just north of Cairo. This was a tremendous opportunity as they all speak German with one another and Arabic with the people who work there. He was exposed to both languages and was able to help them make their English website more accurate. For the second half of his junior year, Carl planned to study for a semester in Heidelberg, Germany. The German universities use a different calendar than those in the United States. His program abroad did not begin until March 1st. We are lucky that we still have connections with the insurance firm that my grandfather founded over one-hundred years ago. My cousin's daughter, Julie, offered to arrange a seven-week internship for Carl. He spent about two weeks each in several of the different offices of the company, being exposed to several aspects of the business as well as learning some business German.

My dear "Carl-le-man," a name I called him when he was still very young, has grown into a sensitive young man whom I love dearly.

Erika, Mumu, and Carl, April 1998

Erika Rose

I had come from Rochester around March 25, 1998, to take care of Carl, then almost two years old. Anna and Bruce were anxiously awaiting the birth of their second child. On March 27, they decided to go to the Aurora

Theater to see Jack Nicholson as a professional malcontent and Helen Hunt as a caring waitress in the movie entitled *As Good as it Gets*.

I was worried and most concerned since Mercy Hospital is not exactly around the corner from East Aurora. Shortly after returning from the movie, Bruce and Anna grabbed the bag containing essentials for Anna and zoomed off. Erika Rose was born at 11:11 p.m., a perfect baby and truly "as good as it gets." Erika was the name of my dear friend and Rose was Bruce's mother's middle name.

Bruce, the beaming father, took Carl and me to visit Anna and Erika the next day. Carl was delighted to see his mother and not quite sure what to do with the baby. He was however fascinated by the many gadgets in the hospital bathroom. He immediately pulled the emergency cord and we heard, "May I help you?" over the loudspeaker. Little Carl ran from the bathroom and jumped on his mother's bed to snuggle up in her protective arms. He could only snuggle into one arm because the other one was taken over by the new member of the family, little Erika.

March 27 has always been an important date for me. I had been celebrating my dear Oma's birthday on this very day for as long as I can remember. Elise Sophie Bartelt lived from 1871 to 1940. I saw my Oma every day and, in retrospect, I think it was she who got me interested in learning languages. Erika sharing her birthday with her great-great grandmother was bound to be a good omen. My hope was that little Erika would be as wise, kind, loving, and giving as Oma. And, twenty years later, she displays all of these wonderful qualities.

Carl never minded drinking his mother's milk from a bottle so she could go to work. Baby Erika had other ideas. No way would she drink from a bottle. We all tried our best. Anna had to take her along when she went to a friend's wedding for three days. Carl stayed with me in Rochester.

Erika had new rules for games that often frustrated her brother. Hide-and-Seek was one of her favorites. I think she was just three years old when she gave these instructions: "You hide, Mumu, but first show me where you are going to hide before you hide. When I am going to hide, I will also tell you the exact place so that you can find me." She most certainly did not want to be lost.

My Grandchildren, Carl Robert and Erika Rose

In the winter of 2002, Erika and Carl visited us for a weekend in Rochester. We were enjoying a quiet evening. The children had their baths and were ready for bed. Carl was busy with Lego blocks and Erika decided to make a chain out of small colorful paperclips. Suddenly, Brigitte shrieked. A mouse had run through the living room. "Do something!" my sister pleaded. Carl and I jumped from the sofa to catch the unwelcome intruder. Little Erika seemed unperturbed and continued with her self-assigned job to link all the paperclips together. When Carl and I returned to the sofa from our unsuccessful hunt, my sister was still rather upset. Erika held up her long, probably about two feet, paperclip chain and said, "Don't worry, Begga, I made this mousetrap for you. You will be safe."

At the end of March of the same year, my sister and I accompanied Bruce, Anna, and the children to Utah for a week of skiing. Brigitte and I were just onlookers. Erika had just turned four. She was wearing a pink snowsuit. Joined by other admiring grandparents, we watched the beginners skiing down the bunny hill. Then I heard someone say, "Oh look at that brave and adorable little pink thing!"

Brigitte and I loved having frequent visits from Anna and the children during the summer months. Picking raspberries in the garden in early July and frequent visits to the small amusement park on Lake Ontario, Sea Breeze, were highlights along with many invented games in our wonderful pool.

Carl, Erika, and Mumu Enjoy the Pool

A chocolate lab joined the Davidson household in early June 2002. Ariel was born in April and little Erika loved to play, hug, and take care of the puppy. She acquired many stuffed puppies. After Erika saw a show about endangered wolves, she decided that she would become a veterinarian and work with wolves. Everybody supported her interest. We even went to a show in Batavia where live wolves were exhibited and Anna painted a mural depicting wolves in Erika's room. Today Erika has outgrown her passion for wolves and her room is redecorated. But Demond, a small stuffed wolf that has been Erika's nightly companion for many years, remains. "I cannot go to sleep without Demond," she once told me.

Erika enjoyed all social activities such as family parties, pre-school, and kindergarten. However, in the following grades, writing sentences with the spelling words of the week appeared to be an insurmountable stumbling block. The little girl steadfastly refused to write. Her parents were exhausted. She put her papers and utensils into her school bag and said, "My teacher loves me anyway." She was right. A wonderful teacher let her tell stories and awakened her interest in reading and writing. Her imagination knows no limits.

I'm pretty sure Erika and I could have been entered into the *Guinness World Records* book in the summer of 2013. There is no doubt in my mind that Erika is the only fifteen-year-old girl who has read *Les Miserables* out loud to her grandmother. Yes, word for word, while also learning to pronounce the many French words, names of streets, people, and events. It was required reading for school, and a chore, but she did it and enjoyed it. Many years have gone by since someone read a story to me. Victor Hugo must have been smiling.

Erika and Mumu

Unlike her brother and parents, Erika does not find golf to her liking, although she always plays at least twice a year: Father's Day and her dad's birthday. According to Bruce, she could be a good golfer if she tried a little.

Erika swam for several years but decided to switch and play lacrosse and soccer. A wonderful music teacher at the high school rekindled her interest and love for playing the French horn. She played in the concert band and in the pit orchestra for musicals at the high school. In college, she is a terrific science student and still plays lacrosse.

To say that I am a happy and proud grandmother would be a huge understatement. Watching Carl and Erika grow into young adults and having the privilege to be a part of their lives has been the driving force of my life since 1996 and I cherish every minute I get to spend with them.

Carl, Mumu, Erika, 2014

Erika and Carl, 2016

My Siblings

Back Row: Hedda, Emmeli, Brigitte
Front: Hinrich and our Mother, Lisa, in 1990

Emmeli

Emmeli was born on November 25, 1922, and died on April 25, 2000. Brigitte was born on December 22, 1923, and died on February 8, 2007. I still grieve for both of them. They were my dearest friends and played a major role in my entire life. Emmeli and Brigitte were kind, generous, and loving toward me, "their little sister." Being just a year apart, there was quite a bit of sibling rivalry and they were often at odds with one another. However, the strongest love for the other sister always overcame all difficulties.

Emmeli and Brigitte, 1926

Emmeli, the first born, was an amazingly gifted child. Always anxious to learn, she taught herself to read at an early age. She retained all the acquired knowledge throughout her life and we always called on her when our memories failed us. Her name was a combination of the two grandmothers' names: EMMa and ELIse. In later years, I used to call her Emmeline or Lina. She was five years my senior, yet we did a lot of things together. Neither one of

Emmeli Reading a Book around 1937

us enjoyed playing with dolls. She did not have any and my two rarely were taken out of their bed. Instead, Emmeli taught me to read and write, play the piano (I never was very good at it), sing all the Christmas carols, and learn to make crafts and presents. We both enjoyed going on hikes. She excelled in school, was good in sports, and a group leader in the Hitler Youth. The latter lasted until she was seventeen, when a serious altercation with her superiors brought her life in the movement to an abrupt halt.

Emmeli was forced to interrupt her medical studies after WWII when the Allies determined that her leadership in the Hitler Youth required some reprimand. She had to take two semesters off from her studies at the university. Emmeli used this year to attend the music school in Lübeck and learn how to play the organ. During that time, she often played at funerals and weddings when the regular organist was busy as director of the choir. Electricity was frequently shut down and my sister needed someone to "pump" the organ. I was usually this "someone," using pedals to pump air for the organ thirty minutes at a time. It was the custom that four trumpeters play from the bell tower on Christmas Eve. In November 1946, Pastor Vorwerk learned that one trumpeter had not returned from the war. My sister volunteered to learn the trumpet. My mother was upset since trumpet practice had to take place in our cramped apartment. But Emmeli was determined and, come Christmas Eve, she was the fourth trumpeter.

Emmeli had enjoyed her music studies but returned to pursue medicine once the year was up. It was difficult at the time to be a student. Little food, an unheated room, and her bed was the best place to read and work. She persevered, finished her medical studies, and began her first year as an assistant in the University Hospital in Kiel. Emmeli buried herself in her work and, we thought at times, she had become a social recluse.

I immigrated to the USA in 1952 and encouraged Emmeli to join me in Rochester, NY. The hospitals needed physicians and Emmeli started her four-year internship at Rochester General Hospital. After completing the required two years of residency in family practice at St. Mary's Hospital, she applied to take the New York State Boards. However, NY limited the number of people who were allowed to take the boards each year and Emmeli would have had to wait at least another year. Instead, she chose to take the State Boards in Illinois which she passed, allowing her to begin practicing there.

In 1959, I drove with her to Jacksonville, IL, where she joined an Ob-Gyn practice, since she needed more experience in that field. After one year, the village of Downs, with six-hundred inhabitants, mostly farmers, invited her to start her practice there. The villagers welcomed their new doctor and built her office on the same lot where she had bought a house. They did the landscaping, planted trees, bushes and flowers, and constructed a big parking lot.

The practice grew quickly. She delivered more than seventy babies in the nearby hospital in Bloomington, assisted in major and minor surgeries involving her patients, and held office hours daily, except Thursday. She was a highly respected and much loved physician. Her charges were low and the majority of patients paid cash when they sought help. When some patients were unable to pay, they mowed her lawn, helped tend her flower beds, cleaned the gutters, and brought her fresh corn, meat, and many other things. It was in many ways a "barter system." My sister was devoted to the families in Downs and she rarely took time off. She visited us in Rochester for a few days at a time, several times a year.

Emmeli did come to celebrate my seventieth birthday in NYC in 1998. We noticed that she was taking pills fairly frequently. I at first thought she had mints and complained when she wouldn't share with me. She shrugged and said they were not for sharing. In April she visited in Rochester to meet Anna's new baby Erika. Anna said to me that she was sure that Emmeli was sick. Brigitte and I approached her and she promised to seek medical advice.

Unfortunately, the news was bad. She had waited too long and the advanced cancer required immediate surgery.

Brigitte and I flew to Illinois and arrived on a Friday. The parking lot was packed and so was the waiting room. While Brigitte started packing Emmeli's suitcases, I went over to the office and told the waiting patients that my sister was very ill and that the office was closed. Emmeli was determined to work until she couldn't anymore. There was complete disbelief when I told the patients that my sister was scheduled to fly with us to Rochester that very evening and that she was scheduled for surgery within three days. I placed a notice in the local IL newspaper and informed her friends there that I would be back soon to dissolve the practice. It was a very sad ending of a long and wonderful life as a physician.

The major operation made it possible for her to live under our care at home until April 2000. She was determined to make it to the new century.

I returned to Downs two weeks later to clear the house and office and put both up for sale. My grand-niece, Lisa, and two of my nephews, Hans and Matthias, came with me to help transport some furniture and my sister's car. The villagers and former patients came with gifts for Emmeli. They also hoped to get some things, also furniture, that had belonged to my sister. We gave most of her belongings away. Lisa had only recently received her driver's license and later revealed to me how absolutely terrified she was to drive across country with me in Emmeli's car although she loved that we needed to stock up on "Knacke" (special snacks) for the long trip.

Emmeli and I became very close during the last two years of her life. She displayed extraordinary courage and willpower and she was able to enjoy family life. We listened to music, primarily J.S. Bach, Verdi, and Mozart, and played daily Scrabble games. We talked about our childhood, people we had known, events we had shared and, of course, our family. She loved it when my daughter Anna came to visit with her two babies, Carl and Erika, and enjoyed the daily visits from Lydia, Brigitte's granddaughter, who lived nearby. One of her favorite things was to watch movies

Emmeli, Erika, Carl, 1999

with Carl about piglet and owl from the Winnie-the-Pooh stories. Carl sat on her bed and they both laughed heartily, again and again, when the wind blew the dishes and piglet out of the window.

Flowers and letters came from her former patients in Illinois and the village built a special bench and planted two trees in her memory in the small park in Downs.

During her lifetime, Emmeli had been frugal and did not afford herself many luxuries. She had saved her money for my brother Hinrich's children, my sister Brigitte's sons, and for my daughter, Anna. I have many precious memories.

Brigitte

Brigitte was a good student and loved the sciences but, unlike Emmeli or me, she really loved dolls. She and her friends would have tea parties with their dolls for hours on end. Her love of dolls remained with her throughout

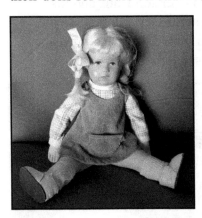

Kathe Kruse Doll

her life and she would go on to collect dolls from different places she visited. During one of our trips to Germany in the eighties, we visited a doll store and Brigitte was in heaven. After long deliberations, she decided to buy a special Käthe Kruse doll. It was expensive, well over one-hundred dollars. She had had one of these dolls as a child and cherished it. It was lost in the bombing of our house. She was thrilled with her purchase and the doll was placed on an important shelf in our house upon our return.

As was required, Brigitte was also a member of the Hitler Youth. She was very athletic which helped her move up in the rankings. Brigitte was a fast runner and loved and excelled at the game of handball. She was very outgoing and had many friends at school. She was much more social than Emmeli. I remember I was often called upon to be Brigitte's change purse. When I was about five or six I started spending a night at my grandfather's house every now and then. It was a special treat. He would give whoever spent the night a little pocket money. I always saved mine, while Brigitte always spent hers right away. As she was four years older than I, she often convinced me to share my money with my "dear sister" so that she could buy some candy from the corner store.

Brigitte followed in Emmeli's footsteps and studied medicine at the university. Her medical studies would of course play a very important role in my future since one of her professors would become my daughter's father many years later. Studying medicine during the war was not an easy task. Many times electricity went out and classes were cancelled. Brigitte had to do a year of service before even beginning at the university.

In the difficult years in Germany following the war, Brigitte ended up immigrating to the United States with her three young sons. Brigitte and I were very compatible and we lived together for over fifty years raising our children and grandchildren.

Once Brigitte and I became financially secure, we liked to travel. Brigitte travelled as often as she could. She went to the Galapagos Islands twice with her sons Christian and Matthias to visit her son Hans and his wife Ellen. She went camping in Alaska with Matthias. She travelled to the Netherlands, Hong Kong, and Australia with our neighbors the Zinmans to attend concerts, sightsee, and also act as the personal pediatrician for the

Zinman's son Raphael. We travelled together to Haiti and Cat Island. She often took my daughter, Anna, along as her roommate. Together, they went sailing in the Caribbean and on an African Safari tour in Kenya, Africa. Of course, we also made several trips back to Germany to visit our relatives and friends. With her grandchildren and their families, she went to Cancun, Florida, and Cape Cod. She even joined Anna's university swim team as the unofficial guest team doctor on training trips to Trinidad and Tobago and the Cayman Islands.

Brigitte and Anna in Trinidad

One of my most favorite memories is the trip that I took with both of my sisters to Maui, Hawaii in 1995. It had always been one place that I wanted to visit. Following the death of our mother in 1994, I finally convinced Brigitte and Emmeli to join me on vacation. It was wonderful to spend two weeks with my sisters. In between sightseeing and other activities, the best part was that we talked and talked and talked about everything, remembering things from our childhood and our lives in America. It was such a special time for us.

Hedda, Brigitte, Emmeli

Brigitte had four grandchildren: Stefan, Lisa, Teresa, and Lydia. I have two grandchildren: Carl and Erika. We loved being grandmothers and having the grandchildren play in our pool, pick raspberries in our yard, and sleep over on special occasions. Brigitte and I made several trips to Sea Breeze amusement park as well as the favorite Toy Fest festival in East Aurora each

Brigitte's Grandchildren: Stefan, Lisa, Teresa in Cancun, 1987   *and Lydia in 2005*

summer. Spending time with our grandchildren and then reminiscing about them when we were back at home gave us great joy.

Jungle Group at Toy Fest
Top Row Faces (L-R): Brigitte, Lydia, Hedda, Christian, Anna, Teresa
Bottom Row Faces (L-R): Matthias, Erika, Carl, Bruce

Brigitte died in February 2007.

I miss my sisters. Not a day goes by without me thinking, "I wish I could call Emmeli, she would remember", or "I wish I could share this with Brigitte."

Hinrich

I was six when my brother was born, and was delighted to have a little brother. I remember helping my mother care for him as a baby. As he grew older, I loved playing school with him. He learned all the capitals of all the countries under my tutelage. He was especially good at math. One day, when he was about five or six, we were sitting at the dining room table and he was carefully studying the chair backs that were lined with decorative gold tacks. He suddenly blurted out, "there are seventy-two tacks in the chair. Eight rows of nine tacks makes seventy-two." He had figured out multiplication on his own.

Fortunately, Hinrich's involvement in the Hitler Youth was limited to a little over a year since he entered in April 1944 when he turned ten and

314

the war was essentially over for him in May 1945. He was a bright boy who excelled in math and science which would serve him well in his chosen career of Engineering and Computer Science. It also made his transition to an American high school easier in 1953 since math and science formulas are universal and the language barrier wasn't as difficult as it was for the other subjects.

Hinrich excelled professionally as a college professor and the director of the computing center at the University of Buffalo. He had four children with his first wife Nancy: David, Philip, Clark, and Polly. He adopted his second wife's, Maria's, two children: Adam and Susan. Together Hinrich and Maria made a beautiful home.

Summers always included some kind of vacation where the family went boating and waterskiing. It was quite a sight to see everyone learning to waterski. My own experience consisted of my brother driving the boat, many people helping me get my skis on, then waiting patiently on the dock. When Hinni started the boat, I successfully got up and everyone was clapping. Almost immediately after getting up, I started to sink into the water. My dear brother's boat had run out of gas. I tried one or two more times, but ended up getting hurt with the tow rope so that put an end to my short-lived waterskiing career. The children all loved it though and there are many stories of trips to the hospital as one tried to outdo another's stunt. Most notably, there was always a contest to see how close you could end up near the dock to avoid having to swim very far. Clark pushed the envelope one year and ended up running into the deck, requiring a trip to the ER and several stitches. This summer tradition continued for many years, first at Kirk Cove and then at Cranberry Lake in the Adirondacks. Even after a long hiatus, the tradition was resurrected in the summer of 1996 when all the children were married and many grandchildren had been born. The picture on the next page has all the family members under age twenty at the time.

Hinrich has fourteen grandchildren: Grant, Brian, Christopher, Amy, Max, Colin, Peter, Katie, Jennifer, Heather, Allison, Elizabeth, Hannah, and Marlena. He thoroughly enjoyed watching them grow and having them visit his wonderful home and pool. When he retired from the University of Buffalo, he began to immerse himself in his hobby of woodworking. After visiting a clock store in Germany, he was inspired to make grandfather clocks. He made a large grandfather clock as well as a mantle sized clock for himself. His children admired them when they visited his house. He then made it a goal to

Grandchildren under age 20 in 1996 at Cranberry Lake
Carl, Teresa, Amy, Grant, Lisa, Max, Peter, Christopher, Brian, Colin, Stefan

make a clock for each of his six children. Some chose full-size grandfather clocks while others chose mantle-size clocks. All are masterpieces.

As we have gotten older, my brother and I have appreciated reminiscing together. His interest in speaking German has also increased. I am glad that I can still share some childhood memories with my brother.

Hinrich's Growing Family, 2001
Back Row from left: David, Kathy, Adam, Jennifer, Annette, Don, Heather, Polly,
Susan, Allison, Tom, Marlena, Carol, Christopher, Philip
Front from left: Brian, Grant, Hinni, Max, Amy, Hannah, Clark, Theresa, Colin,
Peter, Ria, Katie (only granchild missing is Elizabeth who was not yet born)

Memories of Some Special Students

Lisa Purwin Loved the German Language

As a graduate student I became good friends with Bertold Purwin who was getting his master's degree in linguistics. He and his wife, Marianne, had fled from Danzig (Gdansk), formerly East Prussia, when the Nazis closed their restaurant since they were Jewish. Bert's sister, Käthe, had left earlier and settled in Rochester, NY, where she was a practicing psychiatrist. Bert's parents had died some years before, but Marianne's parents stayed behind in East Prussia and died in concentration camps. The Purwins fled to Cuba where both worked in the restaurant business. Their two children, Lisa and her brother, were born there. The Purwins did not practice their religion.

On January 1, 1959, Fidel Castro toppled the Batista regime and prompted many middle- and upper-class people to flee. The Purwins, not yet able to get permission to enter the US, went to the Dominican Republic for some time. Supported by his sister, the family was finally able to settle in Rochester in 1966.

Lisa was fourteen years old at the time. She was fluent in Spanish and German and now had to learn English in high school. Three years later, Lisa's father contacted me at the College of Brockport and asked for my help. Lisa's SAT scores in English were poor and Brockport had declined her admission. I intervened and explained to the admitting officials that English was Lisa's third language and they should make an exception. They did and Lisa did not let me down. She turned out to be a most ambitious and hard-working student and her English improved dramatically.

Lisa took many classes with me: German grammar, composition, and several literature courses. One of the few students who took advantage of my office hours, Lisa confided in me that she wanted to become a teacher of German. While her father was supportive, her mother was adamantly opposed. However, Lisa prevailed. We went ahead and enrolled her in the Junior Year

Abroad program run by SUNY Albany. Her mother reluctantly agreed.

In 1972, Bert, his tearful wife, and I said goodbye to Lisa at the Rochester airport and she flew to Frankfurt, Germany. That night, Brigitte called me out of bed at about 3:00 a.m. (she was often on call and kept her telephone by her bed). "I have an irate woman on the phone who is saying the ugliest words about you." It was Marianne blaming me for putting Lisa in jeopardy. That very day, Israeli athletes had been taken captive at the Olympic Festival in Munich. As soon as I could, I contacted Albany to request that Lisa return immediately to Rochester. Lisa never left the Frankfurt airport. She returned home safely. Despite serious disagreements and arguments in the Purwin household, Lisa prevailed in her desire to teach German.

She continued her study of the German language, but needed a place where she could be a student teacher. I was not able to find a suitable school for her in Rochester, so I wrote to my cousin, Rudolf, a teacher of German in Lübeck. Would he be willing and able to have Lisa work with him for six weeks? He was interested and enthusiastic. Lisa and her father were eager and ready to accept the invitation. The education department here approved of Lisa's student teaching abroad. Now, all she needed was her mother's approval. I invited the Purwins to my house and talked about the childhood I had shared with my dear cousin, Rudolf. He was married to Fidele and they had two daughters, Katharina and Konstanze, and one son, Johannes. I even had photographs to show them. Marianne liked what she heard and saw.

Lisa Purwin, Johannes, Rudolf, Fidele, Katharina,
and Konstanze Hagen in 1973

Lisa loved her stay in Lübeck and, best of all, grew to love the Hagen family. Back home, Lisa graduated from college, as did her boyfriend and the two got married in 1975. Lisa had married into a very orthodox Jewish family, the Isaacsons and, for a while, her parents worried that she and her husband might move to Israel. However, they settled in Ohio, where Lisa also began a successful career as a teacher of German. Lisa became and still is a most successful teacher, taking her students to Germany regularly. She and her husband have two children, Amy and Jeffrey, who have since graduated from the University of Michigan.

The friendship between the Hagens, Purwins, and Isaacsons blossomed. I think it was in 1975 when the Purwins and Isaacsons took a trip to Germany, Lübeck in particular, and stayed with my cousin's family. Everybody was pleased with one another and I was thinking I had done something very good to promote peace among human beings.

Rudolf accepted a most desirable position as a teacher in a German school in Cairo, Egypt, in 1976. This appointment meant a considerable increase in his salary and the opportunity for his family to explore Egypt. (Anna and I visited Egypt for two weeks in 1980. During that time, we met Rudolf's daughter, Konstanze's, future husband, Helmy Abouleisch, a Muslim.) When Rudolf and his family returned to Germany, Konstanze was eighteen and had to finish her Abitur. However, she did not go on to the university. Helmy and his parents came from Cairo and he and Konstanze were soon married in Lübeck.

As soon as Lisa heard of this marriage, she broke off the warm relations she had with the Hagen family and with me. I met Lisa's father, Bert, one day at a store in Rochester. Bert promised me he would change Lisa's attitude toward Muslims. He did. I felt, once again, that I had done something good to promote peace among human beings.

Thelma Freedman Wanted to Marry a German Man

Thelma joined one of my beginning German classes in her last semester of her senior year. I was not particularly fond of students who did that just to get an "easy" three credits for graduation, but Thelma was different. She was a French major and had spent a year with the Peace Corps in Zaire (formerly Congo), Africa. It was there that Thelma met Helmut Krech, the son of a German Protestant minister from Hamburg.

Thelma grew up in an orthodox Jewish family that adhered strictly to their religion. She talked to me about her dilemma. Helmut and Thelma had fallen in love and were hoping to get married. Thelma's mother (her father was dead) and her brother were strongly opposed to this undesirable match. Helmut's parents questioned the choice but were supportive. I agreed to meet with Thelma's mother and brother. They came to see me in my office at the college. "Do you think it is possible for Thelma to live in Germany and be married to a Protestant?" her mother asked. What was I to say? No marriage is a guarantee for everlasting happiness and, in Thelma's case, there was the serious opposition from her mother and her older brother. I liked the soft-spoken, concerned, loving mother, but felt most uncomfortable with Thelma's brother's demeanor. He seemed to hold me personally responsible for the Holocaust. It was not a very productive meeting as far as I was concerned, but I suggested that Helmut come to New York and meet Thelma's family. I agreed to meet them again if it would be helpful.

Helmut and Thelma got married in Hamburg. Her mother attended the wedding while her brother stayed away. The two agreed that their children would study both religions. They did have four: Erika, Richard, Andrea, and Peter. As an engineer, Helmut was able to provide very well for his family and enable Thelma to pursue her many interests. Thelma's mother visited often and the grandchildren visited in New York. Regrettably, I cannot report a happy ending. Helmut and Thelma decided to go their separate ways after almost twenty years of marriage. Thelma is still living in Hamburg, as do their four children.

Michael Dei Anang, a Sad Ending

Michael was born in a small town in Ghana, Africa. After attending a missionary school and a secondary school in Achmota College, he studied in London to obtain his B.A. in philology before WWII. He returned to Ghana to teach English and Latin. He began publishing his poems and emerged as the best-known poet in Ghana.

In 1973, colleges and universities in the United States were encouraged to hire more black faculty and the search went outside our country. When Michael was hired by SUNY Brockport, several colleagues (myself included) resented the fact that his salary was considerably higher than ours, even though he did not hold a doctorate.

One day I received a totally unexpected phone call from him. "Would I be so kind and teach him German?" He was not able to attend my classes, but thought we could meet over lunch. For our first meeting, he came equipped with lunch for both of us and we settled down in my cozy office to become acquainted. I was most pleased to hear only nice things about the Germans and Germany. (German missionaries and linguists had given the people of Ghana a written language for Ashanti, one of several tongues spoken by the various tribes, so the children could learn to read and write Ashanti although English was the official language.) So why his desire to learn German? His son had gone to study medicine in Germany where he was now a practicing surgeon. He had married a German-born nurse and they had two children. He had seen the children when they were infants and was planning to see them again the following summer. His grandchildren would be seven and five years old.

"It is my great wish to be able to talk with them in German," he said. I had a window of about five months to help him learn the language. Not an easy task. Children are not as tolerant as adults when it comes to intonation or pronunciation. In fact, children are very critical. He wanted to learn to read some children's stories. I felt that would be hopeless, so I asked him whether he could sing. His answer was "yes" and I taught him several songs. Students and colleagues stopped in to observe our "singing classes." Although I could teach the songs, my voice was not exactly suitable for performing in public. (My musical brother requested at age three that I please stop singing and tell a story instead.) Michael and I limited his conversational German to just a few sentences which we practiced over and over again.

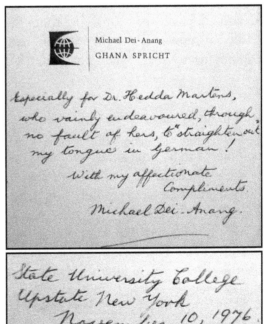

A Note Written on the Inside of the Book Michael Wrote and Gave to Me.

Memories of Some Special Students

By May 1977, my student felt confident and most grateful. He was planning to leave Brockport and return to Ghana with a stop in Frankfurt, Germany. The college was giving a farewell party for Michael and his wife. The faculty lounge was filled with some fifty people and decorated with lovely flowers. Delicious looking food was spread out on the table. Michael's appearance was eagerly awaited, especially by his wife.

Michael never came. He was found in the bathroom. He had suffered a heart attack. I cannot describe the sadness that befell us all. His grief-stricken wife was in shock.

Days later the president held a memorial service. Some of his colleagues in the African-American Studies program gave speeches. I felt like getting up and talking about Michael, the man, and not about a fledgling program that Michael had not liked to teach. However, I did not get up. It was just as well, since I too could not have given him justice.

Kevin Riggs and his Daughter, Lisa

I did not meet Kevin until 1992. It was a few days before Christmas. I had finished correcting twenty final exams for students in my German 101 class at Monroe Community College where I was teaching an evening class as an adjunct professor. Our living room floor was covered with pieces of wood, oodles of screws, and an instruction manual for an "easy-to-assemble" little cabinet for my sister's granddaughter. Then the doorbell rang. It was Kevin.

"Dr. Martens, may I please talk to you? I know that I did not do very well in the course." True. I had just written a failing grade for him. While we were talking, I invited him to work on my do-it-yourself project, which he completed in no time at all while I listened to his story. Kevin told me that he really wanted and needed to learn German to be able to communicate with his daughter and asked me to help him achieve this goal.

It began in 1984 when Kevin traveled with an American choral group to Germany. A pretty German girl named Eva happened to be working as a chef in the inn where the Americans were staying. Kevin and Eva were both in their early twenties and fell in love. Eva decided to follow Kevin to the United States and the two got married. They began their life together in West Palm Beach, FL, where Kevin had a job. Their daughter Lisa was born on February 16, 1987. One day in October of 1988 Kevin came home to an empty apartment and a farewell note from Eva. She had decided to take the baby and return to Germany. Frantic, Kevin drove to the airport, but he was too late. His wife and daughter were gone.

Kevin moved to Rochester in 1992 where he started a job. In order to be able to handle legal problems in German, he enrolled in my German class. After listening to this heartbreaking story, I told him that I would give him a passing grade, provided he would study hard and pass the required tests for German 101 within the next three months. He kept his promise. I assured him of my help in writing letters to the German authorities, as well as to his wife.

We managed to get permission for a supervised visit with his daughter after the divorce was granted by a German court. Kevin's mother went along for the second visit. At that time, Kevin noticed that the child-support money he had sent for Lisa was not spent on her and that she did not wear any of the clothing his mother had sent. Eva had married again and had a son and a daughter. The harsh tone between Kevin and Eva softened somewhat and Lisa was allowed to visit her father for a week when she was eight years old. The language problem between father and daughter was enormous and Kevin came to visit me with his very sweet, but rather confused, little daughter. It was summer and Lisa had a good time in our pool. She was glad she could speak German with me. However, it was a very difficult week for father and daughter.

Time went on. My correspondence with lawyers in Germany continued and Lisa was finally allowed to spend a year of high school in Caledonia, NY, and stay with her father. It was in a French class that she met Travis and the two became fast friends. When the year was up, Lisa returned to complete all requirements for graduation at her German high school. She passed the Abitur (final examination needed to attend the university). Meanwhile, the long-distance love affair between Travis and Lisa had grown so strong that she was given permission to enter SUNY at Geneseo and reside with her father. Needless to say, Kevin was elated. After her graduation, bilingual Lisa found an excellent job with a German-American company and Travis had become a fully established member of the police force. The two seemed destined to become a couple and Kevin called me in January to keep the July 28, 2012, open since Lisa and Travis would be getting married.

Once I received the invitation and was informed that Lisa's German family would also be attending, I began to wonder about meeting her mother, for whom I did not exactly have the warmest feelings. But whenever I expressed my concerns, Anna said in a firm voice, "Mom, you have to go, no matter what."

Kevin introduced me to Lisa's most pleasant stepfather, her two siblings, and the very lovely mother of the groom when Anna and I arrived at the church in Livonia, NY. At the dinner, Eva came to sit down next to me. "I just wanted to tell you how very sorry I am about my downright ugly and dreadful actions and behavior. Kevin and his mother have forgiven me and I hope that you will too." I truly had not realized that I had played such an important role in Kevin and Lisa's life.

Kevin Riggs with Daughter Lisa

Lisa and Travis had a son named Logan in April 2015. They live near Rochester, NY, and Logan's proud grandfather is thrilled to have them nearby. He often sends me updates and photos.

Tom Walker

In the spring of 2018 I received a letter from Tom Walker, a former German 101 student at Brockport in the 1970s. Tom wrote: "I recently viewed your videos from the Holocaust Resource Center of Buffalo (see a link to the videos on page 142) and realized I must finally send you a letter that is long overdue…to thank you for having such a long-lasting impact on my life." Tom went on to teach Mathematics at Pittsford High School and is now getting ready to retire after a forty-year career in information technology at the college of Mount Saint Vincent in the Bronx, NY.

Tom continues: "As I approach retirement age, I reflect a lot on the people who influenced my life. You are at the top of my list. In addition to instilling a desire to learn and know about the German language, you helped me get my first teaching job at Pittsford Sutherland High School.

"You were a most interesting teacher. In learning a language, there is just no way to get around memorizing new vocabulary, grammar, and sentence structure. You often used 'auswending lernen' (learning by memorization) in class. For example, to learn the days of the week, you had us say 'Montag, Dienstag…Sonntag' (Monday, Tuesday…Sunday) in a kind of chant, like in a tempo for marching. Then like a drill sergeant, you had us repeat it again and again and again. For the lesson about certain prepositions that always cause nouns to use the accusative case, you said something like 'durch-für-gegen-ohne-um' (through-for-against-without-around) going faster and faster until we were in unison and you were satisfied. Damned if it didn't work—I still know them now like I was born with the information. Same drill for the prepositions that take the dative case 'aus, außer, bei, mit, nach, seit, von, zu' (out, except, nearby, with, after, since, from, to). When I read how Common Core academic standards, to which many states adhere, is so dead set against rote memorization, I think about my own experience with these three examples and shake my head. My wife does not speak German, but has heard me say the days of the week chant so many times that even she knows them.

"Then there was the task of memorizing Goethe's poem 'Erlkönig' and reciting it in class for a grade. 'Wer reitet so spät durch Nacht und Wind?' (Who's riding so late where winds blow wild?...). That was hard. I must admit that I am not able to recite all of it now, but some parts still stick in my head.

"Many parents tell their children, 'If I've told you once, I've told you a thousand times.' You told us your mother's version was 'wenn Ich Dir einmal gesagt habe, habe Ich Dir 27 mal gesagt…' (if I've told you once, I've told you 27 times). You weren't sure where the 27 came from, but that was the magic number. Your mother also said, 'mach die Tür von draußen zu' (close the door from the outside) when she wanted to get the children out of the room. I have used that line a few times in my life.

"I liked your story about the pediatrician who recited Heinrich Heine's 'Lorelei' to you when you ran into him in the elevator at Strong Memorial Hospital years after having him in class. He had asked you then for one good reason why he, a future pediatrician, needed to memorize that poem. He still knew it by heart. Wouldn't it be amusing to think that there is an army of your former students who still carry that poem in their collective memories?

"After over forty years, I still enjoy immersing myself in the German language. Nobody in my circle of relatives and friends really understands why. The 'why' is you. You gave me the motivation to want to learn German. I think of you when I see this phrase: In Dir muß Brennen, was Du in anderen entzüden willst (In order to share something with others, you have to have a burning desire within yourself).

> "Mit herzlichen Grüßen (with kind regards)
> Tom Walker"

Tom Walker, early 1970s

I have been so lucky to be a teacher and allowed to make a great impact on so many people. My life has been equally enriched by these encounters over the years. I need to mention one other student that I had in Brockport. Irene White took all of my upper level German literature classes. She was a native German speaker, but was studying English literature in school. She was very hardworking and eventually built a company around languages, Language Intelligence. Over the years she has visited me from time to time and I always enjoy our conversations.

Teaching German Again

Confusion at the East Aurora High School made me a very happy
person in 2012. The School Board decided to drop German from the
curriculum. However, there were several students who needed to take the third
year to fulfill the foreign language requirement, so the German teacher was
asked to stay on to teach the third year. My grandson, Carl, had just completed
his first year of German instruction and was looking forward to continuing
his studies. It was suggested that he join the German III class in the fall but
this meant skipping an entire year. I decided that I could help and Carl and I
began to study during the summer months. He made excellent progress, and
I determined that he would be ready to join the other students enrolled in the
third year.

The individual class schedules were sent home in August. It turned
out that German III was scheduled at the same time as jazz band. Carl played
the trumpet and did not want to miss being in the band. His mother met with
the principal and got permission for me to home school Carl in German
throughout the year, on the condition that he take the final examination at
school. Not wanting to lose any precious time, Carl and I began to study
together.

We were soon joined by a fellow classmate and good friend of Carl's,
John Hasselback. John, also a trumpet player, had taken the second year of
German at school; however, he faced the same scheduling conflict as Carl.
John's parents and his paternal grandfather are all musicians and John is
totally immersed in music. His mother learned about Carl's solution and it was
decided that he would join my class. The school approved the plan.

Both Carl and John had German connections. Carl has relatives in
the north, in Hamburg and Lübeck, and John's maternal grandparents live in
the south, in Garmisch. Both boys had visited their respective relatives and
planned to make return visits to Germany in the future. Six weeks of intensive
German studies enabled Carl to be on the same level as John.

The high school German teacher suggested I assign a special project for the boys to complete by the end of the school year. I proposed the names of two composers: Richard Wagner and Richard Strauss, and two artists, the painter Emil Nolde and the graphic artist (grafiker) and sculptor, Ernst Barlach. All four were affected by the Hitler regime in different ways. It did not take the boys long to decide on their topics. John was thrilled to study Strauss since he had visited the home where Strauss had once lived in Germany. Carl opted to write about Ernst Barlach with great enthusiasm. Thanks to Carl's maternal grandfather, I have several works by Barlach in my possession.

As part of their German lessons, I required both boys to memorize two poems: "Der Erlkönig," by Johann Wolfgang von Goethe, and "Ich Weiß nicht was soll es bedueten," by Heinrich Heine. Carl can still recite both poems.

Another poem they memorized was "Die Lorelei" by Heinrich Heine (1797-1856). Heine was born in Düsseldorf. Because he was Jewish, we were told when I was in school in 1938 that his poetry was "written by an unknown poet." Our teacher taught his poems without a book and I learned them by heart. The poems were set to music by Schumann, Liszt, and Mendelssohn. Franz Silcher (1789-1860) composed the melancholy melody for "Die Lorelei." A legendary murmuring rock on the river Rhein is named after the Lorelei, the siren, and the poem tells her story.

> Ich weiss nicht, was soll es bedeuten,
> daß ich so traurig bin;
> ein Märchen aus alten Zeiten,
> das kommt mir nicht aus dem Sinn.
>
> Die Luft ist kühl, und es dunkelt,
> und ruhig fließt der Rhein;
> der Gipfel des Berges funkelt
> im Abendsonnenschein.
>
> Die schönste Jungfrau sitzet
> dort oben wunderbar;
> ihr goldnes Geschmeide blitzet,
> sie kämmt ihr goldnes Haar.

Sie kämmt es mit goldenem Kamme
und singt ein Lied dabei;
das hat eine wundersame,
gewaltige Melodei.

Den Schiffer im kleinen Schiffe
ergreift es mit wildem Weh;
er schaut nicht die Felsenriffe,
er schaut nur hinauf in die Höh'.

Ich glaube die Wellen verschlingen
am Ende Schiffer und Kahn;
und das hat mit ihrem Singen
die Lorelei getan.

I am of the opinion that this poem cannot be properly translated. Translation takes away the music, the magic, and the flow of the carefully crafted words of the original piece. But, since some of my readers may not know German, I have found what I think is an adequate translation that follows here.

I know not if there is a reason
Why I am so sad at heart.
A legend of bygone ages
Haunts me and will not depart.

The air is cool under nightfall.
The calm Rhine courses its way.
The peak of the mountain is sparkling
With evening's final ray.

The fairest of maidens is sitting
So marvelous up there,
Her golden jewels are shining,
She's combing her golden hair.

She combs with a comb also golden,
And sings a song as well
Whose melody binds a wondrous
And overpowering spell.

In his little boat, the boatman
Is seized with a savage woe,
He'd rather look up at the mountain
Than down at the rocks below.

I think that the waves will devour
The boatman and boat as one;
And this by her song's sheer power
Fair Lorelei has done.

My dear father introduced me to the wondrous world of fairy tales where goodness, kindness, and love defeat all evil and the end of each story leaves the listener with relief and hope. At bedtime, he would turn the lights off and begin telling me these wonderful stories. I saw no pictures, but formed my own images from his colorful descriptions and, to this day, remember every detail. When I did not understand the world "astrology," my father led me to the window and we looked at the night sky. Then he told me the scary story of *Aladdin and the Magic Lamp.* I heard about good spirits and evil spirits, God and Allah, the devil and black magic. To this day, I prefer stories without pictures so the listener can form his or her own images.

I thoroughly enjoyed reading German legends, sagas, and fairy tales with my two special German students. While all the fairy tales by the Grimm brothers took place in Germany, the stories told by Wilhelm Hauff took us to the mysterious and less familiar Middle Eastern part of our world. In all of those stories the evil elements, represented by witches, wicked stepmothers, dragons, wolves, giants, and magicians were conquered and severely punished if the perpetrator inflicted terrible harm to another human being. There was little mercy and crimes were not forgiven. Goodness prevailed. I was touched to learn that my seventeen-year-old students were most eager to hear another story when one came to an end. Hauff's tales *Aladdin* and *Ali Baba and the Forty Thieves* go on for one-thousand-and-one nights, and my students listened just as intently and spellbound as the Shah of Persia while the brave young woman told him these stories. In listening, we not only learned a language; we also learned about Islam and Muslims through a fairy tale.

Even cartoons can be a teaching tool. Not only did my students learn German, they learned history and amazing true stories about real people. Erich Ohser was born in 1903 in Plauen, a small town in the southeastern part of

Germany. His father, a custom's officer, decided that his son should learn a proper trade. At age fourteen, Erich Ohser began his apprenticeship with a locksmith. In his free time, he taught himself to sketch and, after three years, he convinced his father to allow him to attend the Academy for Graphic Art and Book Illustration in Leipzig.

Ohser exhibited his work and was awarded numerous first prizes. He befriended the writer, Erich Kästner, and the lector for a book-publishing agency, Erich Knauf. All three men moved to Berlin. Erich Ohser was a cartoonist and illustrated many books (among them those by his friend, Erich Kästner), and sketches of satiric political themes for newspapers and magazines. He married in 1930 and had one son, Christian.

An outspoken anti-communist, he appeared to be not entirely averse to social-democratic ideas. However in 1934, all three friends were suspected of anti-Hitler activities and Kästner's books were banned, Knauf lost his job, and Ohser's political sketches were no longer allowed in newspapers. In desperate need of a livelihood, he was permitted to draw non-political sketches under the pseudonym, "e.o.plauen." Ohser received instant success with his delightful comic strip, *Father and Son.*

Meanwhile, Erich Ohser's father wondered, "Where did my son's extraordinary gift come from?" One day, he remembered that he had had the wish to draw and paint when he was a little boy. However, the need to earn a living quickly eliminated his "outlandish" thoughts and dreams. Now that he could see his son's success, he decided to try painting.

He went into his basement, selected one medium-sized room and painted all four walls white. He then proceeded to draw animals, children, street scenes, family life scenes, trees, flowers, and landscapes—filling all four walls. When Erich Ohser and his son went to visit Erich's father, the elder Ohser was anxious to show them the room in the basement. Erich was stunned and amazed and deeply touched when his father said meekly, "I just wanted you to know where your talents came from."

The bombing of Berlin became so severe in 1944 that Erich Ohser sent his wife and son to safer grounds. He stayed in Berlin with his friends, Erich Kästner and Erich Knauf. They found a place to live in an empty house they shared with others. One other person in the house overheard their anti-Hitler conversations and denounced them. Kästner was able to leave, but Knauf and Ohser were arrested. Two days before their trial, Erich Ohser committed suicide. Erich Knauf was tried and sentenced to death in May 1944.

Kästner's books, (children's literature: *Emil and the Detectives* and *The Flying Classroom*, illustrated by Ohser), and Erich Ohser's best-known comic strip, *Vater und Sohn* (*Father and Son*) series, under the pseudonym e.o.plauen, live on.

Part of my teaching technique included using a penalty box. If either of my students yawned, neglected to do all their homework, seemed distracted, couldn't remember a line of a poem, answered incorrectly, or used improper pronunciation, he had to deposit a dime in the box. Because they were stellar students, I had to add some of my own cash to the penalty box but, by the end of our classes, I was able to buy each boy a handsome new golf shirt.

I cannot describe the joy that I derived from teaching and working with these gifted, talented, eager young men. They were both busy with AP classes, jazz band, and the golf team, yet we managed to enjoy classes in my home two afternoons a week for nine months. Both boys passed their final exam with flying colors and, I like to believe that because of our successful classes, my grandson Carl chose German as his major in college.

John and Carl, 2013

Birthday Celebrations

Throughout my life, October 25th has been a most important date. October 25th was my mother's birthday. It was the one day that my mother allowed me to stay home from school. I would greet her friends as they came to visit for cake and tea or coffee. I was allowed to listen to the wonderful gossip that took place during these visits and, amazingly, I remember many of the conversations in great detail.

In 1957 I started a tradition that became a required, expected, and tasty part of every birthday in my family. My sister, Brigitte, and her two younger sons, Matthias and Christian, arrived from Germany in spring of 1957 on the freighter, *Catharina Oldendorf*. Her oldest son, Hans, was already in America, having come with my mother and uncle in 1956. With the help of a professor at the University of Rochester, Hewitt Kenyon, who gave me a loan without interest, I was able to purchase a small home in Rochester. I was happy to have a place for them all to live on Meigs Street. Christian turned four on May 25, 1957, and I was trying to find some gifts to give him. Money was very tight. In those days, some products sometimes came with toys for the kids. I was lucky that the laundry detergent that I bought came with a small plastic car. So at least I had one gift. I also wanted to bake something. My famous birthday cookies were born. I made up the recipe and formed letters to spell his name and "4" and "Happy Birthday." I used appealing colors to decorate a simple powdered sugar and lemon juice frosting. Christian was very happy. I have baked these birthday cookies for most every birthday for over fifty years.

When I moved to East Aurora, my daughter, Anna, said to me, "Mom you have to teach me how to make the birthday cookies." So I sat next to her as she poured the ingredients on to the counter top until I said, "That looks like the right amount." She then measured and wrote down the exact amounts. After a few tries, she managed to craft a recipe that works every time. I have to confess that some of my birthday batches turned out better than others — the best batches always seemed to include a phone call at the precise moment when my hands would be enveloped in sticky dough. Anna has taken over the tradition and expanded it to include close friends and neighbors. The birthday cookies are always a big hit and everyone always likes them. She even sent them to Germany for Carl's twenty-first birthday. He greatly appreciated this gift from home.

I am glad that I will be known for my birthday cookies.

Cookies From my 90th Birthday Celebration

Carl's 16th Birthday Cookies
I remember using Roman Numerals because he was
studying them in his Latin class.

Hedda's Birthday Letter Cookies (adapted/measured by Anna)

Ingredients:
4 cups flour [1360 g Mehl]
1.5 tsp [TL] baking powder [Back pulver]
3 sticks butter [340g](take out of fridge 45 min - 1 hr prior to baking – it should be firm but not super cold)
1 cup sugar [340 g Zucker]
4 egg yolks [nur Ei gelb]
3 TBS [EL] warm water
2-3 TBS [EL] flour for rolling out dough

Mix flour and baking powder in a bowl.
Put flour mixture onto clean counter in a pile.
Spread flour mixture to about 8-10" in diameter with higher edges to hold
    other ingredients.
Cut up butter into ½ TBS pieces or smaller and spread out in the flour
    bowl on counter.
Sprinkle sugar over butter.
Sprinkle water over sugar and butter.
Add egg yolks.

Using a pastry scraper, begin folding over ingredients and cutting mixture
to combine. After about a minute of combining, use your hands to knead
the mixture until you get a ball – do not over knead (use a little extra flour
as needed until dough doesn't stick to fingers and hands anymore).

Set aside ball of dough and scrape counter surface.
Divide ball into 8 portions.
Using one portion at a time, on a lightly floured surface, roll dough to
form a snake, then make letters out of the snake and place on baking
sheet with parchment paper.

Bake at 350ºF [180ºC] for about 12-15 min — until just beginning to
    darken.
Cool on baking sheet for at least 5 min before transferring to a cookie
    rack.

Icing:

Put a cup or so of powdered confectioner's sugar into a small bowl (or cup)

Add 1-2 tsp lemon juice (best from actual lemon)

Add a little food coloring

Mix with a spoon adding a little more lemon juice or powdered sugar until about the consistency of molasses.

Spread on cookies, allow to dry, and ENJOY!

Hinni (Hinrich) is the Happy Recipient of Birthday Cookies

Sixteen

The age of sixteen often marks an important milestone for a young person. When my grandchildren turned sixteen, I began to reminisce about how things changed or stayed the same when I, my mother, my daughter, and my grandchildren turned sixteen.

When I turned sixteen on February 5, 1944, in Germany, the teachers no longer addressed me with the informal "du," but instead with the formal "sie," signifying adulthood and respect. WWII was raging and nothing was normal or simple. The devastation and misery it brought upon my country were definitely not conducive to religious instructions that were required to be "confirmed" into the Protestant faith which traditionally took place at age sixteen. Although I loved the choral compositions by Bach, Mozart, Verdi, and others, I could not come to terms with the phrase "the Lord is my Shepherd" from Psalm 23 and "Lamb of God" from Agnus Dei, which can be found in many Messiahs and other musical works by these composers. It was hard to fathom how a shepherd could allow the horrors of war that we faced or heard about daily. Nevertheless, I dutifully recited what I had been taught and was confirmed.

My godfather, uncle Arvid Hasselquist (my father's cousin), and his wife, Hertha, had invited a few guests for dinner to celebrate my confirmation. My sisters were away. My godmother, Tante Erna Heddinga-Biehler (my mother's dear friend and our pediatrician) was unable to attend since she had just given birth to her third child, Andreas. Uncle Arvid had neglected to invite my other godmother, Cara Mia von Freidenfeldt, whom I hardly knew. However, she was so insulted that she did the unthinkable. She threw her unwrapped present, an amber necklace, through the mail slot of our apartment door. A small piece of paper resembling a price tag was attached. She had scribbled with barely legible letters "For Hedda, from CMvF." Frau Gaede, a kind neighbor, presented me with a book, *Gabriele von Bülow: Tochter Wilhelm von Humboldts*, which has accompanied me ever since. I have read in it from time to time and, in a way, it gave me the idea for writing about the special age of sixteen. At that time, however, I had put the book, unread, on my shelf.

The book contains some five-hundred pages of correspondence between members of a distinguished Prussian family. They were landed gentry and clearly belonged to the select group of aristocrats. Through original letters, the reader becomes acquainted with Gabriele von Bülow, the daughter of Wilhelm von Humboldt, a philologist and Prussian Minister of Education. By the time Gabriele was sixteen in 1818, she had already said a tearful farewell to her younger sister, Adelaide, who was married at the age of fifteen. Gabriele was sixteen when she got engaged, and was preparing to learn how to preside over a household of a future diplomat. While her husband-to-be was still working on building his career as ambassador, they were separated for long periods of time, a situation that continued throughout their lives. Many letters retrieved from the archives of the Humboldt estate bear witness to the personal lives of the aristocracy in Germany, Italy, and England, as well as the many interesting historical and social events of the nineteenth century. We learn about the death of Napoleon (1821), whose armies had brought much devastation across Europe and the French Revolution (1848). There is a charming account about Victoria's ascension to the throne of Great Britain (1837), as well as of her marriage to the German Prince, Albert. The publications of the *Communist Manifesto* by Karl Marx and Friedrich Engels (1848), and *The Origin of Species* (1859) by Darwin are also mentioned. We also hear about Otto von Bismarck, whose frustration with unsuccessful diplomacy prompted him to make this frightening statement, "Not through speeches and majority resolutions are the great questions of the day decided — that was the great mistake of 1848-49 — but through blood and iron" (1862). Or, more simply stated, "The great questions of the day will not be settled by means of speeches and majority decisions, but by iron and blood."

My mother, then Lisa Bartelt, turned sixteen in 1917 and volunteered for the Red Cross. She tended to the wounded soldiers of WWI. Her schooling had officially ended since she did not plan to enter the university. (Her friend, Erna, had to join the boys' Gymnasium for another two years to enable her to study medicine.) Encouraged to write to prisoners of war, my mother began a correspondence with her best friend's brother, Carl Philipp Martens, who had become a POW in England. My mother told me that the two exchanged letters bi-weekly. By the time Carl Philipp returned and she greeted him at the railroad station, she was certain that she would become his wife. They were married in January 1921. Both Carl Philipp and Lisa saved their letters, but unfortunately they were destroyed in 1942 during the air raid on Lübeck. My mother told me the letters contained mostly accounts of everyday life. Regrettably, they remain unknown to me.

In August of 1944, my thirteen classmates and I were notified that we would be required to "serve" the country. We were about to start the last grade when we were informed that we had to help the war effort. I was first sent to a factory which I despised and then I was sent to take care of the wounded soldiers as an assistant nurse. It was difficult to see the severely wounded soldiers and tend to their injuries. All the boys, ages sixteen and up, were drafted into the armed forces. We were told that our "service" would be equal to our year in school and that we would receive the Abitur, the certificate that would entitle us to enter the university. Amazingly, this important paper did indeed arrive despite the chaotic circumstances in May 1945. Several months later, however, I was informed that the document was declared null and void and that I would have to do another year of school.

Life at the age of sixteen was different indeed when my daughter, Anna, turned sixteen in 1983. In school she displayed a keen interest for and excelled in mathematics and science. She did not enjoy poetry and literature (I tried). She was an outstanding, accomplished swimmer and successfully participated in the National Junior Olympics. The Rochester newspaper called her "the girl with the golden arms" after she won several gold medals at the Empire State Games. She had traveled widely; several times to Germany, with my sister to the Virgin Islands and on a safari to Kenya, as well as a visit in Cairo, Egypt, and Puerto Rico, with me. When some mothers complained about the difficulties they encountered with their teenagers, I could only find in my daughter love, kindness, caring, and concern for the well-being of all family members. She was beginning to look for colleges. After Anna obtained her driver's license, she helped to drive my mother who was beginning to slow down. In short, Anna had grown up. Her future plans centered around attending college and continuing to swim. I was grateful that she was not being forced to marry like Gabriele von Bülow or tend to wounded soldiers like I did at age sixteen.

When my grandchildren, Carl and Erika, turned sixteen in March of 2012 and 2014 respectively, the main source of excitement was obtaining a driver's license and learning to drive. They found it unimaginable that I was twenty-five before actually learning to drive. That seemed like an eternity to them. Like Anna, they were both good in school and enjoyed sports and music. They also were most caring of me. Carl inherited my car when he got his full license and I was happy to no longer have to drive. After always wanting to have a chauffeur, I finally had my grandson and later my granddaughter at my beck and call when I needed a ride somewhere. I thoroughly enjoyed that.

My hope is that the future sixteen-year-olds in my family continue to have a happy coming-of-age and that the politicians of our world resolve all difficulties with diplomacy and NOT with "Blood and Iron" as Bismarck advocated!

Sixteen is a wonderful age!

The Dogs in My Life

Peter, Linda, Juppi (Yoopy), Joshua, Fred, Bill, Peter, Oliver, Ariel, Toby, Nala, and Others

When I was a child living on Hansestrasse, my neighbors, the Franzes, had a little black dog named Peter. We called him "Mohrchen" because he was jet black. I remember asking for a dog, especially after my father died, but our situation did not allow it then.

Linda, Lisa, Emmeli

Fast forward to my mother's life in Mount Morris, NY. In honor of my mother, Lisa, and my uncle, Hans, beginning a new life together, they picked out a beautiful light-brown boxer with a few white markings. She was expensive ($60) and my mother named her Linda. She resided with them on Murray Hill in one of the physician's houses at the Mount Morris Tuberculosis Hospital. My mother took her on her daily walks, exploring the hospital grounds, but her place was right next to my uncle the minute he came home from his work. She was loving, attentive, and obedient. In short, Linda was a wonderful companion. I do not remember her ever being on a leash.

"If she ever has puppies, I would like one," several friends expressed, and my mother and uncle were also inclined to find a suitable mate for this precious dog. Linda was a good mother to her six puppies. Five were as beautiful as their mother, light brown with some white markings. However, the "runt" was darker and did not seem to thrive as well. Anxious future owners picked their puppies and, once they were weaned, the sweet little puppies left, and their first home, the enclosed sun porch, was restored to its actual function with summer furniture and flowerpots. My mother kept the runt of the litter and named her Juppi (Yoopy) after the dachshund her family had owned during her childhood in Germany.

Lisa with Linda's Puppies, Including Juppi

Linda's demeanor changed. She no longer waited for my mother to go on a walk with her. Instead, she took to roaming the countryside, staying out for hours and hours. Then, one day, the police arrived. Linda was accused of raising havoc among peacefully grazing cattle and sheep belonging to a nearby farmer, the husband of one of the nurses. The culprit was easily identified and, unfortunately, a new home for Linda had to be found. It was a hard blow; however, dear little Juppi was successful in consoling the sad family.

Juppi became the best friend and playmate of my three nephews. Hans, Matthias, and Christian spent their summers and many weekends in Mt. Morris and were often joined by my brother's three sons, David, Philip, and Clark. Juppi watched over the boys when they were swimming in the pond or hiking. She alerted my mother with a loud bark when they were fighting with one another.

Lisa with Juppi

Juppi was my mother's dog. There were two cookie jars in her kitchen: one for the children and the other for Juppi. Unaware of this arrangement, my brother once took a cookie from the wrong cookie jar. Not wanting to offend my mother, he politely mentioned that the cookies were stale and a new batch would be advisable.

Juppi loved her frequent trips to Rochester when she and my mother got the boys for the weekend or took them to Mount Morris when either of them was sick or Brigitte and I were working and/or studying. Juppi and my mother were always ready to help. Christian was heartbroken and unable to go to school when Juppi died in the early spring of 1967. All of us were very sad.

Trying to fill the huge void, Brigitte and her sons found Joshua, a sweet little Dalmatian. He was very handsome, black with the trademark white spots, or you could say white with black markings. Either way he looked most attractive. When not romping with the boys, Joshua could be found right next to Anna's crib, guarding my daughter. But Joshua was high strung and easily agitated which is typical of his breed.

Joshua and Christian

We were on very good terms with our immediate neighbors, John and Harriet Hamilton. However, they complained about Joshua, who had begun to cross their front yard to visit a precious Boxer, Penny Pollucio by name. One day, Baron, the Hamilton's Great Dane got so riled up and smashed through his patio window when Joshua had the audacity of passing through Hamilton's property.

While we tried to keep Joshua under lock and key, he somehow managed to find his way back to Penny when she had her alluring scent. The Pollucios called us every name under the sun, when their precious Penny produced a litter of five little Dalmations with Boxer faces. They ordered us to take all of the puppies. My nephew Hans took two puppies and named them

Hans and Fred

Bill and Fred. We kept Joshua, of course. Bill went on to live with one of Hans' friends. We found good homes for the three other puppies as well.

Fred became Hans' most faithful friend. He accompanied his master to his work as a tree surgeon and guarded the tools and the truck. Unfortunately, Joshua exhibited downright animosity when Fred came for a visit. There was no paternal love. Joshua was devoted to us and very protective of Anna. Hans built a fence and the run-away became a model dog. Well, sort of. We worked very hard several times a year to keep Joshua from visiting his girlfriend.

When Joshua died ten years later, Hans and Christian were married and Matthias lived in New York City. Anna, Brigitte, and I very much wanted another dog. Friends recommended a Labrador, a good family dog. It was also recommended that we get two dogs.

We answered an advertisement and were determined to find our new companions. Brigitte immediately liked a cute black puppy, while Anna took to a white one, who was actually a bit less expensive. We named them Oliver and Peter. Once at home, we placed the puppies into Anna's old playpen, which we put into our dining room. Brigitte bought a red leather band for Oliver. He looked very sweet. For blonde Peter, we bought a brown collar, which was equally becoming. During the first weeks, the nights were rather strenuous. When one puppy whined, the other felt obliged to chime in. But they appeared to be happy in their new home and we congratulated ourselves for having made such good use of the playpen.

They had been with us for about three weeks when we came upon a most unfortunate scene when returning home. The playpen was destroyed, the wallpaper was hanging from one wall and part of the pedestal of the dining room table was chewed off. The two culprits were banned into our pantry, where they immediately proceeded to gnaw on the shelves as high as they could reach. The last straw was when Oliver's head got stuck in our watering can while playing outside. We tried desperately to help him get free but, after many unsuccessful attempts, we called the fire department. Thinking that they would cut

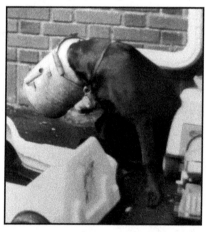

Oliver with his Head Stuck in a Watering Can

the neck of the can, they instead applied gobs of Vaseline to Oliver's neck and head and, with a little maneuvering, he was free. After that dramatic episode, we decided that we were unable to care for two rambunctious rascals. Certain that Oliver was the ringleader, we asked Hans to take him in his care. Oliver was happy in Hilton with Hans, Ellen, and their daughter Lisa.

Since Peter did not care to walk on a leash, we took him to school.

Anna with Oliver (black) and Peter (white)

However, he was not a successful member of the class. Peter loved to swim and Anna and I went frequently to Durand Eastman Park Beach where he thoroughly enjoyed jumping into the waves of Lake Ontario. Peter was the dearest member of our family. He was clearly Anna's dog. The minute she came home during vacations from college, Peter gravitated toward her. He watched over Stefan, Lisa, and Teresa when they came to visit. He was the faithful companion of my uncle and my mother who lived with us after my uncle's heart attack, and he would guard Anna and newborn Carl when they came to Rochester for a visit. Peter shared our lives for thirteen years. It was very difficult to let him go. I remember driving with Peter for the last time to see the veterinarian, Dr. Tom Mullaney, a good friend of mine. Brigitte and I felt that there would never be another dog to replace our Peter.

Once the Davidson children, Carl and Erika, were five and three respectively, the family decided to acquire a pure-bred chocolate American Labrador. She was named Ariel. Ariel was a wonderful companion for the Davidson family. She was always encouraging them to go for hikes and walks. Growing

Ariel Enjoying a Stick

up, her favorite playmate was the neighbor's dog, Phoenix. The two played together nearly every day. She was definitely "daddy's girl," particularly devoted to Bruce, always choosing him to nestle with on the couch. One of her best characteristics was her delight at seeing the children come home from school. Her tail always thumped when anyone said her name. She was nicknamed the "Queen" because she was a bit of a finicky eater and when she decided to dine, everyone had to stop what they were doing so as not to disturb her.

Toby joined the Davidson family in 2007. He was a black American Labrador with a totally different temperament, yet so very lovable. Bruce referred to him as "a Mama's boy." Toby was always under Anna's feet when she prepared dinners, hoping for some left-overs. Not unlike most dogs, Toby was particularly afraid of thunderstorms as well as fireworks. He found protection in Anna and Bruce's closet right under the clothes. I became the protector of the dogs on fireworks nights. We would cling together on the large sofa, comforting one another. Toby was a champion soccer player and learned some hunting skills from his older "sister," Ariel. He loved to swim in the creek and, together with Ariel, he eagerly awaited his twice-daily walks or hikes. In contrast to Ariel, he managed to gulp down his food in about thirty seconds. Both Toby and Ariel had a taste for American cheese and could hear the wrapper being opened from any room in the house.

Toby Prepares to Catch his Soccer Ball

Unfortunately, Toby succumbed to cancer after only six years in June 2014. It was very difficult for the whole family. However, Ariel seemed to be reborn and became much more puppy-like and playful. She seemed to sense that the family needed cheering up. She was much more animated on her daily walks and loved swimming and playing with another neighbor's dog, Abbey. Ariel came with Anna when she visited me at my condo. I enjoyed her visits very much. She was very loving to all of us. After thirteen wonderful years, Ariel died at the end of May 2015. The family was devastated. After only five days, Anna came home and said there was a Labradoodle for sale in Elma and would the family like to take a look.

Of course, "taking a look," meant coming home with a new dog a few days later. Nala joined the Davidson family in June 2015 at ten weeks old. She was a remarkable puppy who seemed to sense that she needed to be very calm and cautious around Bob (Bruce's dad) and me. Both of us were living in Bruce and Anna's home and were on oxygen. Tubing was all over the floor in the house. Nala never once disturbed any of the oxygen tubing or other medical items found throughout the house. Nala is a bundle of happiness and, at fifty pounds, a perfect size. She greets every person with enthusiasm, and I love how she looks out over Cazenovia Creek to survey the

land from my room. She always greets me in the morning as well. She also likes cheese, and every morning when I eat breakfast, she waits patiently beside my chair hoping that I will share a slice of my cheese with her (which of course, I always do). When Bob was not feeling well, she spent her time at his side. She brings a smile to all who encounter her.

Nala joins the Davidson Family

Finally, I have to mention a little puppy named Cleo. My dear friend Debby has been helping me edit this book and I had a desire to find a special gift for her. After watching Debby enjoy Nala everyday and saying how much she missed having a dog of her own, my daughter suggested that I buy her a puppy. Anna spoke with Debby's husband who was supportive of the idea. Anna called a breeder who had a litter of Labradoodles. When Debby came that afternoon to visit and work, I told her about my planned gift to her and I was able to see the joy in her face as she smiled from ear to ear. For the next six weeks, Debby and her husband visited Cleo at the breeder's and then finally were able to bring her home. Their first stop was my house so that I could meet the new puppy. I knew this puppy would provide great joy to Debby and Pat and that meant everything to me. Cleo was the perfect gift.

Dogs have been an important part of my life since moving to America. Our family would definitely be deemed a dog-loving family. Nearly all of my relatives have or have had a dog or dogs. They include: Honey Bunn, Charlie, Emmie, Beverly, Ruth, Stella, Cooper, Asa, Ada, Cordell, Marfa, Bill, Fred, Oliver, Otto, Rosy, Thor, Augie, Timmy, Jaspar, Caddilac, Leo, Blondie, Max, Solo, Kelly, Tika, Chili, Speedy, Foxy, Jaspar, Duncan, Macey, Zedd, and Pootie. The unconditional love and devotion given by each of these dogs

Debby, Pat, and Cleo

mirrors that of our family. I am proud of the support and encouragement that my mother, my uncle, my siblings, and I gave one another and our children, grandchildren, nieces, and nephews, as we built and continue to build our lives in our new country.

Individual dogs may not display all of the following traits, but together you find charisma, a sense of adventure, trust, unconditional love, loyalty, punctuality, dependability, perserverance, protectiveness, a mischievious spirit, and joyfulness. These are all words that also perfectly describe my Onkel Hans in his quest to bring us all to America and nurture our ever-growing family.

Nala and Cleo are Good Friends

A Postcard to Hitler

It was 1986 and my dear Onkel Hans was dying. A heart attack and Parkinson's disease had taken their toll. My uncle lived with us in Rochester and I was his caretaker. Daily activities had come to a standstill. His face had become mask-like due to progressive rigidity and his speech was erratic. He was bedridden. The rented hospital bed was in my former bedroom. I spent many hours by his bedside reading sections of books by his favorite authors to him, repeating many paragraphs when I noticed his frustration because he had been unable to follow.

One day he said, "Hedda, could you please write a postcard for me?" I was delighted and ran to my desk to find a card that depicted a scene from Rochester, NY. Equipped with a pen, I was ready to take dictation. "To whom shall I address this card?"

"To Herrn Adolf Hitler." Thinking that he was delirious, I responded, "Hitler is dead." He raised his upper body and became quite agitated and highly irritated. "I know that, I know that," he retorted in an aggravated voice. Then he began to dictate:

To Herrn Adolf Hitler,

When I was in one of your concentration camps, a gypsy, who was also imprisoned, read my palms and told me my fortune. He predicted that the day would come that I would want to thank you for expelling me from my beloved country, leaving me stateless and homeless. Thanks to your unbelievably cruel action, I am now a grateful citizen of the United States, surrounded by an ever-growing, loving family.

Adolf Hitler

Germany

A Postcard to Hitler

The contents of this postcard left me puzzled and I was determined to find out when he had consulted a gypsy. Interrupted by resting periods and occasional sips of water, he began to tell me his story. Over the next two days, he revealed the following information about his life from 1928 to 1949.

My uncle was a physician, practicing internal medicine in Hamburg. Life was good until he was suddenly arrested in October 1937. His family had trouble finding out anything that might indicate why Hans was arrested. His wife, Dori, later told us that she had heard rumors that he was accused of homosexual activities by prison inmates where he had worked as a physician. Following his arrest, he was transported to the Dachau concentration camp where he shared abysmal living quarters with gypsies. They were called the "scum of the earth" and "a disgrace to Germany." Despite hard, demeaning labor during the day, the gypsies sang and danced in the evening and happily engaged in their expertise of fortune telling.

At this point, I would like to briefly talk about the gypsies. Their name derives from the term "Little Egyptians," when it was incorrectly thought that they originated from Egypt. They are now believed to have originated in India, from where they migrated to Persia (Iran) in the third century. A nomadic people, they were first reported in western Europe around the fifteenth century where they were frequently persecuted by religious and civil authorities. Free spirited, they made their living as dancers, musicians, horse dealers, and fortune tellers. They are short and slightly built, with dark complexions and black hair. They had set up camp at the very end of the long street where I lived in Lübeck and where I spent my childhood. Although it had been strictly prohibited, my sister, Emmeli, had explored the campsite and had been fascinated by the dancing and singing of these people as she would tell me later. (By the time I was old enough to venture out to the end of the very long street, the gypsies were gone.) The National Sozialistische "Nazi" government had removed that group to concentration camps. It is believed that some 600,000 gypsies succumbed in the concentration camps or were killed in gas chambers. Unaware of this tragedy, we sang "Lustig ist das Zigeunerleben, Halli, Halli, Hallo" (Happy is the life of a gypsy). It has a vibrant, happy melody.

Hans' story continues:

After five-to-seven months of incarceration, he was able to contact family and friends. Somehow, an arrangement was made that would allow

Dear Friends Wolfgang and Peter,
who had moved to Austrailia,
visited Hans in 1971.

Hans to buy his freedom, provided he renounce his German citizenship and never step foot in Germany again. Three friends from his university days: Hans Stratz, Wolfgang, and Peter, were able to provide the money he needed since his family could not gain access to his savings. He was put on a bus heading to Holland with German guards who were there to assure that Hans did not exit the bus until arriving in Holland.

Pictured is my grandmother's passport. As you can see, it contains a visa dated July 1938. When I looked at it as I began writing these stories, I remembered accompanying my mother, my uncle Rolf, and grandmother to the railroad station, carrying her small suitcase. My Oma, so I was told at the time, was visiting a friend in Rotterdam. She would be back in a few days. It would be many years later before I learned the truth about the real reason my grandmother travelled to Rotterdam. She had gone to say a final goodbye to her son, Hans.

Elise's Passport
The only time she left Germany
was for this trip.

When the bus entered Holland, Hans was allowed to disembark. He was given twenty minutes to say goodbye to his mother and hand his brother, Rolf, the power of attorney since he had been stripped of his German citizenship and could no longer attend to his own affairs in Germany. German guards then escorted him on board the waiting ship that would take him to Madras, India. My grandmother's one and only trip outside of Germany was one of the most heart-wrenching ordeals any mother can go through. Oma never talked to us children or her friends about her heartbreak. She simply said, "Your uncle is in India working as a physician." She missed her son, especially during the trying times when the insulin did not control her diabetes. The Red Cross informed my grandmother that her son had arrived safely in Madras and that he was working as a physician in an internment camp. His German medical certificate was accepted in India at the time.

Hans' German medical license was valid in India and, after working some months in a hospital, he was once again able to start a private practice in internal medicine. Other German refugees, British officials, and several Indians comprised the majority of his patients. He corresponded with family and friends in Germany and loved getting letters from his mother and sisters. His wife Dori joined him in 1938 and found a job as a graphic designer.

Rolf, Elise, and Onkel Hans
Hans sees his mother for the
last time.

When World War II began and England had declared war on Germany, all German-born refugees in India were immediately sent to an internment camp along with mostly Jewish refugees. Hans was fortunate and allowed to work as one of the camp's physicians. Since Dori was Dutch, she was able to continue working in Madras.

Cloth Envelope Used to Send Mail to Onkel Hans

Hans received sporadic news from his family via the Red Cross. In November 1940 he learned that his mother had died on August 2, 1940. It was almost three months before he finally had a letter from his sister, Lisa (my mother), letting him know that they had all survived the bombing of Lübeck in March 1942. While he was safe in camp, it was most difficult to know his family was stuck in the middle of a horrible war. Once the war in Europe had ended, he was relieved to hear that his family was intact. That was not the case for many of his Jewish friends who were waiting in vain for news of their relatives.

By the summer of 1945, the camp was dissolved and Hans was allowed to practice medicine again. He once again required some financial help from his Austailian friends in order to rebuild his private practice. By the summer of 1947, he was able to repay them. They had insisted that their monetary support was a gift and not a loan, but Hans felt better with his solution.

On January 30, 1948, Mahatma Gandhi was fatally shot by a fanatic. Rules and regulations changed drastically and Hans' German medical license was no longer valid. Fortunately, one of his patients, American Consul Roy Bower, was grateful that Hans had properly diagnosed and treated him and offered to assist him to immigrate to the United States. Roy was able to obtain a visa for Hans. Hans and Dori had separated but, as neither one had any interest in remarrying, they decided not to get a divorce. Dori opted to remain in India at the time. Hans arrived in New York City in the summer of 1948. Roy Bower's sister welcomed him to share her apartment on Riverside Drive. Roy got busy and helped Hans with the necessary paperwork to validate his medical license. They soon learned that he would be admitted to the New York State Board examination without further schooling, since he had received his medical degree in Germany before January 30, 1933, when Hitler came to power. They secured the text books Hans needed, he studied hard for the exam, and passed it in December 1948.

Hans did not have the desire to start another private practice again and decided to take a job as a physician in the Tuberculosis Hospital in Mount Morris, NY. The hospital offered a pleasant apartment on the grounds plus a good, if modest, salary. He was welcomed by all the other physicians and nurses and became good friends with the director, Lynn Armstrong, as well as the pathologist, Dr. Matthias, who had fled Austria in 1938. Life was good. Although he had never been a great fan of athletic activities, he learned how to play golf with the other physicians and even joined the Stafford Country Club. At the persistance of the nurses, he joined them in bowling leagues. He enjoyed the comradery.

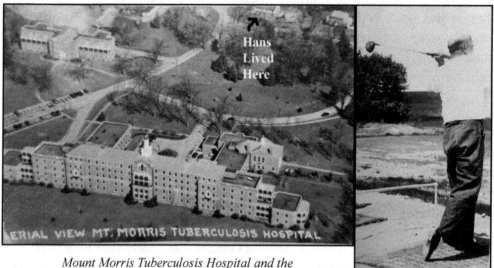

Mount Morris Tuberculosis Hospital and the
House Where Hans Lived

Onkel Hans

October 1985: My Mother's Birthday Celebration
From Left: Dori, Hedda, Hans, Lisa, Stefan, Teresa, Christian, Brigitte

Dori remained in Madras for several years until the situation became difficult for her and she planned to return to Amsterdam. Her family, however, advised her to request that Hans sponsor her to come to the United States. Under the condition that she would look for work elsewhere and that they would not live together, Hans agreed. Dori arrived in the fall of 1951. She worked in Rochester for several years and then moved to Bridgeport, CT. Eventually, Dori returned to the Netherlands and remained there until she died in 1994. She visited us occasionally.

Hans missed his family. Hans and his sister, Lisa, began a regular exchange of letters and were dreaming of a possible life together. Lisa visited him in 1951 and decided that she would also immigrate to the United States. I arrived in the United States in May of 1952. My mother and Hinrich came in December 1952. Emmeli came in 1953 and Brigitte and her sons in 1957. Hans had achieved his goal to bring us all together again.

Lisa and Hans, 1959

My uncle never signed the postcard. He was too tired. He died three days later on February 15, 1986.

Onkel Hans (Far Right Chair) Looking at his Growing Family

A Postcard to Hitler

I had always known that my Onkel Hans was a great man, but my final conversations with him made me realize just how selfless and strong he had been throughout his life. He was arrested for being the man he was, called the "scum of the earth" and a "disgrace to Germany," evicted from his country, survived his time in India, and built a new life in America for himself and his family. He carried no resentment toward Hitler and, despite all the hardship he endured over the years, he lived his life to the fullest, in spite of all that had been done to him. Living his life well and honorably was his ultimate achievement.

For over thirty years, Hans was the most generous, protective patriarch of our ever-growing family which is now five generations strong. Respected and loved by everyone, he was our dear Onkel Hans. It is fortunate for our family that the gypsy's prediction indeed came true.

Onkel Hans, 1969

Maintaining Connections with Relatives Abroad

When I immigrated to the United States in 1952, the internet didn't exist and phone calls were nearly impossible and ridiculously expensive. We were left with old-fashioned letter writing as our only means of communication with the people we had left behind. Fortunately, I loved to write letters and sent many letters abroad. I wrote to Anna's father and my family nearly every day.

My mother was also a great letter writer. She kept in touch with all of her friends and relatives in Germany when she immigrated to America. It is because of my mother and me that we kept in such close contact with our cousins, aunts, uncles, nieces, nephews, and good friends. When the telephone became less prohibitive in the 1970s and 1980s, we occasionally supplemented our letter writing with phone calls.

I stayed in close contact with my dear cousins, Stephan Bartelt and Rudolf Hagen. Actually, most of my correspondence took place with their wives, Nina and Fidele respectively. I also wrote to my dear friends, Erika and Inge Hinrichsen. Meanwhile my mother corresponded with her siblings, Käthe and Rolf, and close friends.

As we became settled in our new country, visitors arrived from Germany. Käthe, Rolf, and his wife Annemarie visited first in Mount Morris. Once we were established in our home on Highland Avenue, we enjoyed visits from my cousins, Christian and Stephan Bartelt, with their families, as well as Rudolf and Fidele Hagen and their children. As their children became teenagers, we hosted several of them for a few weeks or months. This was a great way for them to work on their English and experience life in America. Johannes Hagen worked with my nephew Hans in his landscaping business one summer. Each visitor enjoyed our pool and of course, trips to Niagara Falls.

Of all my mother's grandchildren, Anna knew our relatives abroad the best because they stayed at our house when they visited and she visited Germany every few years. She was also fluent in German which made conversation with relatives very easy. Unfortunately, Hinrich's children did not grow up learning German, which put them at a disadvantage communicating with our older relatives. However, it is interesting that they all eventually found ties with Germany as they grew older. David married Kathy who speaks German and has relatives in southern Germany. They have visited Germany to meet both of their relatives. Philip worked for a company that sent him and his family to Germany for three years and he now speaks some German. Clark also worked with a company that allowed him to take a position in Germany for two years with his family.

Fidele and Rudolf's house was always a most delightful place to stay when we visited in Lübeck. There were occasions, however, when Rudolf and Fidele lived abroad. They spent three years in Greece where their son Johannes was born and they spent five years in Cairo, Egypt. Onkel Hans visited them in Greece and Anna and I visited them in Egypt in May 1980. Brigitte visited that fall when we convinced her she had to take advantage of the opportunity. During our visit, we met Helmy who was about to graduate from the German High School in Cairo. Helmy and Konstanze were married when Konstanze was twenty-one. Helmy's father was Dr. Ibrahim Abouleisch, the founder of SEKEM (a leading business in hydrodynamic agricultural methods). Konstanze and Helmy have been part of building SEKEM from the beginning. They have four daughters and several grandchildren.

As part of our trip abroad in 1980, we travelled to Lübeck, Germany, from Egypt to visit our relatives there. We stayed with my other cousin, Stephan Bartelt, his wife Nina, and children Julie and Felix. Onkel Rolf, Stephan's father, had been the owner Martens and Prahl, the insurance company founded by my grandfather Heinrich Martens. Stephan became the owner of the company upon his father's death. Stephan is fourteen years younger than I and spent many days and weeks with us in Travemünde when his father was a soldier during WWII.

When my niece, Polly, turned forty in 2008, her husband Tom wanted to plan a surprise trip to Italy. He had heard that we had relatives there and asked me to help set up a meeting. The arrangements were made and Polly and Tom visited with Stephan and Nina and met their daughter Julie and her three children at their vacation home south of Florence.

This visit sparked Julie to visit New Hampshire with her family and brother in 2010. Polly had the grand idea to turn the event into a wonderful family reunion at her house in the mountains. Nearly everyone was able to attend. My brother and I loved it, especially being able to watch the younger cousins getting to know one another.

Family Reunion in New Hampshire, 2010

That reunion reinvigorated the connection between Polly, Anna, and Julie. Soon plans were hatched for a grand trip to Europe in the summer of 2011. Carl had made plans to go to Italy with his Latin teacher and class. I suggested that we should all go and make a longer trip of it. Polly and her family asked to join us and so a tremendous trip ensued. We all met in Florence, Italy, where we stayed with my cousin Stephan and his wife Nina in their vacation home and olive grove.

Gathering South of Florence, 2011

For me it was a trip down memory lane as we took the train from Italy to southern Germany. I was so happy to enjoy a genuine knackwurst (knockwurst) on the train. We toured the castle Neuschwanstein. Bruce nearly collapsed pushing my wheelchair up the steep walkway to the castle. I was overcome with joy and excitement when the steeples of the churches in Lübeck came into view as the train drew near. To be able to show and tell Carl, Erika, and all the others the special childhood memories of

Hedda Enjoys a Real Knackwurst, 2011

my hometown, Lübeck, and the surrounding areas was a dream come true. It was a great pleasure to visit with Stephan and Nina, as well as their grown children, Julie and Felix, and their families in their beautiful home that sits on the banks of the Wagnitz river. We also spent time with Rudolf's wife Fidele and their son Johannes and his family. Family ties are wonderful.

Anna, Carl, Bruce, Erika, and Hedda in front of the Hosltentor, 2011

Katherina's daughter Vera came to the US in the spring of 2014 to enrich her studies in agriculture at an organic farm on the Hudson River about five hours from Buffalo. She first spent a week visiting us in East Aurora seeing some of the sites. Erika spent two weeks attending school with Johanna

(Julie's daughter) in Hamburg, Germany, and Johanna came and attended school with Erika for a week. This trip culminated with a visit from Johanna's parents and siblings and we had a wonderful party and family gathering to celebrate. Carl spent several weeks in Germany as a high school graduation present in 2014 to continue his language skills in German.

A great reunion occurred in spring 2016 when Fidele came to visit us with her two daughters, Konstanze who lives in Egypt, and Katharina who lives in southern Germany. I hadn't seen Fidele's daughters in over twenty years so it was wonderful connecting with them again. Konstanze left us with an open invitation to visit her in Egypt any time. Little did we know then that Carl would spend six weeks at the SEKEM farm that very summer speaking German, hearing Arabic, and learning about the sustainable farm and the Muslim culture.

Family Gathering in East Aurora, NY, 2016
Standing from left: Kathy, Hinrich, Teresa, David, Fidele, Katharina, Bruce,
Theresa, Lydia, Matthias
Sitting: Maria, Ellen, Konstanze, Hans, Polly, Clark, Hedda, Carl
In Front: Anna, Erika, Nala

Most recently we had another family reunion at Anna's house in 2017. Julie and two of her children also attended from Germany. It was a wonderful party. Anna now has weekly if not daily contact with her many second cousins abroad with the help of the internet and various apps on her phone. It gives me great pleasure to know that my keeping in touch with everyone has resulted in the younger generation creating bonds that will hopefully continue to grow with relatives across the ocean.

Reunion in East Aurora, 2017

Top Row (l-r): Adam Bell, Christian Boettrich, Susan MacDougall, Don MacDougall, Lisa Gerhardt holding her baby Jane, Teresa Boettrich, Ellen Boettrich, Theresa Martens, Anna Davidson, Clark Martens, Bruce Davidson, David Martens, Tom Culver, Julie Schellack

Row 2: Kathy Martens, **Hedda Martens,** *Hans Boettrich, Philip Gerhardt, Christopher Martens*

Row 3: Colin Martens, Carl Davidson, Peter Davidson, Grant Martens, Hinrich Martens, Polly Martens, Philip Martens

Row 4: Maria Martens, Carol Martens

Row 5: Amy Martens, Leonie Schellack, Hannah Culver, Katie Bell, Heather MacDougall, Lydia Boettrich, Matthias Boettich

Row 6: Erika Davidson, Jennifer Bell, Elizabeth MacDougall, Allison MacDougall, Marlena Culver, Frederick Schellack

Over sixty years have passed since I crossed the Atlantic Ocean and many wonderful things have happened to me.

As I reflect upon the stories I have told in the preceding pages, I am both humbled and grateful to have encountered so many interesting, strong, and insightful people. They have all greatly enriched my life.

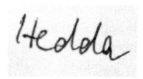

CPSIA information can be obtained
at www.ICGtesting.com
Printed in the USA
FSHW021037030319
56060FS